WIVES AND MOTHERS
IN VICTORIAN INDUSTRY

WIVES & MOTHERS IN VICTORIAN INDUSTRY

by

MARGARET HEWITT

Lecturer in Sociology, University of Exeter

GREENWOOD PRESS, PUBLISHERS
WESTPORT, CONNECTICUT

Library of Congress Cataloging in Publication Data

Hewitt, Margaret, 1928-
    Wives & mothers in Victorian industry.

    Reprint of the ed. published by Rockliff, London.
    Bibliography: p.
    Includes index.
    1. Wives--Employment--Great Britain. 2. Mothers--
Employment--Great Britain. I. Title.
HD6055.H4 1975   331.4'3'0942   73-11623
ISBN 0-8371-7078-8

Originally published in 1958 by Rockliff, London

Reprinted with the permission of Margaret Hewitt

Reprinted in 1975 by Greenwood Press,
a division of Williamhouse-Regency Inc.

Library of Congress Catalog Card Number 73-11623

ISBN 0-8371-7078-8

Printed in the United States of America

To
Dr. Ivy Pinchbeck

This book is dedicated with
gratitude and affection

PREFACE

This study is an amplification of a more restricted investigation which was presented for a higher degree in historical sociology in the University of London. In the course of writing the original thesis and the present book I have become heavily indebted to a number of people for their help and guidance. I should like to take this opportunity of expressing my sincere thanks to Mr. O. R. McGregor of Bedford College, who first encouraged me to investigate this particular problem; and to Professor D. V. Glass of the London School of Economics and Dr. Ivy Pinchbeck of Bedford College, both of whom supervised the work on it for my higher degree and but for whose advice, direction, and encouragement my efforts would have been doomed to failure. My thanks are also due to the Registrar-General for allowing a random sample of 1871 Census schedules, normally unavailable to the public, to be undertaken in his Department and to the Central Research Fund of the University of London for making a grant to cover the cost of this. The publication of the present book has been made possible by the generous assistance of the Publications Fund of the University of Exeter. How greatly I am indebted to all those who have translated my handwriting into typescript only I, they, and other unfortunates who have to decipher my hand can fully appreciate.

MARGARET HEWITT

EXETER.
June 1958

CONTENTS

CHAPTER I

INTRODUCTION

MANY studies have been made of the effects of the growth of the factory system in the nineteenth century on the hours and conditions of employment of women, but scant attention has been paid to the influence of such changes on the homes and families of married women employed in the mills and factories. Yet around this subject the most bitter controversy raged; and to no aspect of it was more fervid writing devoted than the consequences of the employment away from home of the mothers of young children. Indeed, comment on the employment of wives and mothers in the newspapers and journals of our own day—sometimes sweeping enough, in all conscience—appear half-hearted compared with the dramatic pronouncements of the Victorian period. Mrs. Bayley, for example, in a paper read to the National Association for the Promotion of Social Science in 1864, declared "the wife and mother going abroad for work is, with few exceptions, a waste of time, a waste of property, a waste of morals and a waste of health and life and ought in every way to be prevented".[1]

Far from being a consequence of the Industrial Revolution, the employment of married women had become extensive long before the factory had replaced the home as the centre of industry. Some of the work they performed, such as baking, brewing, spinning, and making the clothes for their families, was considered to be part of the normal duties of the housewife and was thus unrewarded. But they had not been merely unpaid housekeepers, dependent on their husbands for support, and with the growth of capitalism and the development of markets there had been increasing opportunities for their gainful employment.[2]

In agriculture, women—married and unmarried alike —had always played an important part. On the large farms the dairy and the care of the poultry were their especial responsibility. The wives and daughters of agricultural labourers were employed in general farm work, such as digging potatoes and beet, gathering furze, and loading pack-horses.[3]

If agriculture was partly dependent on women to provide its labour force, their work was absolutely indispensable to the textile industries, for hand-spinning, the foundation of them all, was traditionally the monopoly of women.[4] The absence of spinning in a district was, in fact, so unusual as to cause comment.[5] Although most of this work was regarded as a spare-time or supplementary occupation, there is evidence that even under the domestic system, in areas such as the West Riding of Yorkshire, the Manchester district, and the West Country, some cottages were often like small factories, the women and children preparing and spinning the wool or cotton for their menfolk to weave on the hand-looms.[6] All women's activity in the textile industries was not confined exclusively to spinning, however, for there are records of women having been engaged in weaving as far back as the fourteenth century.[7]

Many smaller industries, such as lace-making, straw-plaiting, needlework and embroidery of all kinds, button-making, and hat-making, offered employment to numbers of married women. The coal-mining and metal industries employed more again. In the 1840s, the Victorians were horrified to learn that married women were employed in and around the pits in Scotland and parts of England, yet women had traditionally been employed in the mining industry carrying coal from the face at which their menfolk were at work.

Nor were these the only paid employments open to married women. Many were employed in such crafts as jewellery- and fan-making and in retail trade. For, since such businesses were small, it was common for a woman to help her husband during his lifetime, and on his death to continue in business with the aid of skilled men.[8]

There is, in fact, as Barbara Hutchins remarks, "little reason to believe in any decline and fall of women from a golden age in which they did only work which was 'suitable', and that in the bosoms of their families".[9] It had always been expected among the working classes that wives should earn at least sufficient for their own maintenance. "Consider, my dear girl", runs "A Present for a Servant Maid" (1743), " that you have no portions and endeavour to supply the deficiencies of fortune by mind. You cannot expect to marry in such a manner as neither of you shall have occasion to work, and none but a fool will take a wife whose bread must be earned solely by his labour, and who will contribute nothing towards it herself."[10] Not till the home ceased to be the main centre of economic activity did the married woman worker become an object of pity or disapprobation; not till then did she become "news".

Of the many and complex causes of this changed attitude, two may be clearly isolated. First, the long hours of ceaseless toil were less easily overlooked in the factory than in the obscurity of the cottage. Secondly, that women—above all, married women—should work conflicted with the philosophy of the Victorians with its deification of the home. Women ought to marry and married women ought to stay at home to tend their husband's house and bear his children, not toil long hours in factories. "Are we not bound to strive and to hope for a state of things in which men shall be *more* and females shall be *less* employed in the mills?" demands the Rev. Alexander Munro. "That it should be so is simply in accordance with the nature and peculiar powers given to the sexes. Men have powers that fit them for permanent toil: women for slighter and briefer efforts. These are framed for maternal mildness and the watchful offices of affection. All their organs are tender, yielding, and sensitive. Out of home they are, in great measure, out of their sphere, and though nature may be overborne by usage, yet if long thwarted, nature will have its revenge."[11]

Such was the current belief: nevertheless, a great many married women, either through choice or necessity, did go out to work, and in no area was this practice more extensive than in Lancashire, the centre of the cotton industry. Hence it was that Lancashire became the area where Victorian investigation of this problem was mainly concentrated. This book deals largely, therefore, with the Lancashire cotton operative; but we shall show by evidence from the agricultural areas and from other industries, particularly the Staffordshire pottery industry, that the more publicized experiences of the Lancashire cotton districts were by no means unique. Working-class wives and mothers who spent much time away from home, wherever and for whatever reason, experienced the same problems and had to try to solve them as best they might with such resources as their income and ability permitted and such facilities as their locality and Victorian England allowed.

For many reasons it is difficult to give a comprehensive account of how these working wives coped with their domestic responsibilities. Whilst, for example, a great deal was written about the provision made for the care of very young children, practically nothing was recorded about the care of the older children. A great deal of our knowledge of the organization of the homes of middle-class housewives is derived from contemporary novels, but there are few novels which have a factory girl as their heroine. This is scarcely surprising, as Mrs. Neff remarks in her book, *Victorian Working Women*, for "the factory girl was, of all working men and women, the most remote from the experience of both the author and the reader".[12] Few Victorian authors either had or attempted to gain first-hand knowledge of life in the grimy mill-towns of the North. They hesitated to depict for their gentle readers the experiences of women who spent most of their day in the unromantic surroundings of the noise and dirt and, even worse, the mixed company of the mill, and at least some of their leisure in the ale-house.

". . . Other kinds of girls, with cleaner jobs, not so difficult to comprehend, were more attractive. One notes that Disraeli does not make Sybil a worker in Trafford's mill, when in real life she would have been, and Mrs. Gaskell keeps Mary Barton from following the trade of her father, her mother, and her aunt. The factory girl lacked all the qualifications of the Victorian heroine. . . .

". . . Authors desirous of keeping up with the times made a subordinate character a worker, without being too specific about the kind of labour performed. Mrs. Tonna alone described the processes of manufacture and concerned herself with the economic aspects of mill life."[13]

Although the contemporary novel may be neither a rewarding nor a reliable source of information concerning the life of mill folk, there is a great deal of non-literary information from which to draw—Government Blue Books, *Hansard* debates, the reports of royal commissions and of committees of enquiry, the transactions of such societies as the National Society for the Promotion of Social Science—and it is from these sources that we derive most of the information on which the following chapters are based.

Chapters II and III have been placed in a section by themselves, as they are not concerned with the consequences, but with the extent and conditions of married women's employment away from home in mills and factories during the period under review. Whilst some readers may prefer to turn immediately to Part II, the significance of the problems discussed there can only be fully appreciated in the light of the facts presented in Part I.

PART I

THE NATURE OF THE PROBLEM

CHAPTER II

THE NUMBER OF WIVES INVOLVED

THE domestic effects of married women's employment away from their homes, though not mathematically proportionate to the numbers employed, obviously have some relation to it. An important factor contributing to the acrimony of contemporary discussion in the Victorian period was that very few statistics were available of the extent of married women's employment. Even as late as 1893, the Principal Lady Factory Inspectress, Miss Anderson, in her "Report on the Employment of Women" to the Royal Commission on Labour remarked: "It is impossible to assess the extent of married women's employment—though we know that wherever women are employed a proportion of them are married, especially in textiles."[1]

The occupational tables of the 1901 Census, distinguishing for the first time between unmarried and married and widowed women workers, confirmed this view. But since the married and widowed were grouped together, it was still impossible to assess accurately the proportion of married women employed. Miss Anderson, giving further evidence eleven years later to the Interdepartmental Committee on Physical Deterioration, again had to make rough estimates. Asked whether she thought that fewer married women were employed in factories and workshops than was supposed, she replied: "I think so, except in certain districts and in Dundee for instance [where they were extensively employed in the jute mills] and in certain textile districts. . . . The employment of married women probably varies with districts. I think it

is a less serious item as regards the whole than is sometimes supposed."[2]

In the absence of accurate statistics, therefore, those
who wished to arouse the public to the alarming and
disastrous consequences of the industrial employment
of wives and mothers loudly asserted that a large number
—if not the majority—of women employed in factories
and workshops were married; whilst their opponents
insisted with equal confidence that there was little or no
evidence to support such a statement.

Reviewing the social consequences of married women's
employment in the Lancashire mills in the 1840s, for
example, Lord Ashley had no hesitation in stating that
the practice had quite the worst possible implications.
Furthermore, he claimed, "the evil is spreading rapidly
and extensively—desolating like a torrent the peace, the
economy, and the virtue of the mighty masses of the
manufacturing districts. Domestic life and domestic
discipline must soon be at an end; society will consist of
individuals no longer grouped into families; so early is
the separation of husband and wife, of parents and
children."[3]

Sincere as Ashley was in this view, he appears to have
based it on an exaggerated idea of the extent of married
women's employment in the cotton industry. In the
course of the Ten Hours' Debates (1844) he quotes
an informant, who wrote: "Mr. E., a manufacturer,
informs me that he employs women exclusively at his
power-looms; it is so universally; gives a decided preference to married females, especially those with
families at home to support; they are attentive and
docile, more so than unmarried females, and are compelled to use their utmost exertions to procure the
necessities of life."[4] Later in the debates he quotes the
report of a meeting in Manchester: "It was moved by
the Rev. D. Hearne, a Roman Catholic priest of
Manchester, at a meeting at Manchester on 19th April
1844, 'That this meeting is fully convinced that if it was

made known to Her Majesty the Queen that two-thirds and in many instances, three-quarters of the factory workers are females (many of them wives and mothers) she would use her Royal influence for and sympathize with them'."[5]

Ashley's supporters cited similar instances. Lord Wharncliffe claimed: "The system [of employing women instead of men] in some instances had reached its climax, for some of the mills were entirely worked by women— men were entirely excluded. . . . The result had been the demoralization of women . . . and instead of fetching their husbands home from the public house, their husbands came to fetch them."[6]

By such illustrations as these, it was sought to prove that the proportion of married women employed in cotton was extremely high. Those who opposed Ashley, however, were at some pains to prove that he was attempting to generalize from a few, unrepresentative, instances. Quoting the results of an enquiry into the employment of women in 412 textile factories in Lancashire and Yorkshire, Mr. Ward, Member of Parliament for Sheffield, produced figures to show that of 61,000 women, only 10,000—just less than one in six—were married.[7] "If anything is susceptible of proof", he declared, "it is that the number of married women employed in the factories is very small."[8]

In the course of the same debates, Bright contended: "It has been stated that a large proportion of the females employed in mills are married, but the returns to which I will ask your attention will show that this is not the case. If all the noble Lord had said on this subject were true, if the cases he stated, but for which he has no authority, were the rule, instead of being, as I am sure, the exception, such a state of things would go far to justify interference of an extraordinary description on the part of the Legislature."[9]

To support his argument, Bright first called attention to the fact that, in his own mill, out of 249 females employed, only fifty-nine were of twenty-one years and upwards. He then proceeded to adduce evidence from Dr. Mitchell's report to the 1833 Factory Commissioners, where it is stated: ". . . The greatest number of females [employed] is in the period sixteen to twenty-one years of age, but there is a prodigious diminution immediately after: and who can be at a loss to tell the cause?—it is the period when they marry. This is . . . notorious to all the world; and the few documents to the Commission under this head tend still further to establish the fact.

"It is well known by the returns, as well as from the evidence given to the district commissioners, that very few women work in the factories after marriage . . . an inspection of the tables will at once satisfy us that, if we are to search in the registers for the names of these females, it must be in the marriage registers, and not in the registers of the dead."[10]

One of the objections made in 1833 to the limitation of the labour of children in cotton mills had in fact been that it would encourage married women to become employed. The Commissioners, in their Report on the Employment of Children in Factories, commented: "By many others it was stated that the restriction of the hours of infant labour would compel the mothers of families to work in the mills; a consequence which is much deprecated as extremely mischievous."[11] Such evidence suggests that at least at that date the employment of married women was not as extensive as some factory reformers believed it to be.

To prove Ashley and his associates guilty of exaggeration is not to make any startlingly new contribution to the study of nineteenth-century history; yet it is of value here as a caution against too readily accepting contemporary assessments. In the absence of any official national statistics till 1901, it was all too easy to generalize from a few instances carefully selected to illustrate a particular point of view.

There were, however, several attempts to arrive at an

unbiased estimate of the position. In 1847, Mr. Horner, the factory inspector in the Manchester area, at the direction of the Home Secretary, Sir James Graham, visited nine cotton factories; he found that of all the operatives employed, 50% were females; that of these, nearly 70% were over eighteen; that 27% were married.[12]

Three years later a pamphlet circulated by the Association for the Establishment of Day Nurseries in Manchester and Salford[13] stated that 27·31% of the women employed in Manchester and Salford were married,[14] an estimate which seems to corroborate Horner's findings. The proportion of married women, however, was probably exaggerated, since the investigation was based on both cotton and silk mills and the statistics did not include young women known to be temporarily unemployed while some of the cotton mills were closed.

In the early 1860s, Baker, who succeeded Horner, gives us an assessment which does not appear to differ greatly from the two earlier estimates: "The proportions of married women and widows in factories is generally as follows. In the Irish factories 13·6% of the females are over sixteen years of age. In several English factories I have found the proportion more than double that, but I have scarcely sufficient data on which to found a general average."[15]

According to an estimate made ten years later, there would seem to have been a gradual increase in this proportion during the intervening period: Mundella, in the course of the debates on his Factories (Health of Women) Bill in 1873, claimed that one-third of the female operatives in the mills were married.[16] The possible reason for this increase, he suggested, was that "there was a great scarcity of women in Lancashire, and it was quite common when a married worker applied for employment to say: 'We will employ you, but you must bring your wife with you.' "[17]

The Associated Employers of Factory Labour in the Four Counties of Lancashire, York, Derby, and Chester disputed Mundella's figures, claiming that barely 20% of textile operatives were married. To avoid the possibility of State intervention, it was clearly to the Association's interest to underestimate the proportion of married operatives. Mundella's estimate, on the other hand, is supported by the Census returns for 1871, which showed a slight increase in the percentage of women employed who were over twenty years of age—an increase which one would normally expect to include at least some married women. In view of this and of the striking similarity of the results of previous investigations, which revealed a proportion of approximately 27·90% of women operatives married, it seems unlikely that in 1871 the proportion could actually have fallen by as much as 7·90%.

The Percentage of Women Cotton Operatives Who were either Married or Widowed in Seven Registration Districts of Lancashire in 1851

District	% Married	% Widowed
Blackburn	24·14	0·872
Standard error	2·331	0·506
Ashton	25·54	4·296
Standard error	2·130	0·991
Burnley	17·89	2·457
Standard error	2·270	0·917
Chorley	14·45	0·803
Standard error	2·340	0·593
Preston	29·39	2·703
Standard error	2·648	0·946
Oldham	45·51	2·469
Standard error	3·475	0·995
Haslingden	16·13	1·434
Standard error	2·404	0·771
Total	24·73	2·14
Standard error	0·922	0·873

Against the validity of the results of these contemporary investigations, it may justly be argued that they were, with the possible exception of the last, based on small samples, which might or might not have been typical of the whole cotton industry. Analysis of a random sample of 1851 Census household schedules of seven registration districts in Lancashire indicates, however, that they were remarkably accurate.

According to this sample, the average proportion of cotton operatives who were married or widowed in the selected districts was 26·87% (roughly 40,720 women). Since these seven districts appear to have been the main centres of women's employment in the industry (there was scarcely any cotton manufacture in five of the remaining nineteen registration districts of Lancashire— less than 1·00% of all women over twenty years of age were so employed in these districts), it seems reasonable to suppose that the average proportion of operatives who were married in the districts covered by our sample may be taken to be typical of the Lancashire cotton industry as a whole.

A further sample of the 1871 Census household schedules for the Blackburn registration district showed that in this area there had been an increase since 1851 in the proportion of women operatives who were married: in 1851 the proportion was 25·01%, in 1871 34·73%, i.e. in 1851 24·14% of the women operatives were married and 0·872% were widows, and in 1871 30·05% were married women and 4·68% widows.

The Percentage of Women Cotton Operatives Who were either Married or Widowed in the Blackburn Registration District of Lancashire in 1871

% Married	% Widowed
30·05	4·676
Standard error 1·873	Standard error 0·872

As there had also been a slight general increase in Lancashire over the same period (1851–71) in the percentage of all women over twenty years of age who were employed in cotton manufacture, from 57·40% in 1851 to 57·99% in 1871, it seems reasonable to assume that there had been an increase throughout the county in the proportion of women operatives who were married— which would tend to support Mundella's statement.

The occupational tables of the 1881 and 1891 Census do not show the age-structure of particular industries, hence it is difficult to make even a rough estimate for the last three decades of the century of the proportion of women operatives who were married or widowed. But the 1901 Census, distinguishing for the first time between unmarried and married or widowed operatives, showed that the proportion of these latter must have decreased at some date since 1871 to 24·48% (although the actual number had increased to approximately 68,556). This decrease must almost certainly have taken place between 1891–1901, since during the twenty years 1871–91 the total number of women engaged in the Lancashire cotton industry had increased by 9·04% between 1871 and 1881 and by 11·1% between 1881 and 1891. Since the increase of married women's employment in the mills in 1871 was ascribed to the shortage of other female labour,[18] it hardly seems likely that subsequent increases of this magnitude in the total female labour force could have taken place unless a higher proportion of married women were employed.

This hypothesis gains some support from the fact that when the total number of women employed in the cotton industry rose by 11·9% between 1901 and 1911, there was an increase in the proportion of married women employed which was not entirely to be accounted for by an increased rate of marriage among the female operatives.[19]

So far we have only tried to establish the true proportion of women operatives who were married for the middle and later years of the Victorian era. What of the earlier years?

We have seen that Ashley was convinced that this proportion was rapidly increasing, and though he himself undoubtedly thought of this as an increase from a high to an even higher percentage—in which he was mistaken—it is clear that there was an appreciable increase if we take as our criterion the proportion of women operatives over twenty years of age.

Rickard's returns for 1835 show 41·11% of women cotton operatives to be over twenty years of age, the Census returns for 1841, 42·98%. During the next ten years the age structure of the industry changed markedly; the 1851 Census gives a figure of 57·40%.

For this date we have more precise information as, according to the results of the analysis of our random sample, 26% of the total female labour force of the cotton mills were either married or widowed.

During the next ten years, in view of a very slight decrease in the percentage of women over twenty years of age employed in the Lancashire cotton industry, there might well have been a corresponding decrease in the proportion of married women employed. The Census tables show a decrease from 57·4% in 1851 to 57·2% in 1861 in the proportion of women over twenty years so employed.

This fall was more than compensated for in the next decade, by the end of which the proportion of women operatives married or widowed was about 33·33%.

In all probability the proportion continued to increase gradually until the 1890s, during which it declined until, in 1901, only 24% of the women in the Lancashire mills were married or widowed. It may be that this decline dated from about 1895, from which date till 1901 the Registrar-General annually recorded a net decrease in the total number of women employed in the cotton mills.

After 1901, however, the proportion of married

women and widows at work in the industry once more gradually rose.[20]

It has been necessary to devote considerable space to the investigation of the true proportion of married women employed in the cotton industry, in view of the startling nature of many contemporary allegations concerning the effects of their daily absence at the mill, which we shall have to discuss in subsequent chapters.

Moreover, the number and proportion of married women employed in the cotton industry has a peculiar significance. As Miss Anderson's comments indicate, no nineteenth-century factory industry recruited married women on so large a scale as did the textile industries, of which the cotton industry was numerically by far the most important. It is therefore understandable that the Victorians should have devoted so much attention to investigating the implications of married women's employment in that particular industry. It is important that we ourselves, however, should not forget that there are other areas and industries where married women were commonly employed away from home, even if not in such large numbers as Lancashire.

Intent on revealing the social consequences of their employment in the new cotton mills, Victorian commentators were apt to forget that married women were still employed away from home in agriculture, as they had been for centuries before the rise of the factory system. Unfortunately, it is virtually impossible to calculate their number in the Victorian period because of the equivocal manner in which women are described on the Census schedules. The same difficulty does not arise, however, with regard to the Staffordshire pottery industry, which afforded employment to many hundred wives and mothers.

In this particular industry, women were unimportant until the introduction of machinery after 1845. By that date men had begun to fear the competition of female labour, and "the pottery unions were expostulating with women employed for the first time on the new flat-press machinery; and with the widespread use of machinery, the percentage of women employed rose steadily".[21] The following table is based on figures published in the relevant Census reports and compares the proportion of women aged twenty years or more who were engaged in cotton manufacture in Lancashire with the proportion of women of the same age engaged in the manufacture of earthenware in Staffordshire at the same dates:

Date	Percentage of all women engaged in cotton manufacture aged twenty years and above	Percentage of all women engaged in the manufacture of earthenware aged twenty years and above
1851	57·40	52·30
1861	57·29	53·89
1871	57·99	54·76

In view of increases of 12·73% between 1871 and 1881, of 22·10% between 1881 and 1891, and 12·4% between 1891 and 1901 in the total number of women of all ages employed in the Staffordshire potteries, and also of the increasing restrictions on the employment of juvenile labour, it seems reasonable to suppose that the proportion of women aged twenty years and more continued to rise till the end of our period (and with it, almost inevitably, the proportion of married women employed[22]) until in 1901 29%—a higher proportion, though a smaller number (6,159), than in the Lancashire cotton industry—were married or widowed.

An analysis, similar to that for the Lancashire districts, of a sample of the 1851 Census schedules for the registration district of Stoke shows that at that date 37·15% (5,151) of the women engaged in the manufacture of earthenware in this district were married or widowed. This figure certainly exaggerates the true proportion of such women employed in the industry as a whole, since a far higher proportion of women over twenty years of age were engaged in the potteries of the Stoke district than of the other registration district of Staffordshire in which the industry was being developed. Nevertheless, it serves as a salutary reminder that the wives and mothers of Lancashire were not unique in "going abroad to work", and indicates the necessity for us to compare their experiences with those of married women engaged in other factory industries, such as the Staffordshire potteries, and, equally important, with those of married women employed in agriculture.

CHAPTER III

THE LENGTH OF THE WIFE'S ABSENCE

WHILST their middle and upper class contemporaries were heatedly discussing how great a proportion of the female working population they constituted, the working-class wives were themselves inevitably more concerned with the problem of combining their two roles of wage-earner and housewife. How successful they could be in solving this problem naturally depended to some extent on how much, or how little, time these women had to devote to their homes and families after they had discharged their obligations to their employers.

The length of the working day was first regulated in the textile industry—first in cotton and later in all branches of textile manufacture. Even in textile mills, however, nothing was done until 1844 to regulate the hours of women as such. Up to 1841, the factory reformers scarcely alluded to the hours of women operatives: the Ten Hours' movement based its appeal on the overworking of young children.[1]

The hours women worked were often excessively long. In the course of the Ten Hours' debate Lord Ashley refers to Mr. Horner's[2] report for October 1843: "I recently investigated a case in Manchester, in a large mill, where they are now employing workers above eighteen years of age . . . from 5.30 a.m. till eight o'clock at night, with no cessation from work except a quarter of an hour for breakfast and three-quarters of an hour for dinner; so that these persons, having to be out of bed for five o'clock in the morning and not getting home till half-past eight o'clock at night, may fairly be said to labour fifteen hours and a half out of the twenty-four."[3]

Mr. Saunders, another factory inspector, reports in January 1844: "There are among them females who have been employed for some weeks, with one interval of only a few days, from six o'clock in the morning till twelve o'clock at night, with less than two hours off for meals, thus giving them for five nights in the week, six hours out of its twenty-four to go to and from their homes and to obtain rest in bed. . . . A vast majority of the persons employed at night and for long periods during the day are females; their labour is cheaper and they are more easily induced to undergo severe bodily fatigue than men."[4]

What these hours implied for the married woman is best expressed by Mr. Ferrand, who quotes a statement on the organization of the day of the married operative: "Half an hour to dress and suckle her infant and carry it out to nurse; one hour for household duties before leaving home; half an hour for actually travelling to the mill; twelve hours' actual labour; one and a half hours for meals; half an hour for returning home at night; one and a half hours for household duties and preparing for bed, leaving six and a half hours for recreation, seeing and visiting friends and sleep; and in winter, when it is dark, half an hour extra time on the road to the mill and half an hour extra on the road home from the mill."[5]

After 1833, when the "Short Timers" saw that the reduction in the hours of labour of children had not affected the hours of labour of adults, they openly demanded a ten-hour regulation of all factory labour. Even so, there was as yet no specific demand that the hours of work of women operatives should be regulated.

In 1841, however, a Tory Government was returned to power of which great things were expected by the "Short Timers". In the West Riding and several of the manufacturing towns, the elections were fought entirely on factory questions. But it soon became clear that the Tories had only appeared to favour factory legislation to gain support in some of the constituencies; and Ashley, when asked to join Peel's Government, refused on the ground that "the Prime Minister's opinions on factory legislation have not yet matured".[6]

Once more the Short Time committees were stirred into activity, and the West Riding sent a deputation to London to wait on Peel and other Members. They had meetings with Sir James Graham, the Home Secretary, and with Gladstone and others. It was in their Report, issued on their return home, that for the first time there was a demand for the special restriction of women's labour. The "Short Timers" had realized that their demand for a ten-hour day for all would, in effect, increase the working hours of children, which, under the 1833 Act, were to be no more than eight a day or forty-eight a week. Thus they now focused their attention on limiting the hours of women, and accordingly, for the next six years, "the battle for the limitation of the hours of adults in general was fought from behind the women's petticoats".[7]

The deputation from Yorkshire contended that a ten-hour day for all persons between thirteen and twenty-one was more urgent than ever because of the immense number of women working in factories. Behind this there seems also to have been lurking the fear that women were gradually displacing men, for the deputation pressed for the gradual withdrawal of all females from the factories on the ground that "the home, its cares and employments, is the woman's true sphere".

Gladstone, with whom the deputation discussed this, clearly agreed with the last view. He expressed sympathy for the fixing of a higher age for the commencement of what he called "female infant labour"; but, more interesting for us, he also expressed sympathy for the limitation of the number of women in proportion to the number of men employed in one factory and the prohibition of employment of married women during the lifetime of their husbands.[8]

The reward for the manœuvres of the "Short Timers" both in and out of Parliament was the first statutory regulation of the hours of work for women. By the Factory Act of 1844 (7 & 8 Vict., c. 15) the hours of work of women and young persons under eighteen were limited to twelve a day. They were to be worked between 5.30 a.m. and 8.30 p.m., as all night work was prohibited for the operatives affected by the Act.

The stipulation that the work was to be confined to within these particular hours constituted a nominal defeat for the "Short Timers", as Ashley had moved at one stage of the debates on the Bill, and had indeed carried by a majority of nine votes, a motion that the hours between which work should take place should be 6 a.m. and 6 p.m.: this would, in effect, have meant a ten-and-a-half-hour day for the operatives and thus have almost satisfied the demands of the Ten Hours movement. Sir James Graham, however, had reopened the debate on this issue and had defeated Ashley by two votes. Three years later, after several attempts to introduce amending legislation, the Ten Hours movement triumphed: in 1847, by 10 & 11 Victoria, c. 29, the hours of women and children were limited to ten a day, although, for reasons we must presently discuss, the limitation was not effective till 1851.

Most married women operatives had no hesitation in stating their preference for the shorter day. A married weaver remarked to Horner: "I get 10s. with ten hours; and would get 12s. with twelve hours. I prefer ten hours. I have my family and house to look after, and I can go to bed sooner than I used to. I have sometimes been up twenty hours out of the twenty-four."[9]

Horner himself expressed the regret that in some factories "since the shortening of the hours began, they commence at eight o'clock in the morning and continue till seven in the evening, with an interval of one hour for dinner. It is much to be regretted that this change should be made. Until now it has been the almost universal custom to begin work at six in the morning, and in the summer, often at 5.30 a.m. The people are habituated to early rising, and, I believe, would rather do so than lie in bed: they cannot turn to much good any time before going to work: but there are many sources of profit and enjoyment open to them which leisure in the evening would enable them to take advantage of."[10]

Of operatives in general, Horner's criticism was valid: but with regard to married women in particular, the objection is more apparent than real; for the extra hour's freedom from the mill, whether in the morning or the evening, seems to have been almost exclusively devoted to the better care of their homes and families—scrubbing floors is just as easily accomplished in the early morning as at night.

In the ability of the manufacturer to employ women and young persons for any ten hours between 5.30 a.m. and 8.30 p.m. there lay a more serious difficulty, for there were many indications that manufacturers were evading the regulations affecting this class of operative. This they were able to do, as none of the Factory Acts operating at that time limited the hours of work of men over eighteen years of age, and none reduced the length of the working day. It was thus easy for unscrupulous employers to work men for long hours with relays of women to assist them. Where this system was adopted, the hours the women worked were far more than ten a day.[11]

Horner reported in 1849 that in his district (the Manchester district) 114 mills were working women and young persons by shifts. In general, the time of work extended to thirteen and a half hours, from 6 to 7.30, with one and a half hours off for meals, but in some

cases amounting to fifteen hours from 5.30 a.m. to
8.30 p.m. with the same allowance for meals.[12]

A working man wrote to Mr. Sub-Inspector Trimmer:
"If the system must be carried out, the Ten Hours Bill
will be a complete humbug: as many of the women and
children live a long way from the mill, it takes them on
an average one hour to go home and come back again.
I always thought they must work the ten hours between
six and six, so that they might have the night to look
after their domestic affairs, and the proper bringing up
of their children, and that the young might be enabled
to attend school, etc., but I defy any of them to do so
under this system. Besides, what opportunities it affords
to the masters to overwork them; and I defy any
inspector, let him be ever so vigilant, to detect the master
if he does so. An instance of how it will puzzle you, or
any other inspector: one of the overlookers has a lad
who works ten hours in the spinning room and works
the other hours in the weaving room. Now how can you
detect such cases? You cannot, so long as they do not
all give over working at the one time."[13]

It had generally been thought that Section 26 of the
1844 Factory Act, which stated that "the number of
hours shall be reckoned from the time when any child
or young person shall first begin to work in the morning
in such factories", had met this point. From 1844 to
1847 it had, indeed, worked fairly well, but when, in
1847, the ten-hour regulation was enforced, employers
were quick to discover that this clause in the 1844 Act
(which was not amended by the later Act) did not
altogether preclude a relay system.[14] Thus, even with the
widespread depression in Lancashire, the system was
reintroduced.[15]

With the revival of trade in 1849, the relay system
spread. In view of this, Horner brought a test case before
the Court of Exchequer.[16] Baron Parke, giving judgment,
declared that the working of Section 26 of the 1844
Factory Act was not in fact sufficiently stringent to carry

into effect what the court "strongly conjectured" was the intention of the legislature.

The Short Time committees therefore renewed their agitation for statutory regulation of the normal working day. On 14th March 1850 Ashley moved a clause "to introduce a Bill that would carry into effect what had been the intention of Parliament in 1844".[17] As phrased by him, the Bill would have been ineffective: it was thus withdrawn, and Grey introduced a Government Bill to limit the normal working day to the hours of 6 a.m. to 6 p.m. with one and a half hours for meals, and enacting that work should cease for the day at 2 p.m. on Saturdays.[18]

Of this Act Horner wrote: "The great object sought for has been obtained; for young persons and women now have at their disposal a reasonable portion of each day for the purposes of rest, domestic duties, mental improvement, and recreation by the cessation of their work at an early hour in the evening. But one of the greatest boons which the Act of last Session conferred on the working people is the cessation of labour on Saturday afternoon at two o'clock; two and a half hours' continuous time taken off that day from what could be worked under the Ten Hours Act being more valuable to the work people than five separate half-hours from 5.30 to 6 in the evening on to the other days of the week."[19]

Though the manufacturers, as a whole, at first observed the new restrictions, it was not long before they resorted to what the inspectors described as "nibbling". Horner reports: "From the sub-inspectors' reports and from my own observation, I can state that the chief enactments of the law have been found in general to be well observed, with the exception of many encroachments on time beyond the legal hours of work. This is often done by keeping the children, young persons, and women in the mill to clean the machinery during part of the meal times and on Saturdays after two o'clock in place of that work being done within the restricted time, as in the case of well-regulated mills. In other instances, the work is not done to such an extent at any one time as would be sure to excite the attention of neighbours who are obeying the law but, by small instalments, at the times of the day for the commencing and the closing of work, and for meals, each of which is trifling in amount and externally inappreciable but, taken together, amount to so much as to expose the honest mill-owner to very unfair competition."[20]

By the 1870s it was being claimed that, even where mill-owners observed the regulations, ten and a half hours' labour a day was too much for women operatives. In 1873, Bridges and Holmes, reporting to the Local Government Board on "The Proposed Changes in the Hours and Ages of those Employed in Textile Factories", drew attention to the fact that since 1847 there had been a tendency (a) for each operative to be in charge of a greater amount of machinery, (b) for machinery to be driven at a greater speed, and (c) for a development of the practice of giving the overlooker or foreman a premium on the amount of work done. Such conditions, they maintained, increased the strain of work on women generally; and they recommended that the number of hours per week of women's labour should be reduced to fifty-four.[21]

Virtually nothing was done in response to this recommendation: the Factory Act passed the following year did indeed deduct an additional half-hour a day from the statutory hours of work for meals and rest, but the "normal working day" was still left at twelve hours.

An interesting provision in the Act is that it permitted the working day to begin at seven o'clock in the morning instead of six o'clock. Little advantage was taken of this provision by the operatives themselves. Baker reported that "in Lancashire, of 1,053 textile factories, 632 are working from 6 a.m. to 6 p.m., 365 from 6.30 a.m. to 6.30 p.m., and only 7 from 7 a.m. to 7 p.m." "The masters", he says, "determined that work should begin at 6.30 in order to let the women have a longer time in bed, and a longer time to take care of their children before breakfast and leave off at six at night; but there was hardly anyone that would do it, although they [the manufacturers] said everything they possibly could to induce them. One gentleman wrote to me and said, 'The ladies and gentlemen of my establishment will not come to work at half-past six; they have all determined to come at six o'clock.' That was also particularly the case in Blackburn and Manchester, and I may say, all over the cotton districts."[22]

From 1850, then, to the end of our period the married textile operative was absent from her home from before six o'clock in the morning till after six o'clock at night— sometimes later if she was working for an unscrupulous employer. The longest break in the day was at dinner-time—usually 12.30 to 1.30: occasionally, in the larger mill towns, she was able to go home during her dinner-hour; but on the whole it seems that the proportion of women who lived near enough to the mill to be able to do this and thought it worthwhile was not very large.

It is important to realize how many families were affected by this long daily absence of the wife and mother. The analysis of our random sample[23] shows that in 1851 in the main cotton districts slightly fewer than one in three (30·02%) of all married women of all social classes were employed; and of these more than half (17·00%) were employed in cotton manufacture. Moreover, a certain number of married women recorded as "cotton hand-loom weavers" were actually working in factories, and not in their own homes.[24] Yet another 2·697% of the 30·02% of all married women occupied in these districts were employed in other branches of textile manufacture—silk, wool, worsted, and flax— where the hours of work were identical. Thus almost two in every three occupied married women, or nearly one in five of all married women in these districts, were textile operatives, of whom cotton operatives formed by far the largest single group.

Twenty years later, at least in the registration district of Blackburn, the number of families affected by the employment of married women in the mills appears to have increased.[25] In all probability, since there was, between 1851 and 1871, a general increase in the proportion of women living in Lancashire of over twenty years of age who were engaged in cotton textiles, this experience was shared by the county as a whole. In fact, it was most likely typical for the following two decades as well, since during those years there was a general increase in the proportion of women of all ages living in Lancashire engaged in the mills[26]—a trend which was reversed in the following ten years.[27]

It is interesting, incidentally, that the proportion of families "desolated" in Staffordshire by the absence of the wife and mother in the main local industry was very nearly as great as the proportion affected by married women's employment in the Lancashire cotton mills.[28] And in the potteries, no attempt was made to limit the number of hours women worked till 1864, when the ten-and-a-half-hour day prevailing for women operatives in the cotton mills was imposed in this industry also.

Whilst the hours of work in many other factories and workshops where married women were reported to be at work—such as bleaching and dyeing works, lace works, and nailing "shops"—were also regulated by the series of statutes of 1860 to 1867, which established some sort of control over the hours of work in nearly all manufacturing industry, the married-woman cotton operative had certain advantages as regards hours of work over her counterpart in other "regulated" industries. For example, although the hours of work in women's workshops were nominally limited to ten and a half hours a day, the failure to introduce in the original statute of 1867 the principle of "the normal working day" meant that until 1878—and, in the case of workshops where no child or young person was employed, until 1891—the limitation was not effective.

The Factory Act of 1874 relating to textile industries reduced the working day in the mills to ten hours, thus placing the women cotton operatives in an even more advantageous position compared to the other women factory workers.

But perhaps their greatest advantage, which they had possessed since 1850, was that they had Saturday afternoon completely free from work, whereas women employed in regulated non-textile factories and workshops might legally be asked to work eight hours on that day, with one and a half hours off for meals, though, by the beginning of the twentieth century, in many of the non-textile factories, employers had adopted the practice of releasing the women at 2 p.m.[29]

Yet with all her advantages in respect of the length of the day she might herself be expected to work, the married woman cotton operative still shared with married women working in other factories and workshops the basic problem of how to reconcile the demands of her employer with those of her husband and home.

Reviewing the hours of work prevailing in the cotton industry in 1844, Ashley demanded: "Where, sir, under these conditions are the possibilities of domestic life? How can its obligations be fulfilled? Regard the woman as a wife and mother—how can she accomplish any portion of her calling? And if she cannot do that which Providence has assigned to her, what must be the effect on the whole surface of society?"[30]

To this problem we must now turn.

PART II

THE PROBLEM CONSIDERED

CHAPTER IV

THE EFFECT ON THE
AGE OF MARRIAGE

OF the many consequences alleged to be the inevitable result of offering employment to women after marriage, one of the least disputed was that the practice encouraged early ·marriage. It was claimed, for example, that in the factory districts "it often occurs that the united ages of married couples do not exceed thirty-four years; and a very considerable proportion of our female population are mothers before they have completed their seventeenth year".[1] The result was a high rate of infant mortality among the operatives' children and a deplorably low standard of household management. No woman operative was deemed capable, at seventeen years of age, of bearing a live and healthy child, and ". . . the evil consequences of early marriages are not confined to the birth of the child. The judgment and experience necessary for the economical management of household affairs are seldom acquired before the age of twenty-one; and in no department of domestic duty does the young mother of sixteen or seventeen fail more egregiously than in the treatment and bringing up of her children. . . ."[2]

The causes of such marriages were, to the Victorian mind, only too obvious. Partly they were thought to be the outcome of the "roving and independent cast of mind"[3] of the mill girls, who, self-supporting and thus independent of parental control and advice to a degree unknown in middle and upper class families,[4] might well be expected to commit such folly, "being too little

35

aware of their deficiencies" as potential housewives.[5] But more especially were they thought to be directly attributable to the cupidity of the working-class man. "I have alluded before", wrote Mr. Baker, a factory inspector, "to the early marriages of factory girls; and, without wishing to be censorious, no doubt the large wages which these girls of seventeen and eighteen years of age receive make them to be thought desirable as wives by young men who have no very great desire to work hard themselves. In the cotton districts of this country there were in 1860 399,992 power looms; and as the rate of minding four looms varies from 15s. to 24s. per week, for three looms 14s. to 16s., and for two looms 10s. to 12s., the amount of the weekly earnings of these young women becomes an absolute independence. Hence their early disregard of their parents and parental home, which is to be lamented; and hence too the early possession of homes of their own before they have been instructed in the duties of the homes they have left."[6]

There was commonly thought to be an essential connexion between the employment of the wife and the idleness of the husband. For example, in a paper read to the National Association for the Promotion of Social Science in 1868 on "The Social Results of the Employment of Girls and Women in Factories", the view Baker had expressed in his report as factory inspector was reiterated to a wider public:

"From the same cause—namely, high wages—many very early and improvident marriages take place. It is not an uncommon thing at all, because she can keep him without working, for a man to propose to a factory worker and be accepted. She works for the home afterwards and he minds it. Why should he work when her wages are enough for both? So he reasons, and so she continues to work."[7]

How valid this contention was we shall need to consider later, since it has an obvious bearing on the causes of married women's employment. At this point we shall confine ourselves to examining such evidence as was adduced purporting to prove the general thesis that not only was the age of marriage in factory districts low, but that it was so because women were able to continue in employment after marriage.

In 1833, in evidence to the Royal Commission on the Employment of Children in Factories, it was stated that, "in a general way", factory men and women marry before they are twenty years of age;[8] and Playfair, in 1845, quotes the evidence of Dr. Strange of Ashton, who states: "It is . . . no uncommon thing to meet with married females of fifteen years of age. . . ."[9]

Statements such as these, based on personal experience, it is virtually impossible to prove or disprove. Others of the same opinion, however, determined to prove their case beyond doubt, produced figures and tables extracted from the Census reports. These figures, it was claimed, not only showed that in areas such as Lancashire where there was large-scale employment of married women in the major local industry, the operatives actually did marry earlier than the rest of the community, but also justified Dr. Strange's contention that many of them married by the time they were fifteen years of age. Unfortunately, the critics' indignation appears to have made them oblivious to the correct interpretation of the Census material. R. Arthur Arnold, for example, in a paper read to the National Association for the Promotion of Social Science, adduced the following statistical evidence: "As might be expected where labour is in such great demand, juvenile marriages [in Lancashire] are more common than in any other of the English counties. The Census returns of 1861 show that among the population of Bolton, 45 husbands and 172 wives were coupled at the early age of '15 and under'; in Burnley, there were 51 husbands and 147 wives; in Stockport 59 husbands and 179 wives in the same category."[10]

This evidence is entirely valueless, since the figures

are not related to the total number of people living in
the age group to which they are alleged to refer, nor is
comparison made with similar data for other districts.
On the other hand, one of the factory inspectors, in a
half-yearly report, produced an elaborate table (also
based on the 1861 Census figures) which was supposed
to establish conclusively the truth of these assertions
regarding the influence of married women's work on
the age of marriage. It is characteristic of the interest of
the members of the N.A.P.S.Sc. in Government publications—however routine—that this table should have
been discussed in yet another paper read before the same
Annual Congress. W. D. Husband, F.R.C.S., refers to
"A tabular statement of Mr. Baker, factory inspector,
whose district included Ireland, Chester, Warwick, and
Leicester", claiming that it showed "in the cotton, silk,
iron and pottery district" (in all of which there were
opportunities for women to continue in employment
after marriage) "early marriages of boys and girls, but
more especially the latter, are exceedingly numerous,
whilst in agricultural districts they are comparatively
rare".[11]

It so happens that there is not the slightest justification
for such a deduction from these figures, for the simple
reason that the numbers quoted are not of people married
under fifteen years of age, but of marriages between
fifteen and twenty years of age. It is quite impossible to
ascertain from the 1861 Census, or from any of the other
Census returns of our period, the number of people
married under fifteen years of age, as the Registrar-
General specifically states in a footnote to each table concerning the "Civil Condition of the People" in each
district that the number of people married or widowed at
this age is so small that they are included in the numbers
of people married between fifteen and twenty years of
age. Furthermore, the number of married people described by Baker as of between fifteen and twenty years
of age is in fact the number of married people recorded

in the 1861 Census as aged between twenty to twenty-five years of age.

Another curious feature of this table is that Baker's "centesimal proportions" of men and women married in the lower age group—incorrectly styled by him "minus fifteen years of age"—are calculated in an orthodox manner on the total number of men and women living in the various districts between fifteen and twenty years of age; but the percentages of men and women in the higher age group, which should be headed "twenty to twenty-five years of age", are also calculated on the number of men and women living between fifteen and twenty years of age—an unorthodox procedure, to say no more.

The Centesimal Proportions of Marriage by Persons under Fifteen Years of Age, and between Fifteen and Twenty Years of Age; and of Widows of All Ages in Certain Registration Districts of Lancashire and Staffordshire compared with the Same Proportions in Agricultural Districts of Devonshire and Hertfordshire (1861)[12]

Place	Population 1861*	Married 15 years and under Head	Married 15 years and under Wife	Centesimal Proportion	Married 15-20 years Head	Married 15-20 years Wife	Centesimal Proportion	Widowed Male	Widowed Female	Centesimal Proportion	Main Industry
Stockport	94,360	59	179	0·2	1,285	1,815	3·2	1,789	3,328	4·0	Cotton
Wigan	94,561	28	186	0·2	1,290	1,927	3·4	1,648	2,854	3·0	
Bolton	130,269	45	172	0·1	1,682	2,305	3·4	2,203	4,529	3·5	
Bury	101,135	28	108	0·1	1,230	1,746	2·9	1,787	3,299	3·2	
Burnley	79,595	51	147	0·2	1,060	1,381	3·2	1,380	2,189	2·8	
Macclesfield	61,543	23	75	0·1	534	889	2·3	1,366	2,289	3·7	Silk
Congleton	34,328	12	65	0·2	383	696	3·1	629	1,053	3·0	
Wolverhampton	126,902	31	252	0·2	1,519	2,572	3·2	1,880	3,363	2·6	Iron
Wolstanton Stoke	125,664	56	323	0·2	1,938	3,008	3·9	1,966	3,878	3·0	Pottery
Totnes Stoke Damerel South Molton Bideford Holsworthy	130,257	26	167	0·1	999	1,815	2·1	2,385	5,515	5·2	Agriculture (Devon)
Ware Bishop's Stortford Royston Hitchin Hertford Hatfield St. Albans Watford	177,452	28	144	0·09	1,470	2,337	2·0	3,634	6,442	3·6	Agriculture (Hertford)

* I.e. the total population aged fifteen to twenty years.

Even Baker's own calculations, however, show that the proportion of men and women married in the lower age group in Bolton, Bury, and Macclesfield, which constitute one-third of the districts he gives as illustrating the effects of the industrial employment of women on the age of marriage, is no larger than the group of Devonshire agricultural districts; and only slightly higher than the group of Hertfordshire agricultural districts.

If the percentage of married men and women of between fifteen and twenty years of age in different counties and districts are calculated correctly from the Census returns,[13] it will be found that throughout the nineteenth century the proportion of people married and widowed in the population of Lancashire between fifteen and twenty years of age was in fact above the proportion prevailing in England and Wales throughout our period. As regards Staffordshire, which also showed an excessive proportion of young people married or widowed at all but one of the Census dates, the result is clearly influenced by the very high proportion of such marriages in the registration district of Stoke, where there were many women employed after marriage in the pottery industry. There is also support for the view that the proportion of such marriages in agricultural counties was smaller than in the country as a whole, and noticeably smaller than in counties which were, on the whole, industrial. But these results may or may not have been connected with the possibilities of the employment of women after marriage, for the interesting fact that emerges from an examination of the Census figures is that the county which consistently showed the highest proportion of young people married was Durham, where the major industry of mining offered scarcely any employment to women, married or unmarried—a result which corroborates the statement made by one of the Poor Law Commissioners in 1834 that "miners assumed the most important office of manhood at the earliest age

at which nature and passion prompted".[14] In Bedfordshire and Buckinghamshire, where married women
could augment the family income by working in the
straw plait and lace-making industries of these two
counties, the proportion of such marriages only exceeded
the proportion for England and Wales once—in 1851.

If similar calculations are made for each separate
registration district of Lancashire from the Census
returns of 1861, in which Baker showed such an interest,
and from the returns of the following Census in 1871, the
districts showing the highest proportion of young married people are not necessarily the centres of the cotton
industry. In 1861, Warrington, where the employment
of women in cotton was negligible and where there was
no other particular industry employing women, had the
highest proportion of persons married at an early age;
moreover, the cotton district of Bury showed a lower
proportion of such marriages than Ulverston: ten years
later, the main cotton districts still failed to compare
unfavourably with Liverpool, Prescot, Wigan, Warrington, Salford, and Manchester. The country districts do
indeed show a lower proportion of early marriages than
was average for Lancashire; but so do the cotton districts, Chorley, Clitheroe, and Bolton; and in 1871
Chorley and Haslingden (one of the main cotton districts) had a proportion of such marriages less than the
average for the county as a whole. When the proportion
of women married and widowed is considered separately,
several of the main cotton districts had a proportion less
than the average for England and Wales at these dates;
and the districts with the largest excesses were not the
centres of the textile industry.

As regards marriages of men and women between
twenty and twenty-five years of age, Durham continued
to show a higher proportion than Lancashire, though
Staffordshire showed the highest proportion at each
Census.[6]

In the districts of Lancashire itself, in 1861 Blackburn showed the highest proportion and Oldham the next highest; this might appear to indicate that marriage between these ages was more common in cotton districts than elsewhere in Lancashire, yet Wigan and Warrington showed a proportion not much less than Oldham: Prescot, with little industry of any kind, still ranked among the highest proportion—a distinction it retained in 1871.

Such calculations thus fail to prove that the industrial employment of women was directly responsible for early marriages: certainly they do not substantiate Arnold's claim that there was a larger proportion of such marriages in Lancashire than in any other county.

It may be argued that calculations such as these could never, by their very nature, be used to prove Baker's original contention, since they make no allowance whatsoever for class structure—a serious defect, since it was perfectly well known that the age of marriage amongst the working classes was lower than amongst the middle and upper classes.

In the reports of the 1833 Factory Commissioners the early age of marriage of the lower classes had been a matter for comment;[15] and in evidence to the Health of Towns Commission some ten years later it had been specifically stated that "it must be borne in mind that the poorer classes usually marry and have families at an earlier age than among the middle and upper classes, the great majority at least of women being married at twenty".[16] The average age at marriage of spinsters at this time, according to the Registrar-General, was 24·3 years.[17]

Again, in 1840, referring to the age of men in particular, Commissioner Hickson reported that "marriages are always later among the middle classes than among the working classes; and latest of all, perhaps, amongst the most educated part of the community, those who follow the law".[18] Nor did this comment cease to be true as the century progressed. In 1886 the Registrar-General commented on "the very early ages at which working men undertake the experience of marriage, and how much later the prudent classes venture to do so".[19] Clearly, such a practice would have obvious repercussions on the combined age at marriage of husband and wife.

It is clear that an excess of people married between fifteen and twenty years of age in a given population might be merely a reflection of the class structure of the district—a possibility which was never investigated by Baker and those who shared his views.

They might possibly have tried to argue that, although it was true that the working classes as a whole married earlier than the upper and middle classes, the factory operatives married at an earlier age than was general among their own class in the same district. In fact, however, such an argument and the evidence to support it was never produced: the comparison, where it was made, was always with *the other classes* in the same district.

There is little evidence from other sources. Such as it is, it fails to show that the factory women married any earlier than other women in their own station of life.

In Dr. Mitchell's report to the Factory Commissioners is printed a table giving the age at marriage of 110 women workers from textile factories in Catrine, Ayrshire, and of 109 other women of the same district.[20]

The average age at marriage of women employed in the textile factories previous to marriage was 23·68 years and for those not so employed 22·61 years.

The interesting point to note is that the lower age at marriage in the second class of women was due to the fact that, whereas forty-one of their number married between sixteen and twenty-one years of age, only twenty-eight of the women employed in factories previous to marriage had done so.

Age at marriage	Women who worked in factories	Women who did not work in factories
16	–	3
17	4	4
18	3	14
19	11	7
20	10	13
21	13	12
22	8	9
23	17	8
24	9	9
25	5	5
26	4	9
27	7	3
28	2	2
29	1	2
30	7	2
31	–	1
32	3	2
33	1	–
34	3	–
35	–	2
36	1	1
37	–	–
38	1	1
	110	109

In the same report, the age at marriage of 130 women workers in the Staffordshire pottery industry is given.[21] The average age at marriage of these women is 20·82 years. This is lower than the age of marriage of the women employed in the textile factories at Catrine and it is unfortunate that no comparative figures are given of the age at marriage of other women in Staffordshire not employed in the pottery industry prior to marriage, yet it is no lower than that stated to be usual among the working-class women generally.[22]

More than fifty years later, the Registrar-General, in

his Annual Reports for 1886 (when the average age at marriage of bachelors was 26·1 years and of spinsters 24·6 years), published the following table, based on the statistics relating to marriages contracted in the twelve months 1884–5:

Average Ages at Marriage of Bachelors and Spinsters in Occupational Groups, 1884-5[23]

Occupational group	Bachelors, years	Spinsters, years
Miners	24·06	22·46
Textile hands	24·38	23·43
Shoemakers and tailors . . .	24·92	24·31
Artisans	25·35	23·70
Labourers	25·56	23·66
Commercial clerks	26·25	24·43
Shopkeepers and shopmen .	26·67	24·22
Farmers and farmers' sons . .	29·23	26·91
Professional and independent class	31·22	26·40

It will be seen from this table that women in the textile hands occupational group married at much the same age as women in the other working class groups, with the notable exception of women in the mining group, who married earlier.

Since this table only refers to the experience of one year, it cannot, of course, be used as a basis for generalization. A later enquiry of a similar nature, however, connected with the 1911 Fertility Census, extended over a far longer period. Investigating the age at marriage of all women recorded as married in 1911 in various social classes and occupational groups, the earliest of which marriages took place in 1861, it was found that "generally speaking, the proportion of early marriages increased and of late marriages decreased as we descend the social scale: but miners marry particularly early, and textile workers later than the bulk of skilled artisans"[24]—a result which considerably modifies such conclusions as might be drawn from the Registrar's figures for 1884–5

and casts further doubt on the allegation we are considering.

Moreover, the results of the 1911 enquiry give added
point to an observation made many years before by
Commissioner Hickson. Writing of the potential earnings of women textile operatives, he declares: "I believe
it is to the interest of the community that every young
woman should have this in her power. She is not then
driven into an early marriage by the necessity of seeking
a home."[25]

Those whose opinions we have been assessing in this
chapter, coming from those sections of Victorian society
which judged a woman's social status by her relationship
to some man—be he her husband, father, or brother—
and her success in life by the degree of her success in the
marriage market in a world where "marriage was the
only provision for well-educated women of small
fortune their pleasantest preservative from want", seem
to have been oblivious to the fact that all their contemporaries might not share such views. They appear
to have entirely overlooked the fact that a girl capable of
supporting herself in tolerable comfort might not wish
to assume the burdens of marriage, still less the burden
of an indolent husband, at an early age.

The whole evidence on which the particular alleged
effect of married women's employment was based is
both insufficient and inconclusive: such statistical evidence as was adduced was both invalid and entirely
misleading. The impression given by the investigators in
this field is not merely that they were incompetent; and
not merely that they overestimated the extent of married
women's employment in the cotton industry, which most
certainly they did; but that they were also extremely
biased, judging the working classes by the rules of conduct of the middle and upper classes to which they themselves belonged, disregarding the fact that the conditions
and standards of life of these "two nations" were quite
dissimilar.

Thus, when we come to consider the alleged incompetence of the married woman operative as a wife and mother, it should be remembered that contemporary allegations that her incompetence in these roles was due to her premature marriage were both ill-founded and non-proven.

CHAPTER V

COTTON–MILL MORALITY

NINETEENTH-CENTURY accounts reveal with what
agitation of spirit the Victorians viewed the moral
consequences of the employment of women in factories.
The frequent and impassioned appeals for "the nearer
and more urgent concern of the governing and employing class" were almost exclusively based on evidence
relating to the woman cotton operative of Lancashire.
Their alleged lack of virtue and sense of shame was
deplored alike in Parliamentary debates, in Government Blue Books, in contemporary novels, and in
newspapers—media, for the most part, of middle and
upper class opinion.

The horror with which contemporary observers
viewed even the suggestion of unchastity in these
women reflected their attitude to sex in general, for
Victorian society, as they would have understood the
term, differed morally from that of the eighteenth
century and its aftermath in that it was accepted as
socially expedient that the institution of the family
should be the means of controlling sexual relations. To
this, however, should be added the major qualification,
"as far as women were concerned". Sexual irregularities
persisted, but they were driven underground; society
made special arrangements for the "different" and
"stronger" passions of men, but they were not mentioned
in conversation, still less blazoned forth in print. The
tacit acceptance of this double moral standard is
reflected in the words of Anthony Trollope's Mrs.
Wortle: "Anything wrong about a man was of little

moment; but anything about a woman . . . Oh dear!"
Social ostracism was the correct treatment for "fallen
women" when they attempted to make a claim on the
society responsible for their misfortunes. "It is useful.
It keeps women from going astray." But which women?
Mrs. Grundy epitomized the beliefs and attitudes of the
Victorian middle and upper classes in these matters:
whether she also epitomized the beliefs and attitudes of
the lower social strata was never considered.

Ashley proclaims of the moral effect of women's
labour in cotton mills: "You are poisoning the very
sources of order and happiness and virtue; you are
tearing up root and branch all relations of families to
one another; you are annulling, as it were, the institution
of domestic life decreed by Providence Himself, the
wisest and kindest of all earthly ordinancers, the main-
stay of peace and virtue and therein of national
security."[1]

Many were the allegations of profligacy and vice
among the unmarried operatives. In evidence to the
Royal Commission on the Employment of Children in
Factories, 1833, a witness claimed that "it would be no
strain on his conscience to say that three-quarters of the
girls between fourteen and twenty years of age were
unchaste".[2] In reports to the same Commission it can
also be read that "many of the women operatives had
natural children", and that "they did not seem to think
much about it".[3]

Both Mrs. Tonna and Mrs. Gaskell, in their novels,
represent the factory girl as being too low to be taken
into a lady's house as a servant. When Helen Fleetwood's
health was threatened by the confinement of the mill,
domestic service was thought of, unhappily too late, for
"there isn't a small tradesman's wife would not think
herself disgraced to take a factory girl as a servant".[4]
Because Bess in Mrs. Gaskell's North and South wanted
her younger sister to become a household servant, she
keeps her out of the mills. In Mary Barton the same

authoress makes John Barton unwilling to have his daughter in the mills, and she shows Esther going from the factory to become the mistress of a man who later brought her to a life on the streets.

This immorality was claimed to be rooted in the conditions of work in cotton mills. "We complain", writes one of the factory inspectors, "of the low state of morality amongst the working classes without remembering to what late hours the sexes are congregated together, and to what influences they are exposed in going to and returning from work, and that they are almost without moral supervision; and we will not see that female labour in factories, even though it be necessary, is at variance with domestic teaching, and that, for the sake of the wages it brings, everything that is good and holy in the female character is often sacrificed."[5]

It was maintained that these influences exerted a deleterious effect, not merely on the morals of the unmarried woman operative, but on those of the married woman as well. "Some of the married women were as bad as the girls", it was said;[6] and Gaskell claims of the operatives: "The chastity of marriage is but little known or exercised among them: husband and wife sin equally, and a habitual indifference to sexual rights is generated which adds one other item to the destruction of domestic habits."[7]

One cause of the immorality of cotton mills was said to be the seduction of the women operatives by their employers: "There is alive today (or was not long ago) not far from Manchester, an employer who makes seduction one of the conditions on which women may work at his establishment", writes Allen Clarke. "If they decline, they must quit. Single or married makes no difference, and the same rule applies to the girl of sixteen as to the woman of thirty. How many victims have fallen to this gentleman it would be difficult to estimate, but he has been enforcing this game for many

years. There are many employers like him; I knew two
or three myself some years ago."[8]

Alternatively, the overlooker was charged with de-
grading the married women under his supervision. It
was reported to the Royal Commission on Labour in
1893 that an overlooker in a Nelson mill had been dis-
missed for making immoral proposals to the married
women and using indecent language to the others—"an
offence not uncommon amongst men who have the
oversight of the female operatives of the mills".[9]

We may infer from such allegations of immorality that
observers considered that the morals of the cotton
operatives differed from those of the working classes in
general; and that the social and moral habits observed
by the women of the middle and upper classes were
observed by the majority of women of the working classes
also. If it could be proved that such was indeed the case,
if the morals of the women in the cotton textile districts
were in fact worse than the morals of women of the
same class elsewhere, and if the cause of this difference
was that alleged, then there would be some truth in the
allegation that conditions of women's employment in
the cotton mills were breaking up the moral structure
of the home in these areas: and this would be as true
of the special aspect of women's employment—the
employment of married women—which interests us
here as of women's employment in the cotton industry
generally.

National statistics cannot be used to throw light on
this problem. We shall have to refer in detail in a
subsequent chapter to the deficiencies of the registration
of births during our period: the registration of illegitimate births was even more unsatisfactory. Farr, in
evidence before the Select Committee on the Best Means
of Protecting Infants put out to Nurse, 1871, remarks of
the statistics relating to illegitimate births: "In Cumber-
land, for instance, the proportion [of illegitimate births
to legitimate births registered] is 104 in 1,000, and in

Norfolk 97 in 1,000 for the year 1869. These are the two highest counties in this particular year. The lowest is Middlesex, including all London; but it is rather lower in the parts of Middlesex out of London than the figure of 40 in 1,000, which applies to London. . . . Two explanations have been offered. The one is that in consequence of the number of prostitutes being considerable, prostitutes being often infertile, the proportion of births does not bear any proportion to the immorality in London; the other is that the registration of illegitimate children is defective. The mother has the power of representing the birth as legitimate when it is really illegitimate. She is not asked whether she has been married or whether she was married, or any other particulars. I proposed myself a more complete registration, and took the trouble of applying it in London, and by additional questions which I asked, I ascertained that many cases that would have otherwise escaped observation were really cases of illegitimate births. The Registration Act, if they make a false statement, subjects them to the same pains as perjury; but it would be difficult in some parts of London to convict informants of perjury."[10]

Similar explanations could be, and indeed were, offered of the low rate of illegitimate births in Lancashire, a densely populated area, which includes the large towns of Liverpool and Manchester, and yet showed for almost the whole of Victoria's reign a lower rate than was general for England and Wales as a whole.

Because of this, it is necessary to examine such other evidence relevant to this issue as can be adduced. It should, in the first place, be remembered that the allegations of Ashley and his friends concerning profligacy and vice in the cotton mills can be matched again and again by similar statements relating to other trades. Mr. Ward, in the Ten Hours debates, demanded: "When the noble lord, the Member for Dorsetshire asked for interference in the case of factory labourers, had he enquired into the case of the female nailors, employed at Sedgely and Birmingham, of whom his own Commissioners had said that 'morality was nothing among them; in fact, that they had no morals at all'. Look at the lace-making by hand in Nottinghamshire and Bedfordshire, look at the weavers in Bethnal Green and Spitalfield, look at the maids of all work in London and elsewhere."[11] We might also add, "Look at the women employed in the potteries in North Stafford-shire", where it was claimed that the throwing-rooms were "emporiums of profligacy", and "the young girls have no sense of the sin of whoredom or of the bestiality of uncleanliness".[12]

Ashley never compared the morals of the cotton operatives with those of women employed in agriculture; yet of these last we may read: "I remark also a particular deficiency in the feelings of the women as to chastity; in many instances they seem hardly to comprehend or value it as a virtue."[13] The immorality of the agricul-tural "gangs" was proverbial; "the immorality caused by the 'gang system' has caused it to be put an end to in many parishes, and it is universally reprobated by those who are independent of its profits", wrote Dr. Hunter.[14] The Chaplain of Swaffham Prison, in his Annual Report for 1866, wrote of the employment of girls in the fields as "at best a questionable occupation, unfitting them for home duties in after-life, burdening our Union poorhouses with illegitimate offspring and young wretched mothers".[15]

Moreover, the detractors of the factory system commonly misunderstood and misrepresented the causes of such immorality as they detected among cotton operatives. Those whose views we have quoted above belonged to those classes of society where free association of the sexes was viewed with horror as a certain temp-tation to vice. Confronted with a system where men and women worked day after day in the same building, sometimes the same room, it is not unnatural that they should conclude that such factories must be hot-beds of immorality.

Natural as this conclusion might be, it was too often arrived at independently of the facts. "They speak as if men and women were herded together the whole day, subject to no superintendence, with opportunities and facilities for licentious conversation", writes Cooke Taylor. "Now conversation in a mill is all but physically impossible; the operatives are separated from each other by frames of working machinery which require their constant attendance, and the overseers would soon dismiss tenters who abandoned the care of their frames to indulge in idle gossip. On this subject it is not easy to obtain accurate information in town factories, because it is impossible for the masters to have a strict surveillance over operatives whose dwellings are dispersed over a wide and crowded surface. In the country mills it is possible to make some approach to accuracy, and here the returns show that seductions are of rare occurrence and take place in the evenings after work when they do occur; and that in nine cases out of ten the seduced do not belong to the same mill as the seducers."[16]

Even of what might appear at first sight to be immorality amongst the operatives, a certain amount must be discounted. Gaskell, comparing the morals of factory workers unfavourably with those who lived and worked in agricultural districts, writes: "Some surprise may be excited probably by the assertion, in those whose attention has never been directed to the subject, but it is none the less true, that sexual intercourse was almost universal prior to marriage in the agricultural districts. This intercourse must not be confounded with that promiscuous and indecent concourse of the sexes which is so prevalent in towns and which is ruinous alike to health and morals. It existed only between parties where a tacit understanding had all the weight of obligation— and this was that marriage should be the result."[17] In point of fact, however, there was this "understanding" between factory workers also. "Though there is a good deal of sexual intercourse between young persons", writes Allen Clarke of Lancashire at the end of the century, "this is not promiscuous, but between courting couples, before marriage."[18] Nor should it be imagined that this was a practice peculiar to the factory workers of the Lancashire cotton towns. Evidence from Staffordshire and elsewhere shows that "in the labouring class, though seduction is too often the result of keeping company, marriage usually precedes the birth of the child, and no stigma in such cases attaches even to the woman".[19, 20]

A very great deal of the evidence of immorality among cotton operatives is based on the statements of witnesses connected with the mills in and around Manchester: but Manchester was far from being a typical cotton town. As Cooke Taylor is at pains to show, there existed in Manchester other causes conducive to a low state of morality, causes which were common to all large towns and not connected with the life of the cotton mill at all: "About 40,000 strangers arrive weekly in Manchester by railway and other means of conveyance; such an influence must necessarily have a perturbing effect on the tables of crime and morality, for a very large proportion must become tenants of the low and filthy lodging-houses, where both sexes are huddled indiscriminately together, and where there can be no doubt that crimes and profligacy of every description are both planned and perpetrated. In the statistics of the Manchester police for 1846, we find 109 lodging-houses returned as places where the sexes sleep indiscriminately together; and 91 mendicant lodging-houses. But the nuisance exists to a still greater extent in London, Liverpool, and Glasgow, and in the lodging-houses frequented by the travelling poor along the main roads of England. It is sad to find the want of domestic accommodation and of means for separating the sexes exists not merely in towns, where the great value of the ground, the expense of building, and many similar causes, may render the evil to some extent unavoidable; but it also prevails to a frightful extent among the agricultural population of the south of England."[21]

In support of this last point we might quote the agent of the Marquis of Lansdowne on the effects of the housing conditions of agricultural labourers in Wiltshire. "What is your opinion as to the effect of the mixing with men in their occupations upon their morals [i.e. the morals of women agricultural workers]?" he is asked. "I have never perceived any particular effect, or any immoral consequences from it; the character of the women in this respect depends much more upon the way they have been brought up at home." He continues: "I don't think this state of things is attributable to people working in the fields, but more to the want of proper accommodation in the cottages."[22] Nearly twenty years later, Mr. Long also reported: "I have already observed that the depravity of gang workers in some districts has been attributed to the debilitating influences of their homes; more particularly to the crowding of persons of different sexes and all ages in their sleeping rooms. Dr. Morris states that the crowding of labourers' houses is a great evil in Spalding."[23, 24]

In no decade of our period, in town or country, were the working classes adequately housed: in the overcrowded conditions under which many of them lived, it can have been difficult indeed to retain the moral refinement demanded by the upper strata of society. How far immorality among the working classes was due to the physical conditions under which they lived is a matter of opinion; but in so far as it was a cause, it would exert an influence on the whole of the working classes, and not merely on the cotton operatives.

Whatsoever evidence we examine, it is clear that the so-called "cotton-mill morality" was indicative of a morality which prevailed generally among the lower

classes. The Factory Commissioners of 1833 reported:
"In regard to morals, we find that though statements
and depositions of the different witnesses that have been
examined are to a considerable degree conflicting, yet
there is no evidence to show that vice and immorality
are more prevalent amongst these people [i.e. the cotton
operatives] considered as a class than amongst other
portions of the community in the same station."[25] The
later evidence of our period, far from disproving this
statement, gives it overwhelming support. A pen manufacturer, for example, advised in 1843 to place a respectable older woman in charge of the morals of the
girls in his employ, retorted that he would be willing if
he could find such a woman among his workpeople.[26]
The Superintendent of Police, Burslem, was asked in
the same year whether there was any reason to believe
that the women employed in the potteries were any less
chaste than other women. He replied that "there are as
virtuous women to be found there [i.e. in the potteries]
as in the world again".[27] Similarly, a Vicar remarks
sadly in 1867: "I used to think that field labour had a
bad effect on the morals of females, but I doubt whether
they are at all worse than those who do not go out.
Morality is at low ebb."[28] Three years later, the Medical
Officer of Health for Salford gave evidence of the fact
that in the "rural mining" districts of Wath, near
Rotherham, where there was little employment of
women save at harvest-time, they "thought little of
immorality".[29]

Some of the working classes vigorously denied the
persisting allegations that the employment of women in
mixed factories and workshops was threatening the
moral virtue of "the mighty masses". "I have been
working for twenty-seven or twenty-eight years,"
declared a representative of the Bradford and District
Power Loom Overlookers' Society to the Royal Commission on Labour in 1893, "and I would stand up for
the morality of the female portion of mill life in

opposition to that of any other grade of society from the top to the bottom."[30] Witnesses from the Staffordshire pottery industry went so far as to claim that "the introduction of women had anyhow improved the men".[31]

Those who had most to say against the employment of women in factories occasionally admitted, probably without realizing the implication of their words, that they had in fact met factory women with the very highest moral standards. "Some of our Lancashire girls are remarkable for the high view they take of life", writes James Haslam in an article in *The Englishwoman* in 1912.[32] "I remember that I used to owe some of my finest aspirations in life to their good influence, and the more I have seen of people in other grades of life, the more my mind goes back to them with the thought of what commendable women some of them were."

A revealing comment made during the Ten Hours debates by some who refused to accept on their face value the lurid pictures of "cotton-mill morality" painted by Ashley and others was that what was denounced in the cotton districts was tolerated in others. Mr. Warburton claimed that "His right honourable friend [Sir James Graham], formerly First Lord of the Admiralty, could tell the House something of the morality of Portsmouth Hard if he chose to be communicative on so delicate a subject. Yet no one, because the morals of sailors were lax, and those of their female subjects abandoned, proposed a Commission to scrutinize and lay bare their frailties. Why this abstinence from such an . attempt? Because all men know the paramount importance of keeping up the Navy, and that our commercial and political greatness depends on our maintaining it."[33] The immorality that was exposed by various commissions is not only a comment on the behaviour of the working classes, but also on the behaviour of contemporary society as a whole: "Behind the barricade of Victorian rectitude", says Mr. Beales, "is the vast reality of prostitution."[34]

According to the 1833 Factory Commission, "the number of factory girls who finally recruit the ranks of professional prostitutes is perhaps small; at least, out of fifty prostitutes who have entered Manchester Penitentiary during the last four years, only eight proceeded from factories, while twenty-nine had been in service."[35] A similar result was noted by some observers in other towns.[36] Obviously a woman can be immoral without being a professional prostitute. Furthermore, these figures are clearly too small to permit any generalization to be made from them. It is significant of the contemporary determination to defile the character of the women cotton operatives, however, that this, one of the few existing attempts to estimate the chief sources from which professional prostitutes were drawn, was almost completely ignored.

Evidence of a slightly different nature also failed to prove that women operatives were more flagrantly immoral than other women of their social class. Before the Select Committee on the Best Means of Protecting Infants put out to Nurse, for example, it was stated time after time that the majority of mothers of illegitimate children were domestic servants.[37]

Mr. Whitehead, a surgeon at St. Mary's Hospital, Manchester, where a register of wet-nurses was kept, gave evidence that "in six months of 1868, the whole of 1869 and three months of 1871, there were 207 applications to be entered on this register. Of this number, only twenty-five were married and two were widows—the rest being single women." He continued: "Seventy-five of the applicants were domestic servants, ninety-nine worked in warehouses, shops, restaurants, or were living at home." Mill operatives, he told the Select Committee, seldom made application to be entered on the register.[38]

This evidence does not in any way prove that the women cotton operatives were pillars of virtue compared with other women of their own class, since it is known that unmarried cotton operatives with illegitimate children frequently continued to work at the mill, leaving their babies, as did the mothers of legitimate children, with a local nurse during the day.[39] For these women there was no necessity to eke out a living as wet-nurses to the children of the well-to-do. This is no doubt part of the explanation of the figures of "chargeable bastards" in various parts of England quoted by Cooke Taylor as showing that there was no connexion between women's employment and a high rate of illegitimate births.[40] Furthermore, not all cotton manufacturers were prepared to employ in their mills mothers of illegitimate children.[41]

Even so, facts such as these call for rather more convincing evidence of the inferior morals of the women cotton operatives compared with other women of their own class than detractors of the factory system could adduce.

In the absence of such evidence, and in the light of the comparative data presented in the foregoing pages, it seems impossible to maintain the view that the employment of women in the cotton mills was breaking up the moral structure of the working-class family; and there appears to be no reason why this should be less true of woman's employment in other industries.

Viewing the whole of the evidence, the only reasonable conclusion is that of a witness to the Interdepartmental Committee on Physical Deterioration in 1904: "The standard of morals in a factory very largely reflects the standard outside it."[42]

Quite certainly, for a variety of reasons, the standards of moral conduct for unmarried women of the upper classes did not, or could not, apply generally lower down the social scale: how far their standards concerning the conduct of the married women applied to the working classes is much less certain, for the whole matter is concealed by a conspiracy of silence. Such evidence as has been found on this point is inconclusive. For example, one of the witnesses to the Royal Commission on the Employment of Children, 1843, the Vicar of Tunstall, Staffordshire, relates the following story:

"A woman said to me a few days ago, 'You have one of my sons in your school.' 'Have I?' I replied. 'Yes. I had him by another man.' Her husband stood by."[43]

Again, Mr. Fowler of Wakefield repeated the following anecdote to the Committee of the Obstetrical Society of London in 1873:

"A woman was asked, on her applying for medical aid in her approaching confinement, how many children she had had before. She volunteered the following statement: 'Let's see. First was a chance 'un; second was a chance 'un; third was all right; this is the fourth.' It was known that she herself was a bastard, and, as her mother was there, the question was put to her, 'Have you ever had any illegitimate children?' 'Yes, your honour; six.' "[44]

It is impossible to ascertain from these statements whether the illegitimate children of these women were born to them after marriage. Thus it may be that such statements are only significant of the husband's disregard of the wife's unchastity before marriage.

Since it cannot be proved, however, that during our period working in the mill or factory *per se* made the unmarried women more depraved than other unmarried women of their own class, it is difficult to maintain the related view that the married woman worker was more depraved than other married women of her own class.

CHAPTER VI

THE MARRIED OPERATIVE AS A HOME-MAKER

COMMENTING on the impact of industrialism on the working-class home, Dr. Pinchbeck writes: "It has generally been admitted that women gained greatly by the transference of manufacture from the home to the factory. As Commissioner Hickson stated in his report in 1840, 'domestic happiness is not promoted but impaired by all members of the family muddling together and jostling each other in the same room'.[1] Moreover, dust and oil and offensive smells were often the necessary accompaniments of domestic industry; hence, however the Industrial Revolution may have affected the married woman's economic position, it cannot be denied that it immensely improved her domestic conditions. Now that the home was no longer a workshop, many women were able for the first time in the history of the industrial classes to devote their energies to the business of home-making and the care of their children, who stood to benefit greatly by the changed conditions."[2]

True as this is, the married woman who was absent daily from her home from early morning till early evening was scarcely able to benefit by the change to the same degree; certainly she could not devote her energies solely, or even mainly, to the business of home-making. In 1833, Dr. Hawkins had written of the Lancashire cotton districts that "the married women fell remarkably short of the usual characteristics of the English wife; in fact, in addition to the labour of twelve hours daily, they often have cares which engaged almost the undivided attention of married women in other classes of life".[3] The result, according to the factory inspector for the north-west nearly thirty years later, was clear and inevitable: "I scarcely need argue", he wrote "that there can be comparatively no comfort in the dwelling of a working man whose wife is away from home from half-past five in the morning till half-past six in the evening, except at mealtimes, for she is compelled to leave her children and her household to other hands; and, having so little experience of her own, is quite unable to teach her daughter those attractive qualifications which are to keep their husbands from disreputable associations."[4] Criticism indeed in an era when it was accepted that "the great privilege of women in domestic life is certainly that of making a man's home so attractive as to counteract the many inducements that may cross his path to become a rover from it".[5]

The delegation of domestic duties was simple enough where there was a young daughter of seven, eight, or nine years of age who could be kept at home to clean the house, run the errands, and look after any younger children. Some women with no young daughters of their own to perform these duties would often hire another's child. Not every woman, however, possessed one of these diminutive "home-helps"; nor could every domestic duty be delegated to them by those who had.

Ellen Barlee records in her *Visit to Lancashire in December 1862*: "I learned that high as were the wages which the operatives earn, they are considerably reduced by the outlay which is necessarily a consequence of the absence of the wife and mother from her domestic duties, which must be deputed to others or be performed at night. The former plan is generally adopted and a very large class of women derive their maintenance entirely by providing for the wants of mill hands and often earn more than the operatives themselves.

"I noted down some of these women's trades, if I may

so term them. There is a body of women called 'tea-women'. These take up their abode near the mill and receive from the hands as they pass in to their early labour small packets of tea, etc. It is their business to provide hot water and make the tea or perhaps coffee against the breakfast hour. For this accommodation they received 4*d*. a head per week, and a larger sum if they are likewise called upon to provide a dinner. One tea-woman can prepare breakfast for 200 hands. There are generally six or eight such persons belonging to a mill.

"The washerwomen in the manufacturing districts form another class. Their earnings usually average 1*s*. per week for every couple they wash for.

"The needlewomen and dressmakers are again a distinct body, and thrive upon such an occupied female population, for the Lancashire lassies rarely make their own dresses. They can, however, pay well to have them done, and it is therefore worthwhile for the dressmakers to study fashions and fits; so that on Sundays and holidays, I was told, it was quite surprising to see the elegant appearance these girls made.

"Shoemakers also abound and drive a good trade. But the most thriving business in these districts appears to be that of nursing; as the children must be looked after, they are committed to a class of artificial mothers who make child-nursing a trade."[6]

The obvious omission from this list is the body of women who undertook to clean for the married operatives, one such woman often cleaning for a group of neighbouring operatives. Whether these women also undertook to prepare a midday meal is not clear from contemporary accounts. Where this was not the case, there must have been yet another group of women who earned a pittance by preparing a meal for those operatives who lived near enough to the mill to go home for their dinner. Gaskell described the operatives rushing from the mill at noon to a meal that "has been imperfectly cooked by someone left for that purpose, not unusually a mere child or a superannuated man or woman".[7]

Much as this delegation of domestic duties was decried by the factory inspectors, it was by no means an innovation in the working-class home. The married cotton hand-loom weaver, whose factory was her own home, had little if any more time to devote to cleaning and cooking. In 1840 Muggeridge, reporting on the conditions of the hand-loom weavers of Lancashire, states that "in many instances" he found children of from seven to ten years of age deputizing for the mother while she was occupied at the loom.[8] Hickson, in the same year, reported that "in Bethnal Green Road [Spitalfields] there is held every Monday and Tuesday morning between the hours of six and eight, a children's labour market—that is to say, there is an open space to which children of both sexes from the age of seven upwards resort to be hired by the week or month by any person who may require their services. Many of the girls who accept these situations are between seven and nine years of age, and are paid from 1s. 8d. to 2s. per week. In a weaver's family, where the wife is employed at the loom, she requires a servant to nurse the child, make the beds, and help cook the victuals; and, as a strong girl would be too expensive for the purpose, a mere child of seven, nine, ten, or eleven is hired instead. A child thus hired comes to work before eight in the morning, having had her breakfast, returns home to dinner, and at night again returns to sleep. On Saturday night she receives the 20d. she has earned and gives it to her parents."[9]

Mrs. Barlee failed to estimate how much the factory operative paid in all per week to those whom she hired to perform some service for her; but some idea may be gleaned from the calculations of others. Mr. Hawes, for example, in the course of a debate in the House of Commons in 1844, quoted some statistics compiled by the Mayor of Manchester of the expenditure of a spinner's family of five persons; from these it was calculated that, "by allowing the married woman one and a half hours per day longer at home, 2s. per week would be saved on nursing, cooking, and mending which would otherwise have had to be paid for".[10]

Lord Ashley had already, in the same debates, given a more detailed and, needless to say, more dramatic estimate of the amount spent per week on such services: "He would refer to the expenses of a family of five persons, three of whom worked in the mill twelve hours a day, the father being out of employment, and the mother and two children working in the mill. The mother obtains 10s. per week, the eldest child 4s. and the other 3s., making the total receipt of the family 17s. But what were the outgoings under the present system? The expense of washing which they were obliged to send out, and mangling, was 2s. per week." (A reasonable enough estimate in the light of a statement made to a factory inspector by a woman weaver to the effect that for her own *personal* washing she paid 9d. per week.[11]) "It cost them 1s. per week to employ a woman to assist the husband—who remained at home performing the domestic work—in cleaning the house; and a further expense of 1s. per week was incurred by the necessity of sending meals out to the mill. But there was another source of loss to be taken into account—that which arose from the cooking being performed by the husband. He [Lord Ashley] believed that no man, whether Frenchman or Englishman, could cook so economically as a woman. The loss from this source might be calculated at 1s. per week. The total loss of the family was therefore 12s. per week." Once again the assumption is that the husbands of the married women workers were unemployed. Without necessarily accepting this assumption, since the midday meal was frequently prepared by a young child or an old woman, not necessarily more competent, it seems reasonable to allow this estimate.

Even though many of the operatives paid for some of their household tasks to be performed for them, few could have afforded to delegate all such work, and the remainder still found a great deal to do at the week-end. "On Saturday the mills are closed at midday and the men and single women make real holiday", writes Mrs. Barlee. "Then the town is all alive; it is quite a gala day; the men appearing in good broadcloth suits, and the girls as smart as wages can make them. The married women, who seem the slaves of Lancashire society, are obliged then, however, to set to work harder than ever. They have only this day to clean their houses, provide for the week, bake for the family, mend clothes, beside doing any washing that is not put out, and attend the market to purchase the Sunday's dinner (quite a business in itself). The market is kept open very late at night for this purpose. Then there is also washing the children and setting them to rights—always the Saturday night's business in every cottage, so that the poor mother seldom gets a rest ere the Sabbath dawns if, indeed, she is not up all night."[13]

Where the family income was so low that the wife had to organize her home unaided, the life of the conscientious married operative was one of unceasing drudgery. Charlotte Tonna describes the lot of Alice Smith: "by working every night herself and fixing for Polly [her eldest daughter] she had kept her mending pretty well done; and on Friday evening she had, much against her will, washed out the linen, filling her little room with damp discomfort while drying it, an annoyance so new to Smith [her husband] that he could not help grumbling about it a little, and declaring that she must in future put it out to a neighbour to wash, or he should be obliged to leave home till it was over."[14] The cleaning and baking were reserved for the week-end "holiday".

It is scarcely surprising that Alice's standards of housewifery gradually deteriorated and that her house became neglected; woman's energies are not, after all, limitless.

Scant sympathy, however, was extended to the

married operative. Whether she struggled to perform all or part of her domestic duties in addition to her factory work, or whether, by choice or force of circumstances, her home became neglected, to the contemporary observer the net result was the same—a cheerless and uninviting home.

"No clean and tidy wife appears to welcome her husband—no smiling and affectionate mother to welcome her children—no home, cheerful and inviting, to make it regarded", writes Gaskell. "On the contrary, all assemble there equally jaded; it is miserably furnished, dirty, and squalid in its appearance."[15] "Glorious life this working in the mill, carrying an unborn baby and coming home to drudge at housework till bedtime", observes Allen Clarke. "Finding no home comforts, the natural thing follows. The husband, after the day's work is done, and finding his wife helping to keep the home, goes off to the ale-house."[16]

Mrs. Gaskell emphasized the fact that the women themselves saw the domestic difficulties which followed the employment of married women. In a conversation in *Mary Barton*, Mrs. Wilson and her elderly sister-in-law, Alice, brought out their view of the case: "Father does not like girls to work in factories," said Mary. "No, I know he does not; and reason good," replies Mrs. Wilson. "They oughtn't to go out after they're married, that I'm very clear about. I could reckon up"—counting on her fingers—"aye nine men I know as has been driven to the public house by having wives as worked in factories; good folk too, as thought there was no harm in putting their little ones out to nurse and letting their homes go all dirty and their fires all out; and that was a place as was tempting for a husband to stay in, was it? He soon finds out gin-shops where all is clear and bright and where the fire blazes cheerfully and gives a man a welcome, as it were."

Alice, who was standing near for the convenience of hearing, had caught much of this speech, and it was evident the subject had previously been discussed by the women, for she chimed in:

"I wish our Jem could speak a word to th' Queen, about factory work for married women. Eh but he comes it strong when once yo get him to speak about it. Wife o' his'n will never work away fra' home."

"I say as it's Prince Albert as ought to be asked how he'd like his missis to be from home when he comes in, tired and worn, and wanting someone to cheer him; and, maybe her to come in by-and-by, just as tired and down in the mouth; and how he'd like for her never to be at home to see to th' cleaning of his house or keep his fire bright. Let alone his meals being all hugger-mugger and comfortless. I'd be bound, prince as he is, if his missis served him so he'd be off to a gin palace, or sommat o' that kind. So why can't he make a law again poor folk's wives working in factories?"

Mary ventured to say that she thought the Queen and Prince could not make laws, but the answer was, "Pooh, don't tell me it's not the Queen as makes laws; and isn't she bound to obey Prince Albert? And if he said they mustn't, why, she'd say they mustn't, and then all folk would say, 'Oh, no, we shall never do any such things no more.' "[17]

Prince Albert's legislation, however, would have had to have been of wider application than merely to the cotton mills of Lancashire. For although the condition of the married operative's home received greater publicity, the same "painful" tales of neglect came to light on enquiry into the domestic conditions of other workers where the wife was also employed away from home. Married women workers would have to have been excluded from the Staffordshire pottery industry, for example, where their homes were described as "very nearly desolate";[18] from the factories and workshops of the nail- and chain-making districts, where the result of their employment was "everything being neglected at home, and when a man goes into his little palace, his

little castle as it should be, there is nothing clean and
tidy. It drives him to the public house and all that kind
of thing."[19] They would have to have been driven from
the jute mills of Dundee, where, although the women
attempted to do the family washing, cleaning, and
mending on their Saturday afternoon "off", we are
assured that "dirt and discomfort abounded", and that
the factory inspectress "never saw any attempt at
cooking".[20] Certainly they would have had to have
been excluded from agriculture, where a generally low
level of wages prevailed and thus, as in the last three
industries mentioned, in the absence of a child of her
own whom she could leave to take care of the house,
little is heard of hiring other children or old women to
wash and clean for the absent housewife,[21] save where
a child had to be hired to nurse the baby in the mother's
absence. In such cases she was usually expected to help
in the house.

Only a few years after Baker had inveighed against
the standard of domestic comfort in Lancashire when
the wife was employed in the mills an almost identical
account is given of the effects on the home when the
wife was employed in the fields:

"Being employed from eight in the morning till five
in the evening, they [i.e. the married women] return
home tired and wearied, and unwilling to make any
further exertion to render the cottage comfortable",
the Children's Employment Commission was told in
1867. "When the husband returns, he finds everything
uncomfortable, the cottage dirty, no meal prepared, the
children tiresome and quarrelsome, the wife slatternly
and cross, and his home so unpleasant to him that he
not rarely betakes himself to the public house and
becomes a drunkard."[22]

Nor was this an isolated opinion, as other reports on
agricultural workers show. The home of the agricultural
labourer in south Northumberland, for example, is
contrasted unfavourably, in one of these reports, with

that of his counterpart in the north of the county, where married women were but rarely employed in the fields: "South Northumberland presents some remarkable contrasts with the northern part of the county, such as the extensive employment of married women in farm labour, neglecting their homes, and leaving a child that ought to be at school to look after the house."[23] As the agricultural labourer's wage was insufficient to pay for the preparation of a midday meal, "the diet when the women are at work and therefore have no time to cook a dinner is generally bread and cheese or bread with a little butter. When they have time to prepare a dinner, it generally consists of flour dumplings and potatoes. Sometimes a little fat pork is chopped up and put into the dumplings."[24]

How bad a housewife the married woman employed away from home was, however, depended on how good her counterpart was who stayed at home all day. Precisely the same group of observers who condemned the former at the same time decried the latter: "Out of thirteen married females taken at one mill, it was claimed that only one knew how to make her husband a shirt, and only four knew how to mend one. I have the evidence of several females who declare their own ignorance of every domestic accomplishment—the unmarried declare—'not a single qualification of any sort for household servants'. The married, 'untidy, slovenly, dirty, cannot wash, sew, take care of their children or their houses; cannot manage expenses; perpetual waste and extravagances'."[25]

The "improvidence" of the married operative as a housekeeper was illustrated by Mrs. Gaskell in *Libbie Marsh's Three Eras*:

"Mrs. Dixon set out the tea things and put the kettle on, fetched home the youngest child (boarded out on weekdays with a neighbour), which added to the commotion. Then she called Anne downstairs, and sent her for this thing and that; eggs to be put in the cream, it was so thin; ham to give a relish to the bread and butter, some new bread, hot if she could get it. Libbie heard all these orders given at full pitch of Mrs. Dixon's voice, and wondered at their extravagance, so different from the place where she had last lodged. But they were fine spinners, in receipt of good wages, and confined all day in an atmosphere ranging from 55 to 80 degrees. They had lost all natural healthy appetite for simple food, and, having no higher tastes, found their greatest enjoyment in their luxurious meals."[26]

On the other hand, it seems, the operative who stayed at home after marriage did little better. "It has been made apparent of late years", wrote a factory inspector, "that one of the reasons why the beer-shop has been more attractive than the worker's home is the want of domestic qualification on the part of the 'factory girls' as wives; their utter incapacity to make a home, however poor, more desirable from its comforts than external amusements and associations; their extravagance in purchasing new and tawdry articles of dress, partly from a love of finery, partly from their incapableness of mending old clothes; their general waste or misapplication of their earnings in the purchase of provisions once only to be seen in the homes of the wealthy, but now on most Sundays in theirs, and from their general ignorance of how to put their income to the best advantage.[27] These evils", he continues, "arise in the first instance by withdrawing female children from home at a very early age, then by exposing them to the danger of bad examples and which are augmented by the absence of domestic training when the hours of work are over."

It was claimed that in the manufacturing districts "God forbid that I should marry a girl out of the mill" was a common saying.[28] Lord Ashley quoted Robert Sutcliffe, an operative, who, at a meeting at Halifax on 13th April 1844, was reported as saying: "With regard to their own families, he would say as the father of several girls, that Lord Ashley's Bill was well worth struggling for alone. If they did not wish their daughters to grow up completely unfit for every domestic duty which, as wives and mothers, they would be called on in after life to discharge, they must insist on the curtailment of the excessive and protracted toil they endured in the factories. He had daughters at work in the factories; they were required to get up at five o'clock in the morning in the factories and they did not get home till eight o'clock in the evening and they were in such a state of exhaustion both of body and mind they were altogether unfit to learn any kind of domestic economy."[29]

Mrs. Wilson, in *Mary Barton*, says: "If you'll believe me, Mary, there never was such a born goose at housekeeping as I were, and yet he married me. I had been in the factory sin' five years old a'most, and I knew nought about cleaning or cooking, let alone washing and such-like work. The day after we were married he goes to his work after breakfast and says he, 'Jenny, we'll ha' the cold beef and potatoes, and that is a dinner for a Prince.' I were anxious to make him comfortable, God knows how anxious. And yet I'd no notion how to cook a potato. I know'd they were boiled, and I know'd their skins were taken off, and that were all. So I tidied my house, in a rough kind o' way, then I looked at that very clock yonder (pointing at one that hung against the wall), and I seed it were nine o'clock, so think I, th' potatoes shall be well boiled at any rate, and I gets 'em on the fire in a jiffy (that's to say, as soon as I could peel 'em, which were a tough job at first), and then I fell to unpacking my boxes. And at twenty minutes past twelve, he comes home, and I had the beef ready on the table, and I went to take the potatoes out o' the pot; and Oh! Mary, th' water had all boiled away and they were all a nasty brown mess and smelt through all the house. He said nought and were very gentle; but Oh! Mary, I cried so that afternoon."[30]

On the other hand, working-class people themselves

are sometimes recorded as emphatically denying the incompetence of factory girls as wives. One witness to the 1833 Factory Commission, a spinner, stated: "A daughter of mine began work between nine and ten; is now married; nineteen; can make her own clothes. In my family, missing my coat, everything else is made for myself and the young men and young women by my wife and daughter."[31] Another man, being asked whether the women factory operatives make bad wives, replied: "I have heard it said so, but I know to the contrary, because I married three wives out of the factory, and I take that as proof. I am certain that as good wives may be had from the factories as from any other occupation."[32]

The suggestion that they were less competent in the home was actively resented by some of the women witnesses: "You think we can do nought but work at factories," said one of them, "neither brew, nor bake nor sew."[33]

An investigation carried out into "the educational and other conditions of a district in Ancoats", a mill area in Manchester, by the Manchester Statistical Society in 1865-6 yielded no evidence that the dirtiest houses in the district were those of the cotton operatives.[34]

The same accusations and denials were being made concerning the effects of the employment of women and girls elsewhere. It was claimed, for example, that "the employment of girls from an early age in the Staffordshire pottery industry made them 'very bad wives', knowing nothing of domestic economy, comfort, and cleanliness; but leave their duties to be performed as they may".[35] The employment of girls in agriculture was said to have the same effect. "It is quite evident", writes an Overseer and Relieving Officer in 1843, "that field labour spoils them for house service, as it renders them less cleanly."[36] In a later report it was said that "the chief objection to the work is on moral grounds. The effect is unfitting girls to look after a house and for domestic life, is very bad, and that is a very important consideration now."[37]

The truth of the matter was that amongst the working classes generally the standard of domestic accomplishment was deplorably low. G. W. Hastings, in a paper read to the National Association for the Promotion of Social Science, remarked: "There is a widespread feeling that the industrial employment of women is prejudicial to the domestic happiness of the working classes; and that it hinders women from acquiring a knowledge of domestic economy; that their houses are therefore comfortless, their husbands driven to the gin-shops, their children brought up in squalor, and they themselves thriftless and depraved.

"The justice of this idea, however, is disproved out and out, by comparing the districts where the industrial employment of women prevails with those districts where it is scarcely known. Take for example, colliery districts, mining districts, towns of metal manufacture, seaport towns without fisheries, and there you find that the squalor, the thriftlessness, the ignorance, and the dissipation are far more universal than in towns and districts devoted to the manufacture of cotton, linen, lace, and suchlike products. In the latter instances, woman has abundant work; in the former she has none. Slatternly habits, therefore, in the lower orders are not a consequence of the industrial employment of women, but constitute an evil to be dealt with on its own grounds."[38]

Of the prevailing low standard of housewifery in the mid-nineteenth century, Dr. Pinchbeck writes: "It is exceedingly difficult to see how this could have been otherwise, or how the standard could ever have been much higher. Not only were the women of the eighteenth century busily engaged in earning their living in agriculture or industry, but their facilities for acquiring any measure of skill in domestic matters were exceedingly limited. Cottage accommodation was often of the meanest; food in many homes was limited to oatmeal porridge, milk, bread, cheese and potatoes, with meat a rare luxury; cooking utensils were few and turf and furze were the common fuel used by a great proportion of the population. Brick ovens, though common in farmhouses, were by no means general in use among the cottages, and iron grates only began to be supplied at the end of the eighteenth century after the expansion of the iron trade. In these circumstances it is inconceivable that the standard of culinary skill could ever have been higher, or that the training of children in domestic affairs could have been much superior to that of children who spent their early lives in the factories. Knowledge was limited to the economy practised in the humble homes of their parents."[39]

The housing conditions of the "labouring and industrial classes" continued to be deplorable throughout the nineteenth century. In Manchester in 1861 some of them were still forced to live in two-roomed cellar dwellings through the chronic lack of small houses;[40] in the smaller mill towns conditions were not much better.[41] Fifty years later, though there were no longer cellar dwellings in Manchester, there were still back-to-back houses, and 34,137 people were reported as living in overcrowded conditions.[42] In the Potteries, it was claimed in 1897, "you hardly ever find more than two bedrooms, and sometimes you have eight adults. It is extraordinary how many people you have in one house."[43] Some time before it had been stated that "for years the overcrowding of rural labourers' dwelling has been a matter of deep concern, not only to persons who are for sanitary good, but to persons who care for decent and moral life".[44]

Nor was there any marked improvement in working class diet. In 1864 a Committee appointed to report on the state of prisons had been asked by the Home Secretary to report on the state of prisoners' diet in the light of the meals required by a free labourer. "It is extremely difficult to ascertain what the ordinary food of the free labourer is", the Committee found, "even if the enquiry was limited to that class of free labourer which is known to be the worst fed, namely, agricultural labourers, the true facts of the case would not be readily obtained."[45] Such evidence as exists on the diet of the working classes during our period is not encouraging. Edwin Smith, who had studied the diets of the poorer people, said in 1864 that most farm labourers enjoyed one hot meal a week;[46] and his records of the diet of the Lancashire cotton operatives show that they lived largely on bread, oatmeal, bacon, a very little butter, treacle and tea and coffee.[47]

Forty years later the Interdepartmental Committee on Physical Deterioration tried to elicit further information on this subject, and found that "a diet of bread and butter for breakfast, potatoes and herring for dinner, and bread and butter for tea", enlivened by some cheap cuts of meat on Sunday and purchases from the fried-fish shop during the week, when funds permitted, was the normal working-class diet.[48, 49] Tinned foods, a boon to the busy housewife, were still too dear to be much used by the working class, and for the same reason milk was used very sparingly.[50]

It was, in short, quite unrealistic for the upper and middle class Victorian observers to dilate upon the dirt, squalor, lack of domestic pride, and skill of the working class housewife—whether employed away from home or not—without considering how their own wives would have conducted domestic life under such unpromising circumstances.

It is significant that, throughout our period, domestic servants were said to make the most suitable wives. This was simply and solely because they had received some domestic training in households where there was sufficient wealth to support a higher standard of living. "Where any knowledge is possessed by the wife of a labourer", wrote Mr. Austin in 1843, "it is generally to be traced to the circumstance of her having, before marriage, lived as a servant in a farmhouse or elsewhere. A girl brought up in a cottage until she marries is generally ignorant of nearly everything she ought to be acquainted with for the comfortable and economical management of a cottage—she marries, and brings up her daughters in the same ignorance and their lives are a repetition of her own."[51] Again and again during the following years it was said that "the only training of this kind open to them is domestic service".[52, 53] "This most important branch of female education is as a rule wholly neglected in elementary schools", declared Dr. Rumsey in 1871, "nor do I perceive any signs of greater attention to the subject under the new school boards."[54]

In 1876, attention was paid to the subject at last: domestic economy, as a compulsory specific subject for girls in board schools, was introduced by the new Education Code of that year. The value of this instruction may be judged by the fact that there was no financial provision for practical training in any branch of the subject—a shortcoming which drew the justifiable comment from the School Board of Wolverhampton that "abstract teaching in the branch of domestic economy connected with the subject of food and its preparation would prove more useful if accompanied with practical instruction in cookery, with such utensils as might be used in the homes of the working classes".[55]

Yet even had there been provision for practical instruction in cookery, there would still have remained the fundamental difficulty of finding teachers adequately qualified to teach this, or indeed any, branch of domestic economy. Furthermore, as one of the school inspectors reported in 1879: "At present, very many girls attend mixed schools in which the staff and teachers consist exclusively of men, who, by their training and habits, must be and are practically ignorant of anything but a book knowledge of the mysteries of food and its preparation, washing materials and their uses, or the management of the sick-room." The combined effect of lack of practical instruction and lack of qualified teachers, maintained this inspector, was that "the girls stumble through a mixture of learned nonsense concerning carbonaceous and nitrogenous products, but they cannot tell you how to boil a potato or cook a roast of beef".[56]

In the very rare instances where the inspectors reported a high standard of instruction in domestic subjects, it usually transpires that this was owing to the personal interest and supervision of some local patroness, such as Mrs. Leach, who personally instructed the girls of Hob Hill Girls' School, Stalybridge, Manchester.[57]

No better provision was made in the independent schools. Here, as in the public schools, inspectors lament the poor quality of needlework produced for approval. The Industrial Department of St. Philip's Girls' School, Hulme, appears to have been exceptional among Church of England schools in Lancashire in providing practical instruction in laundry, cooking, and sewing—the cost of the necessary materials being met out of the offertory.[58]

During the 1890s, fortified by the "whisky money", some of the technical education committees decided to provide practical domestic instruction for the working classes. But if the complaint of the 1870s had been the lack of practical instruction and qualified teachers, the complaint now was that the teachers demonstrated their skill on equipment and materials rarely to be found in the working class home. *The Englishwoman* acidly comments that "the dairy instructress did roses and statuary in butter to *épater le bourjeois*, and the laundress showed how to wash chiffon frills, silk blouses, and quilted tea-cosies. . . . The pupils cost 10s. per head per lecture and learned little or nothing."[59]

Shortly after the sporadic and not very successful attempts of the technical education committees to start domestic science courses, practical lessons in domestic subjects were introduced in public elementary schools. These again, apparently, were not initially a success, and for exactly the same reason. According to the

Report of the Chief Inspector of Schools for 1906, the lessons were "expensive, unsuited to the needs of the locality, and unpopular with parents and children".[60]

Nothing perhaps so clearly indicates the profound ignorance of the middle and upper class Victorian of the domestic needs and conditions of the working classes than the unreality with which they attempted to improve the level of housewifery of their social inferiors. This was as true of most local philanthropic action as of the efforts made in State schools.

For some years before the Education Code of 1876 there had been a growing concern among the middle and upper classes that some instruction in domestic economy should be provided for the women of the working classes. An article in *Household Words* in 1852, entitled "The New School for Wives", describes the opening of the first evening schools for women in Birmingham in September 1847, where instruction was given in the three Rs, sewing, including mending, and religion, for which the pupils paid 13*d*. per quarter.[61] Similar institutions were opened in other manufacturing areas. The Dowager Lady Ellesmere set up a kitchen at Worsley, Lancashire, where working class girls could be instructed by practical demonstration in the art of cookery, and in the same building which housed the kitchen she also organized needlework classes.[62] Never did this philanthropic movement receive such an impetus in the cotton districts as during the Cotton Famine, 1861–5, when "sewing schools" were established by private benefactors, attendance at which qualified the women and girls for relief. It is recorded that the four Blackburn sewing schools produced in the year 1862–3 3,013 chemises, 2,949 petticoats, 1,698 shirts, and 829 flannel waistcoats.[63]

Laudable as such efforts were, their emphasis on the actual making of clothes was ill-chosen; it was based on a misconception of the functions of the home in an industrial society. Professor Clapham long ago drew attention to the fact that, by the end of the eighteenth century, the labourer in agricultural districts—still, at that time, the typical working class figure—was buying "a considerable portion, if not the whole of his clothes, from a shopkeeper".[64] It is thus not surprising to find a Commissioner writing in 1843: "The arts of weaving and spinning and knitting have left the cottage, and most of the necessities of life are still commanded by money alone.[65] . . . The agricultural labourer who was too poor to buy clothes outright joined clothing clubs which were partly, and in some cases wholly, supported by the contributions of his richer neighbour."[66]

Those who criticized the factory girl, and particularly the factory mother, for not making the clothes worn by herself and her family, and attempted by instruction to remedy her shortcomings, failed to perceive the folly of spending precious hours over garments which the shop-worker, in co-operation with the manufacturer, was turning out cheaper—and not infrequently better—made.

We have compared the domestic skill of the factory woman with the skill of other women of her own social class: in fairness to the working class woman, however, it is worth remembering that the domestic skill of their social superior was not above criticism. On 27th April 1859 an article appeared in *Household Words* entitled "A Good Plain Cook".[67] The writer lamented the fact that "the young ladies of the leisure classes are educated to become uncommonly acute critics of all that pertains to personal blandishments. They keep an uncompromisingly tight hand over the milliners and lady's maid. They can tell to a thread when a flounce is too narrow or a tuck too deep. . . . But her 'good plain cook'—when the damsel is promoted to wedlock and owns one—passes unreproached for the most heinous offences. . . . These crimes, from their frequency and the ignorance of 'the lady of the house', remain unpunished. Whereupon husbands, tired of their Barmecide feasts—which disappoint the taste more because they often have a promising look to the eye—prefer better fare at their clubs: and escape the Scylla of bad digestion, to be wrecked on the Charybdis of domestic discord. All this owing to the wife's culinary ignorance and to your 'good plain cook'."[68]

A German observer of the level of culinary skill generally obtaining in England at the time affirmed: "The culinary condition of the English is so bad that nothing but a root-and-branch reform will ever do them any good!"[69]

Throughout the nineteenth century there were numerous magazines and journals, published weekly or monthly, which contained advice on all aspects of home management. Some, as their titles suggest—*The House and Home* and *The Household*—were entirely devoted to the subject. Others, such as *The Penny Scrap Book*, *Household Words*, *The People's Journal*, included special articles of particular interest to housewives—usually on cooking and child-care. The Religious Tract Society issued numbers of pamphlets, later collected into two volumes, *Homes Homely and Happy* and *Household Truths for Mothers and Daughters*, in which, either directly by "Old Chatty Cheerful" or indirectly by moral tales, women were given advice on how best to manage their homes and households. But, with the exception of these pamphlets, the advice given in all this literature was not to educate the working class housewife, but the married women of the higher social classes. How many working class housewives employed a cook to whom it was their duty "to furnish with convenient apartments and sufficient variety of utensils"[70] for the performance of her tasks? Again, how many factory women could afford to experiment with the recipe for fig cake given in an issue of *House and Home* (23rd June 1882) which required two cups of sugar, one cup of butter, three cups of flour, half a cup of sweet milk and the whites of seven eggs?

The Preface to *The Practical Housewife* (1855) explains that—"Almost before the echoes of the wedding-bells have ceased to vibrate, how many ladies there are who, assuming the honourable distinction of wife, discover their unfitness to meet its attendant duties—duties so important that future peace or misery depends upon them! More especially for these has this Book been prepared. . . . With *The Practical Housewife* at hand, no domestic head of the domicile need be alarmed to hear her husband intends giving a dinner-party; for in it she will learn at a glance what to provide and how to prepare it, from the cooking of a potato to the tasteful folding of a dinner napkin. . . ." Clearly, unless the editors imagined that the working class housewife was in the habit of giving dinner-parties, such advice as *The Practical Housewife* had to offer was not for her.

In the light of these considerations, much of the condemnation during our period of the married worker as a housewife appears both misconceived and exaggerated. It is obviously futile, when the production of clothes was no longer the function of the household nor the necessary duty of the wife, to condemn a woman for buying her husband's shirts ready made. At the root of much of the criticism was the contemporary doctrine that the woman's place was in the home: even had the young girls or old women to whom some gave the care of their homes been exemplary housekeepers, the wife would still have been upbraided for her daily absence at the factory; for the delegation of domestic duties can hardly have been the fundamental criticism of such a woman, since the homes of those who most found fault with her were precisely those where as many irksome domestic tasks as possible were left to servants.

Obviously, the home left to the care of an unsupervised hireling was scarcely likely to be well tended; and where no one was hired for this purpose, the house must have been even less inviting to the family returning tired from the mill at night. On the other hand, in view of the low standard of housewifery prevailing during our period throughout the working classes—and indeed among some sections of the middle and upper classes, where the higher level of comfort attained seems on the whole to have reflected not a greater efficiency on the part of the housewife, but the larger amount of money available for expenditure on domestic help, furnishing, and food—the terms of comparison between the standard of domestic comfort in the working class home where the wife was in employment and the standard of domestic comfort where she was not are more accurately described, not as good and bad, but as bad and worse.

CHAPTER VII

THE COMPARATIVE SIZE OF THE MARRIED OPERATIVE'S FAMILY

"REGARD the woman operative as a wife and mother . . ." exhorts Ashley.[1] In the previous chapters we have considered her primarily as a wife. Before discussing how her children were cared for during her daily absence at the mill, and how this compared with arrangements made by mothers employed in other industries, it is worth enquiring whether the occupation of married women in the cotton industry influenced the number of children they bore, and if so, whether this was an illustration of the effect on family size of the industrial employment of married women generally.

The evidence on this point for the early years of our period is very slight. The main source of our early information is the evidence incidental to the 1833 Royal Commission on the employment of women and children in factories;[2] and, in particular, the testimony of twenty-eight surgeons contained in the medical evidence.[3] Of these twenty-eight surgeons only one dissented from the general opinion that the employment of wives in cotton mills had no effect on their fertility. A Manchester surgeon, for example, states: "I have never made an estimate of the comparative fecundity of families employed in different trades. My enquiries, however, enable me to say that the married operatives of this town are generally prolific. In the case of 160 married women (taken without selection), patients of the Lying-in-Charity, whose average age was thirty years and a half, and the average age at marriage was twenty years and nine months, I found that they had borne 686 children (about 4¼ for each woman) of which number 512 (about 3⅛ for each) lived to be weaned at the age, on average, of fifteen months and a half. The duration of fruitfulness, too, would seem to be in no degree shorter here than elsewhere; of 10,000 pregnant women who had presented themselves to the Board of the Lying-in-Charity, I ascertained that 436 were upwards of forty years of age and that, of this number 51 had attained their forty-sixth year and upward."[4]

Testimony that depends on personal, general impressions and on such small numbers as we have quoted above must be of dubious validity. For the later years of our period, the situation is much clearer, for the Fertility Commission of 1911 recorded the history of married women of eight "social classes" on the basis of their husband's occupation. Classes I–V form a kind of social scale, beginning with professional workers and ending with the unskilled labourers; three special industrial groups—textile workers, miners, and agricultural labourers—form Classes VI, VII, and VIII respectively. Within each group the couples were divided according to the period in which they were married.

The relation between the different social classes is conveniently shown by expressing their average size as a proportion of the average for all classes together. In the following tables are given the figures for the groups who married between 1851 and 1886.

It will be seen from these tables that even for the earliest group, where differences in fertility between the social groups were not so marked as later, the wives of textile workers were less fertile than either of the other two major occupational groups and were indeed to be ranked with Classes I and II as the most infertile of the eight classes over the whole period for which our tables apply. This was a distinction which in point of fact they never lost for the entire period covered by the Fertility Commission, 1851–1911.[5]

Fertility in Relation to Social Class. Children born to Marriages of Various Dates in Each Social Class, percentage of the Corresponding Rates for Occupied Persons of all Classes jointly in Marriages of Similar Dates[6]

Social class		Total No. of children born (crude)			
		1851–	1861–	1871–	1881–6
I.	Professional and higher administrative in finance	86	85	78	72
II.	Employers in industry and retail trade . . .	98	95	90	86
III.	Skilled workers . . .	101	102	102	102
IV.	Intermediate between III and V	100	100	101	102
V.	Unskilled	105	105	109	112
VI.	Textile workers . . .	98	96	95	93
VII.	Miners	110	118	125	132
VIII.	Agricultural labourers .	106	104	108	113

Social class	No. of children born (standardized)			
	1851–	1861–	1871–	1881–6
I	89	88	81	76
II	99	96	93	89
III	101	101	101	100
IV	99	100	101	101
V	103	104	107	116
VI	94	94	93	92
VII	108	113	117	124
VIII	105	104	109	114

It would be incorrect to infer from this that it was the infertility of married women operatives which largely influenced this result, as not every male operative was married to a woman similarly occupied. But that the result was at least in part influenced by the employment of married women in textiles becomes apparent from the analysis of a more detailed table also published in the Report of the Commission—"Fertility in Relation to Husband's Occupation"[7]—in which the fertility of the Census subdivisions of occupations was recorded.

Commenting on this table, the Registrar-General wrote: "Textile workers . . . furnish no instance among

their subdivisions dealt with of even average reproduc-
tiveness, the ratios for standardized continuing fertility
ranging from 93% for lace workers to 79% for wool
and worsted weavers. For completed fertility, their ratios,
though also low, run a little higher, ranging from 83%
for wool spinners and weavers to 96% for hosiery
workers. One of the most interesting points brought out",
he continued, "is the superiority of the spinners over the
weavers of cotton. Both branches of industry are centred
chiefly in the same county [Lancashire], though to a
great extent in different localities, so at first a marked
difference of 8% and 9% of defect [of wives of under
forty-five years of age at the time of the Census] seems
surprising. There may, of course, be economic factors,
but the explanation is probably to be found largely in the
difference between the two occupations in regard to the
occupation of wives. Cotton spinning is mainly a man's
job, and weaving a woman's. The number of married
males returned as engaged in cotton spinning is 32,474,
and of married females 10,637; whereas for weaving
processes the numbers are 38,626 and 53,691 respectively.
And most male weavers are employed in districts where
weaving is so far the predominant branch of industry
that the demand for female labour is especially great. It
may fairly be inferred from these facts that a much
larger proportion of the wives of cotton-weaving husbands than of cotton spinners work in the mills, which
would account for their lower fertility. For, as will be
seen when the fertility of occupied married women is
discussed, occupation of the wife entails, as might be
expected, considerable reduction of fertility. But that
there is some other reason for the greater fertility of
cotton spinners is shown by the fact that in Table XLIX[8]
—'Fertility of Wives of less than Forty-five Years of Age
and returned as following Gainful Occupations'—the
continuing fertility of wives themselves occupied in
cotton spinning is shown to be 82% as against only 72%
for weavers—a defect in the one case of 18% and in the

other of 28%. The difference is not so great as that between 8% and 19% for men, but it is still very substantial, and cotton spinners stand out as considerably more fertile than any other section of the cotton or woollen industries, whether the men or women employed are considered."[9]

The existence of other factors cannot, of course, be denied, and it is perhaps best illustrated by an extract from the Registrar-General's comments on the wool and worsted industries. This evidence, however, does not invalidate the contention that the occupation of married women tended to lower their fertility. It merely serves as a caution against emphasizing this factor to the exclusion of all others. The Registrar-General remarks:

"Wool and worsted are only slightly less fertile than cotton workers, the total standardized continuing fertility being 86% for cotton and 84% for wool,[10] while, in consequence of the lower child mortality in the West Riding than in Lancashire, wool holds a slight advantage in regard to effective fertility. But for completed fertility the difference is greater—showing a ratio of 92% for cotton and only 85% for wool.[11]

"In this connexion, it is to be remembered that wool is very much less handicapped than cotton by the mill employment of wives, married women employed in the cotton industry amounting to 90% of married men, against only 50% for wool, so that there can be little doubt that if the fertility of the two industries was compared for those families where the husband alone works in the mill, the advantage of cotton would be considerably increased. Probably Table XLIX (where the fertility of gainfully occupied married women is recorded) may be taken as approximately representative of the cases where the husband and wife both work in the mill, and in it the woollen workers are seen to be decidedly less fertile than the cotton, the total standardized fertility ratio being 66% for wool against 74% for cotton, a difference which is far from being

compensated for by the slightly lower mortality of the
woollen worker's children. It thus appears that comparison of like with like in the two cases where the wife
does and does not work in the mill as well as the husband
would definitely be to the advantage of cotton."[12]

Of the remaining branches of the textile trades the
Registrar-General noted: "Hosiery and lace manufacture, both of which employed almost as much married
female labour, return higher standardized continuing
fertility than for the great textile trades; and for hosiery,
but not for lace, the completed fertility is also higher.
The lace trade is exceptional in showing a higher rate
for the married women than for the married men
employed. It differs from the other textile industries in
being to some extent carried on at home, but the bulk of
women employed work away from home. The influence
of locality has no doubt to be considered, as these trades
can hardly dominate their centres as the larger industries. The comparatively high fertility of the dyeing and
finishing trades, on the other hand, is readily explicable
as a result of the small proportion of married female
labour employed. In those cases where married women
are employed, their fertility is rather below that of
married female cotton operatives."[13]

Was the diminished fertility related to the occupation
of wives a phenomenon peculiar to the textile industries?
The evidence proves quite clearly that it was not. "The
shopkeeping occupations", remarks the Registrar-
General, "present some rather striking contrasts in
fertility, as recorded in these same tables. Some of the
goods distributing trades—butchers, fishmongers, green-
grocers—return rates little below the general average,
while other trades, of apparently much the same social
standing—tobacconists, grocers, drapers, boot and shoe
dealers, etc.—are greatly in defect. These differences
appear to be well established, applying, though—except
in the case of tobacconists—in somewhat less degree to
completed as well as continuing fertility. The differences

in the extent to which married female labour is employed in these trades (married females forming 18% of married males in the more fertile, and 27% in the less fertile of the two groups named) are too small to go far in accounting for the contrast. Still, it may not be altogether without significance that the least fertile of the seven trades quoted, tobacco distribution, employs the largest proportion of married female to married male labour—42%."[14]

Most of the evidence we have quoted so far is of groups classified by the occupation of the husband. When the table of fertility to which we have already referred (Table XLIX[15]) is considered, the low fertility of occupied married women is strikingly illustrated. Brushmakers and costermongers alone returned a standardized continuing fertility rate as high as that of the general population; and of all the occupations which can be compared with those in the tables where fertility is related to the occupation of the husband, lace-making alone returns a higher fertility for married women than for married males. In some instances the differences are very great, as of teachers, with a standardized total ratio of 70% for males and 52% for females; musicians, 78 and 54; clerks, 76 and 55; farmers, 101 and 83; woollen weavers, 79 and 59; textile dyers and finishers, 92 and 72; and barmen and barmaids, 100 and 63 respectively. Even in the case of persons returned as living on private means, the fertility is only 50% of average where the wife is so returned as against 59% where the description applies to the husband.

The opportunity of directly contrasting the fertility within occupational groups where the husband alone was employed with the fertility where both the husband and the wife were employed was lost when this Census material was being analysed; thus although this last table may be taken as illustrating the effect on fertility when both husband and wife were occupied, the tables where occupational classification is by the husband's occupation must also have included some instances where the wife was occupied also. The difference in fertility between the spinners and the weavers of cotton is therefore the best illustration of the diminished fertility of occupied married women contained in the report.

An attempt was made in the course of this same report to compare the fertility of the three occupational groups—agriculturalists, textile operatives, and miners in certain localities—with that of the remaining population in the same locality. The Registrar-General commented on the results of his comparisons:

"The result of the comparison as expressed in Table LI shows that the high fertility attached to mining and agriculture is largely or altogether peculiar to these industries, and shared only in a minor degree by the other inhabitants of the districts in which they are centred. On the other hand, the low fertility of the textile industry is very largely shared by the general population of the areas in which it is carried on. It would seem that while, generally speaking, there is some direct relation between the excess or deficiency in fertility of these important sections of the population dealt with and that of their neighbours (the order in rank of fertility of the latter being the same as that of the former, though the differences on which it depends are very much less), the excesses for mining and agriculture are chiefly dependent on the circumstances of these employments themselves. That this is not so in the case of textile production may be very largely because factory work by married women (which, as we have seen, is accompanied by low fertility) is open to the wives of men engaged in other occupations equally with those of male textile workers. Where the wife works little, as in agriculture, or not at all, as in mining, the husband's occupation alone can influence fertility; but where the wife works as much in textile production, it may be that her work largely, or even mainly, governs the situation."[16]

The evidence of the Fertility Commission therefore indicates that, at least during the later years of our period, the employment of married women in the cotton districts diminished their fertility. It is equally clear, as the diminution of fertility was common to all married women occupied away from home, that this was not conceivably due to the conditions of work in cotton mills.

This lower recorded fertility cannot be explained by one factor alone. Some mothers gave up their outside employment "when their families grew so large as to demand their attention at home";[17, 18] others were women deserted by their husbands; yet others may have worked in the mills and factories precisely because they were unable to have children for physiological reasons. Whether these factors were the entire explanation of the lower fertility of the married women factory worker during our period is, however, doubtful. As we shall see in subsequent chapters, the practice of leaving young children in the care of a local nurse while the mother worked in the mill was both expensive and dangerous. As the mothers can scarcely have been unaware of this, it is difficult to believe that their attitude to bearing children was unaffected by it; and it seems reasonable to believe that the lower fertility of the mother employed away from home was, in part at least, the almost inevitable result of the conflict between motherhood and the claims of her job.

It is not altogether certain how far the smaller family of the married woman worker was the result of "moral restraint" or contraceptive measures. Historical accounts of family limitation sometimes overlook the fact that birth-control literature had been quietly circulating in England many years before the Bradlaugh-Besant Trial of 1877–9. Francis Place had published his *Illustration and Proofs of Principles of Population* more than fifty years earlier (1822). Though many preceded Place in discussing methods, he seems to have been the first to venture upon an organized attempt to educate the masses, arguing that restriction of births would raise wages and end the necessity for child labour.[19] By clever and sometimes subterranean methods, he and his assistants succeeded in widely distributing medical handbills, such as "To the Married of Both Sexes" and "To the Married of Both Sexes of the Working Population", both published in 1823. The discussion that ensued caused them to be reprinted in several Radical journals of the period—Carlile's *Republican* and T. V. Wooler's *The Black Dwarf*. Two years later, Carlile published his *What is Love?* which was reprinted the following year as *Every Woman's Book: or What is Love?*, which enjoyed a huge circulation. In 1834, a reprint of Knowlton's *Fruits of Philosophy* was issued as a 6*d*. paper-bound pamphlet. For the next forty years this pamphlet, with other literature brought out in the intervening period, some of it directed specifically towards the working classes, enjoyed a quite large circulation— Knowlton's pamphlet selling 42,000 copies.[20]

Given the conflict between motherhood and money-earning, it would be highly unlikely that the operatives had not acquainted themselves with the information contained in these handbills and articles. This supposition gains support from the wide circulation enjoyed by Place's handbill in the manufacturing districts of the North and from a survey by the Manchester Statistical Society in 1835, *On Immoral and Irreligious Works sold in Manchester*. The results of this enquiry showed that 600 copies had been sold during the previous twelve months of *The Bridal Gem, Fruits of Philosophy*, and *Moral Physiology*. The true significance of these sales is perhaps best demonstrated by comparison with the sales of other works—with Paine's *Age of Reason*, for example, which had only sold 400 copies during the three years previous to the enquiry, and with his *Rights of Man*, which had sold 800 copies during the same period. Moreover, "in the 1830s, at the same time that immorality in the factory districts was being computed according to off-spring born out of wedlock, the charge was made that the fact that no unlawful children could be produced for the records was attributable to the wide circulation of books on birth-control by Carlile".[21] There is no reason to suppose that the reading of Carlile was confined to potential prostitutes.

This is borne out in the preface to a collection of letters from working women all over the country published in 1915 by the Women's Co-operative Guild. The editor states emphatically: "it is absolutely certain that the decline in the birth-rate during the past forty years amongst textile workers is mainly due to the deliberate limitation of the family".[22] Many of the letters themselves contain clear evidence that methods of artificial birth-control were indeed known and practised amongst married women working not only in the mills but elsewhere. These women deliberately controlled their own fertility partly to avoid the physical rigours of bearing children in quick succession, but partly also that the standard of living made possible by the wife's contribution to the family income might not be imperilled by a large family, whose demands might force the mother to give up her employment.[23]

It is important to bear in mind that a large number of the married women were out at work in the factories and workshops because their husbands were unable, for one reason or another, to provide an income adequate to the needs of their households. In these cases, the incentive to limit the size of their family was particularly strong. That this is rather more than idle speculation is proved by evidence given before the Interdepartmental Committee on Physical Deterioration.[24]

Whether or not, during our period, the size of the working wife's family was diminished by means of abortion can only be a matter of conjecture in the absence of reliable material. In the course of their enquiries, the 1833 Factory Commissioners asked an overseer of the poor at Stockport:

"Are you aware whether any means are used to procure abortion in Stockport?"—"Some instances there are, but I have no reason to believe that they are more frequent in Stockport than in any other places."

"Have you any reason to believe that attempts to procure abortion are more frequently made by the factory women than non-factory women?"—"No, I have not observed that; the cases are so very rare."

"Are you aware whether any means are employed among factory females in Stockport to prevent conception?"—"I am not."

"Do you suspect there are?"—"I do not."

"Do you think any such means could be generally used without your knowledge?"—"I do not."[25]

Be this as it may, allegations of the prevalence of abortion among operatives caused some concern in later years. When, for example, in the late 1890s it was proposed that one month's compulsory absence from work after their confinement for women employed in factories and workshops should be extended to at least three months, the factory inspectresses urged that "if married women were forced to forgo the money they earned for many months, the allegation that there is increasing use of unlawful means to prevent child-bearing . . . would have further to be considered. Some of the notes on bad influences in Burnley refer to the presence there of this debasing and disintegrating factor, and similar evidence is forthcoming from Nottingham, Leicester, etc."[26] How far these assertions were justified and how far abortion was prevalent among operatives compared with other groups it is impossible to judge. Nevertheless, the matter was deemed grave enough to be included in a Board of Health investigation into the causes of infant mortality in Lancashire in 1912.

Dr. Copeman, one of the investigators, whose area included Burnley, Colne, and Nelson, reported:

"At an early state of my investigation I found the prevalent belief that the use of abortification drugs, and also of various procedures directed towards the prevention of pregnancy or, in the alternative, of procuring a miscarriage or abortion has greatly increased in Burnley and Nelson, especially during the last few years.

"I found a fairly general consensus of opinion that among the cotton operatives a considerable proportion of married women are desirous of avoiding pregnancy if possible . . . by one means or another.

"Both in Burnley and Nelson, during the past few years, certain individuals have come under suspicion of practising abortion, and I was informed that in each of those towns a prosecution has been followed by conviction and a sentence of penal servitude."[27]

In Wigan the investigator was assured that "abortion by operative interference is not uncommon in the town, and that the practice of 'drug-taking', usually of dialehyn pills, which were supposed to contain lead, in the hope of terminating pregnancy, is widely practised among married women.

"This statement was confirmed by a number of mid-wives who conferred with the medical officer and myself. . . . They testified that the practice of taking abortificant drugs was common among the married women in Wigan. They gave the names of five persons, including a herbalist and a grocer, who were known to traffic in drugs, the composition of which was stated to me. A woman who was formerly a midwife with a large practice in the town is now in penal servitude, having been convicted as an abortionist, and I was informed that after her arrest several women in the neighbourhood were suffering from severe haemorrhage, but dared not call in medical assistance."[28]

Similar evidence was produced for Stockport.[29]

Whether the method of limitation chosen was contraception or abortion, there can be little doubt that active measures on the part of the operatives to limit the

size of their family increased over our period, as will be
seen from the marked decrease in the size of families
among couples married 1881–6 as compared with those
married 1851–61 shown in the following figures taken
from the Report of the 1911 Fertility Commission:

*Average Size of Completed Families of Women in Various
Social Classes who married 1851–61 and 1881–6 as a
Percentage of the Average for All Classes*

	I	II	III	IV	V	VI	VII	VIII
1851–61	86	98	101	100	105	99	110	106
1881–6	72	86	102	102	112	93	132	113
% reduction	33	30	21	20	15	22	10	15

It is thus quite certainly true that the employment of
married women away from home during the late years
of our period resulted in their diminished fertility. In
view of the unreliability of the earliest contemporary
records, it may well be equally true of the earlier years
also.

It should, however, be clearly understood that the
fertility referred to in this chapter is total fertility—that
is to say, the number of children born to employed
married women. When effective fertility is considered—
the total number of children surviving in each family—
other considerations and factors come into operation.
These we must now discuss.

CHAPTER VIII

THE SACRIFICE OF INFANTS

"What do they do," asked Charles Dickens of the Rector of a parish in a large English town, "what do they do with the infants of the mothers who work in the mills?" "Oh," replied the clergyman, "they bring them to me, and I take care of them in the churchyard!"[1]

Fielden, introducing the 1847 Factory Bill in the House of Commons, referred to the effect of the long hours of work of the married cotton operatives on the lives of their youngest children in the following terms: "I hear men talk glibly of the 'horrors of war'; and I believe there is in this country a 'Peace Preservation Society', whose object is to show mankind that nations, to avoid such horrors, should always remain at peace. I applaud their efforts; but let me ask what are the 'horrors of war' but a wholesale sacrifice of human life now and then occurring? They are horrors, and I respect those who bestow the energy of their minds in endeavours to convince the world of their futility and wickedness: but when the Registrar-General in the document I have just quoted [viz. A Table of Deaths Registered in 115 Districts in England during the Quarter ending 30th September 1846] notifies to us the horrible sacrifice of human life that is annually perpetrated in our manufacturing towns, far exceeding the average sacrifice of life by war, I think we should give an earnest of our desire to avoid such horrors by immediately setting to work, in every practical form, to effect the object at home."[2]

Others expressed the same view with less reference to

statistics and considerably more literary embellishment. "When mothers work away from home, families must be neglected at home; and as most plants die when they have neither food nor sunshine, so children die as the chords of maternal affection slacken into indifference, by separation, and disappear altogether as the domestic hearth grows colder and colder, and the ashes, the only things which never contain fire, accumulate in it."[3] Thus R. Smith Baker depicts the results of the employment of mothers.

These are but a few illustrations from the discussions of our period[4]—a problem that was still absorbing the interest of many at the beginning of this present century, and indeed even later.[5]

The deleterious influence of a mother's employment on the life of her baby was first heard of in this country in connexion with the employment of married women in the Lancashire mills. As the years passed, however, it became clear that this was a problem that could neither be properly discussed nor remedied in terms of Lancashire alone, and by the end of the century sufficient proof of this had accumulated for some sort of general statutory restriction to be placed on the employment of mothers. But this is to anticipate the following chapters.

Clearly this alleged connexion between the employment of married women in cotton mills and the high infant death-rate prevailing in Lancashire towns was dependent on the prolonged absence of the mothers from home during the day. Equally it was dependent on the relative number of married and unmarried women operatives; and, more particularly upon the proportion of married women who had children under one year of age.

These proportions were often grossly exaggerated by the statesmen, politicians, and philanthropists who lent their eloquence to the contemporary debates on the subject. Ashley, though one of the earliest, and perhaps the most notorious offender in this respect, was by no means the only one to err. There were many who assumed (and wrongly so, as we have already seen) that by far the greater number of women factory operatives were married; and further assumed that most, if not all, of the married women were the mothers of young children. This they did on little or no evidence.

Reference has already been made to the estimates, published in a pamphlet circulated in the middle of the last century, which showed the proportion of married to unmarried women cotton operatives employed in Manchester and Salford.[6] Here it was stated that these married women were "for the most part young and having young families":[7] a statement for which no authority was cited or forthcoming.

Mr. Herford, the Coroner for Manchester, had to refute a suggestion put to him some years later, in 1871, "that maybe in his district there were 30,000 to 40,000 mothers working in textiles".[8] It is illuminating to compare this estimate with figures published in the occupational tables in the Registrar-General's returns for the Census of 1861,[9] where it will be found that the total number of women over twenty years married and unmarried employed in cotton manufacture in the Manchester district in 1861 was 10,983.

Mundella, in the debates in the House of Commons on the Factory Amendment Bill, 1873, claims that statistics showed that of 557,377 women and girls employed in cotton mills, 184,000 were the mothers of families.[10] It soon transpired, however, in subsequent discussion both in the House and elsewhere, that these "statistics", the source of which was never disclosed, really referred to the estimated proportion of married women; and the construction put on them by Mundella, that all these married women were mothers of families, was without any foundation whatsoever save in his own imagination.[11]

A more realistic estimate of the proportion of married women mill operatives who were the mothers of very young children may be derived from the data collected in the course of the random sample of the 1851 Census household schedules referred to in Chapter II.

The results of this sample show that, in the seven Lancashire registration districts investigated, the proportion of married women operatives with children under one year of age in 1851 ranged from 14·95% to 27·45%, the average for the seven districts being 21·03%.

These figures exclude mothers employed in the hand-loom weaving of cotton and are thus a conservative estimate, since "weaving is not invariably a domestic occupation among the hand-loom weavers as it is among the silk weavers: in most cases they work at home; but the practice is beginning to extend itself of assembling them in factories".[12] There is some reason to believe that it was the younger weavers, which would include women with young children, who formed the majority of hand-loom factory workers.

Philanthropists and politicians were not alone in maintaining that the employment of mothers in Lancashire had a direct, and deleterious, effect on the infant death-rate. The Registrar-General, in his introduction to the 1851 Census tables, comments, not for the first time: "The duties of a wife and mother and a mistress of a family can only be performed by unremitting attention; accordingly, it is found that where the women are much employed away from home the children . . . perish in large numbers."[13] Similarly, the Medical Officer of the Privy Council (John Simon), writing of the causes of infant mortality, refers to "there being certain large manufacturing towns where women are greatly engaged in branches of industry away from home".[14]

Moreover, the factory inspectors for the Lancashire area, the local medical officers of health and general practitioners in the mill towns, all of whom were able to judge from first-hand professional experience, subscribed to the same view. After pointing out the "grave moral dangers" of having women employed in factories, a factory inspector for part of the north-west of England writes in one of his reports for 1864: "But I think there is still greater danger consecutive on the employment of young mothers in congregational labour, the result of which is a considerable loss of infant life annually, a loss which might be saved to the country, and in lives which are literally thrown away."[15] Dr. J. Brown, Medical Officer of Health for Bacup, speaking at the Liverpool Congress of the Sanitary Science and Preventive Medicine Association in 1895, agrees: "Most of the medical officers who were engaged in the manufacturing towns in Lancashire were perfectly cognisant of the evils which caused the high rate of infant mortality. Speaking as a medical officer of health in north-east Lancashire for seventeen years, he felt that the sacrifice of innocents was something lamentable."[16, 17]

Perhaps the following comment best sums up the prevailing informed opinion. "The result of the enquiry approaches unanimity only on one point, but on that point we submit that the medical evidence is conclusive, viz. the great damage and loss of life caused by the employment of suckling women as they are now employed in factories . . . nor is this, as far as we can learn, doubted by any person, medical or not, who has any experience of the factory system as it prevails in large towns. Those of our correspondents who see no evidence of increased mortality reside chiefly in country districts or in parts of the county where suckling women do not generally work."[18]

The graph on p. 104 illustrates why it was that the causes of the infant death-rate in Lancashire called for such detailed investigation. Further graphs are appended for the period 1855–74, the years during which the basic data were collected, illustrating the infant mortality of Lancashire as compared with that prevailing in various agricultural counties, of the mining and industrial county of Staffordshire, and of the mining county of Durham.[19] All these graphs are based on the figures published in the annual reports of the Registrar-General.

As most of the investigations we propose to discuss also derive their statistical data from the same source, a word must be said on their accuracy.

The accurate calculation of an infant death-rate clearly depends primarily on the accuracy of the registration of births and deaths; in this period, such registration was far from complete. This deficiency was

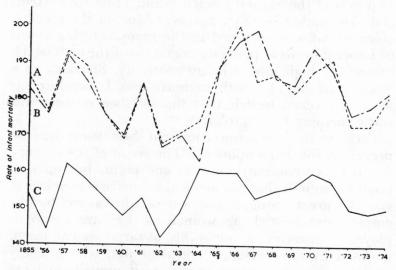

Graph 1, the Mortality of infants — 1 year per 1,000 births in the entire County of Lancaster (A), in the Districts of that County affected by the Cotton Famine (B), and in England and Wales (C), 1855-74.

perhaps better recognized and assessed by Dr. William Farr, who was Head of the Statistical Department of the Registrar-General's office, than by any other contemporary observer. On several occasions in his "Annual Letter to the Registrar-General", printed as an appendix to the Registrar-General's reports, he draws attention to it.[20] Again, in his evidence to the Select Committee on the Best Means of Protecting Infants put out to Nurse, 1871, he gives a very full statement on the system of registration then operating: "Under the Act, 6 & 7 Will. IV, c. 86,[21] no one is bound to give information of the birth having occurred; there is no penalty attached to negligence of this kind in England."[22] This being so, there is no possible clue to the exact number of births escaping registration, though it is known that, over the whole period, this deficiency declined.[23]

Still-born children were not registered at all, "in fact, the registrar is not authorized to register still-born children".[24] It was possible, even if a child died many days after its birth, for a person to take it to an undertaker and declare it still-born, and for it to be buried "lawfully" without its having been certified in either the records of births or deaths. It was thought by some that the number of children being thus born and buried was extremely large—sufficiently large to make a difference of as much as 6% in the death-rate in the first year of life in England.[25] Farr himself certainly would not have shared this view, but that such burials were possible at all he admitted to be a grave defect in the system.

With regard to the registration of deaths in general, it was compulsory in so far as no person could bury another without a certificate of death. Or, more properly stated, they could bury, but the clergyman was bound to give the information to the registrar of the district within seven days; if he failed to give information, he subjected himself to a penalty not exceeding £10, "but that is very difficult to work".[26] In cases of concealment of death, there was no penalty at all.[27]

Yet another source of error was the manner in which notification of death was given to the registrar: "A person present at the death, or in attendance during the last illness of the deceased person, goes to or sends for the registrar of his district in which the death happens, gives the requisite information and signs the register book as the informant either in writing or by mark. The qualification implies that the informant has seen the deceased person alive during the last illness, but beyond that there is no restriction in the Act on capacity, character, sex, and age."[28] A medical certificate of death could be asked for, but was not legally required, and the informant could not be compelled to produce such a document.[29] A great number were buried without one, and this was particularly the case with regard to children.[30] That this was open to the gravest abuse is beyond question.[31]

In view of these admitted deficiencies of the statistics, their value as evidence is much diminished; and yet, because they are the only official statistics, they are not without interest; nor are they altogether without value, particularly if care is taken to collect them for a lengthy period so as to minimize extraordinary local conditions, such as epidemics.

With these reservations in mind, therefore, when we come to examine the graphs and compare the infant death-rate prevailing in Lancashire, as compared with that prevailing in England and Wales generally and in other particular counties, it is obvious that there must be some special causes operating in Lancashire to produce so high a rate. It is not surprising, in view of the geographical concentration in the county of the cotton industry, which employed many thousands of women, that it should be maintained that one of these causes was the absence during the day of mothers who were employed in the mills.

Against this hypothesis it was naturally argued that the inadequate solution to the problems of public health posed by the aggregation of large numbers of people in the industrial towns, large and small, of Lancashire harmed adults and children alike and sufficiently explained the high infant death-rate.[32]

Of the rate of general mortality in Lancashire, the Registrar-General in his Report for the first quarter of 1864 writes: "the mortality of the counties which are now suffering from the cotton crisis has always been higher than the mortality of the rest of the kingdom, owing chiefly to the sanitary defects of the towns. . . . Mr. Rawlinson, in his intelligent report, justly says, 'the high death-rate prevailing in the Lancashire towns has its main cause in the foul cottage cess-pit. The inspection of any town in the district will show this.' "[33]

That the physical conditions of town life in the nineteenth century exerted an influence detrimental to the health of young and old alike was never disputed. John Simon, for example, specifically states: "It cannot be too distinctly recognized that a high local death-rate of children must also necessarily denote a local prevalence of those causes which determine a degeneration of the race."[34] What was disputed, however, was the contention that sanitary defects were the sole important explanation of the deaths of infants in Lancashire.

The Rev. J. Clay, in his "Report on the Sanitary Condition of Preston", writes: "The filthiness, want of drainage, bad air, etc., already described will account for very much of the infantile death; but there is reason to fear that in addition to those causes which are alike obnoxious to adult and infant health, there are others operating peculiarly against the latter."[35]

Among those other causes, the employment of mothers in the cotton mills was claimed to be of great importance. Clay draws attention to the results of a study by Messrs. Harrison and Ewing on the health of the families of the 749 married men employed in factories, which showed that of 100 children dying under eleven and a half years of age, 76 died before they were five years old; among the "dressers"—the better-paid section of the group—the loss of children under five years was only 62·2%. From the figures for all England and Wales, it was shown that of 100 children dying under fifteen years, 84 died before they reached their fifth year. "May the lower death-rate of the children in the group be because the majority of the mothers were at home?" asks Clay. Only 133 of the wives of the 749 men operatives were employed away from home.[36]

Of a similar nature, and supporting Clay's suggestion, is the evidence of Mr. Fletcher, a surgeon at Bury, who wrote to Lord John Manners: ". . . While preparing a report for the Health of Towns Commission, my attention had been attracted to the great mortality, especially among infants, in the factory districts of the town [viz. Bury] and its neighbourhood, compared with those in which few mills existed." In calculating the death-rates of infants under two years, the better- and worse-conditioned localities were carefully distinguished; and in each district the factory operatives were distinguished from the other working classes. "I give below the deaths under two years of age of the children of factory operatives and other operatives in three districts which, differing materially in their sanitary conditions and containing a large proportion of factory people, afford a fair comparison. The first is a town district extremely ill-conditioned as regards ventilation, draining and cleaning. In this locality, the deaths of infants under two years of factory operatives amounted to $61\frac{1}{5}\%$; other operatives, $32\frac{3}{4}\%$. In the registration district of Bury North, exclusive of the above, the average deaths of infants under two years of factory operatives amounted to $54\frac{3}{5}\%$; other operatives, $33\frac{1}{3}\%$. In Woodhill district, lying a short distance from the town and particularly well situated as regards the health of its population, the general mortality of the northern suburb of which it forms a part being 1 in $44\frac{3}{10}\%$, which is, I believe, the average of all England, and being in this particular locality 1 in 40, the cottages of the operatives being also more roomy, better ventilated and more cleanly than is generally the case, we find that the deaths of infants under two years of factory operatives amount to 56%; other operatives, 33%. In other districts, the disparity appears even greater, but the proportion of operatives who work in factories is so small that I do not consider that the comparison is a fair one. I have only further to state that these calculations are made on the average of seven years, and include every death that has occurred under two years of age in these localities. They appear calculated to rebut the assumption that it is the condition of large towns and not the employment in factories which produces . . . the mortality of the infant population in manufacturing districts. This, as you are aware, has been strongly maintained by several medical practitioners and others."[37]

This type of investigation was later carried out elsewhere, with similar results. Holmes and Bridges, to whose report we have already referred, quote a speech made by a member of Bradford Town Council:

"In September 1872," he said, "178 infants under five years of age died in Bradford: 115 of these deaths, or 64·6% were of children −1 year of age; 47, or 26·4%, were of children above 1 year and −2 years; leaving 9% of children over 2 years of age.

"These 178 children had 172 mothers. Of these, 62 went away from home to work, principally, of course, to the factories; 110 did not go out to work. An inquiry was instituted as to the number of children that each of these sets of mothers had borne, and the proportion of them which had died. The 110 mothers who did not go out to work had borne 544 children, of whom 248, or 45·5%, had died.

"The 62 mothers who went out to work had borne 185 children, of whom 127, or 68·6%, had died."[38]

The results of these investigations are based on very small numbers, and do not by themselves constitute conclusive evidence that the employment of mothers in the cotton mills was one of the causes of the high infant death-rate of Lancashire; yet later evidence produced by other investigations of a similar nature corroborated them as also did the results of contemporary investigations of a somewhat different nature.

Dr. Greenhow, summing up the results of his investigations into the factors affecting the health of people in England and Wales, as reflected in the vital statistics for 1847–54, writes: "One of the most evident facts brought to light by the present investigation is the influence of occupation on health. This influence is either direct, as in the case of cutlers in Sheffield, the lead-miners of Ashton, the lace-makers of Towcester and Bedford, or the silk manufacturers of Macclesfield; or it is indirect, as where the employment of women seems to aggravate the infant mortality."[39] This conclusion was confirmed by his later investigation, under the auspices of the Medical Officer of the Privy Council, into "The Circumstances under which there is Excessive Mortality of Young Children among Certain Manufacturing Populations".[40] To the evidence on which these two similar enquiries was based, we shall return presently.

At this point it is worth paying some attention to the Report published in 1864 on an enquiry into "The Excessive Mortality of Infants in Some Rural Districts of England", conducted by Dr. Julian Hunter, which not only contains further evidence to support the case that infant mortality was not merely the result of the overcrowded conditions of town life, but also throws some light on the effect of a mother's employment in the fields on the life of her infant.

This enquiry was instituted after a general enquiry into "the extent of marsh diseases in those districts which have a reputation for breeding it" had revealed that in some entirely rural marsh districts, the mortality of infants, on the evidence of the previous ten years, was almost as high as that of some of the large towns: that the infant mortality of Wisbech, for example, was within a fraction as high as that of Manchester. Hunter writes:

"If the rural districts be turned to, it will be found that throughout the pastoral districts of Bellingham, Glendale, and Rothbury . . . a low infant death-rate prevails . . . but, on the other hand, it is apparent that some few of the thoroughly rural districts, having no extraordinary mortality at all ages, and no factories whatever, still have an infant mortality which is equalled by only a few of the large towns.

"If those districts distinguished by a high rate of infant mortality, not to be explained by the presence of factories or mines, be selected from the list, it is found that those in which the mortality is above 20,000 in 100,000 living at the age, are but the centres of a large country in which the rate is above the English average and lie in five districts or clusters of districts . . . they all lie on or near the mouth of the large rivers pouring into the North Sea.

"(1) At the point where the Ouse, Aire, Don, and Trent meet to form the Humber Estuary, Howden, Goole, and Thorne have an infantile death-rate of 23,375, 21,815, 20,744.

"(2) Around the Wash, a large part of Norfolk, Lincolnshire, and Cambridgeshire is involved in the same character, together with the banks of the Lower Ouse, Nene, Welland, and Fossdyke. This area contains the following districts: Wisbech (26,001), King's Lynn (22,561), Ely (22,016), North Witchford (22,601), Downham (23,106), Whittlesey (23,772), Walsingham (21,778), Docking (22,273), Spalding (21,845), Holbeach (23,495), Freebridge Lynn (19,606).

"(3) A third country consists of the mouth of the Wansum, Yare, Bure, and Waveney, containing the districts of Yarmouth and Mutford. Yarmouth has an infant mortality rate of 22,486; it is, however, a manufacturing town, containing a silk mill and many women employed in net-making. If it stood alone, therefore, it might, like Norwich, which itself presents an infant death-rate of 23,517, be excepted from the present enquiry; but with Yarmouth is included a small area adjoining the rural district of Mutford, which itself has an infant mortality rate of 21,101.

"(4) A fourth scene of infant death is inland; but except for the parish of Buckenham, scarcely above the level of the sea, Wayland, 20,711, and Guiltcross, 21,508, are mostly low, fenny districts lying in the middle of East Anglia and are of no great extent of population.

"(5) The small district of Hoo on the Medway,

opposite to Chatham, which has an infant death-rate of 24,452.''[41]

The significance of these death-rates is perhaps best appreciated when related to those of other districts of different densities of population. Ely and North Witchford, for example, had an infant death-rate equal to that of Salford and Blackburn; Spalding was equal in this respect to Whitechapel, and, as we have already seen, Wisbech was on a par with Manchester. Yet the density of population in Ely and North Witchford was 3·57 and 3·86 acres to a person respectively; the density in Salford and Blackburn was 0·05 and 0·48 acres to a person; in Spalding, the density was 3·32 acres to a person; in Whitechapel, 0·246; in Wisbech, 3·78 acres to a person; in Manchester, 0·05 acres.[42]

"The opinions of about seventy medical practitioners, with those of other gentlemen", were obtained concerning this phenomenon. "With wonderful accord, the cause of mortality was traced by nearly all those well qualified to witness to the bringing of the land under tillage—that is, to the cause which has banished malaria, and has substituted a fertile though unsightly garden for the winter marshes and summer pastures of fifty or a hundred years ago. It was generally thought that the infants no longer received any injury from soil, climate, or malarious influences, but that a more fatal enemy had been introduced by the employment of mothers in the fields. . . . It appears that the land in these districts is generally light, and that the recently reclaimed 'black lands' are very light indeed, and may be submitted to women's work to a far greater extent than anywhere else in the kingdom. . . . A party of women will often come from several miles off to work at a village. . . . One source of profit in the employment of women is the superior management and consideration they show in combining their work with that of boys and girls, and this quality has led to the frequent formation of what are called 'gangs' of women and children who work together for a stated sum paid by the farmer to a man called the undertaker, who contracts for the whole gang. These gangs will often travel many miles from their own village; they are to be met, morning and evening, on the roads . . . looking wonderfully strong and healthy, but . . . heedless of the fatal results which their love of this busy independent life is bringing on their unfortunate offspring, who are left pining at home.''[43]

Such was the evidence that could be adduced to refute the contention that the high infant death-rate of Lancashire was adequately explained by the over-crowded conditions of the towns.

Further evidence was collected to prove that, in Lancashire at least, the excessive infant mortality was also not a reflection of the social structure of the population. Such evidence was essential for those who sought to prove that the employment of mothers in cotton mills increased the infant death-rate, since various calculations were published during the period of the different rates of infant mortality prevailing in different social classes which showed that among children of the working classes the rate was higher than that of the middle and upper classes.

The Rev. J. Clay, in his "Report on the Sanitary Condition of Preston", constructed tables based on the entries in the Superintendent Registrar's books for the years 1832–43,[44] in which he showed that the death-rate for children under five years of age of gentlemen and professional men was about 17%; among tradesmen 38% and among operatives 55%.

From another of his tables, it is found that, of every 100 children born among the gentry, 91 reach their first year; of every 100 born among the tradespeople, 80 reach their first year; whilst among the operatives 68 survive so long.

To similar effect may be quoted the results of an enquiry, published in 1874, by Mr. C. Ansell into the death-rate among 49,099 English children of the upper and professional classes: he found that the infant death-rate among these was 80·5 per 1,000, whereas the general infant death-rate for England and Wales in 1875 was 158.[45, 46]

The disparity between the infant death-rate of the operatives and that of the well-to-do was said to be caused "partly from possessing less ample means of treatment of disease, partly from inadequate food, but mainly through the impure atmosphere which commonly surrounds their overcrowded and unventilated dwellings".[47]

It was possible to admit the general validity of such statements, however, and still feel that the complete explanation had not yet been found. "I am not satisfied with the general allegation that the excess of deaths are due to the poverty so often experienced in the manufacturing districts", says Lyon Playfair.[48] . . . "I have already stated in the low-waged counties of Wiltshire only 11% of all the children born were swept off before they attained one year of age; whilst 17% are removed by death in Lancashire; and Mrs. Robertson adduces similar facts by a comparison of the county of Dorsetshire. The pauperism is also greater in agricultural counties than in Lancashire—in the latter being one in two of inhabitants, in the former county referred to one in eight. Mr. Farr coincides with the opinion that pauperism is not the cause of the excessive mortality in our cities, for in his first letter to the Registrar-General he says: 'The occupations in cities are not more laborious than those in agriculture, and the great mass of the people of the town population has constant exercise and employment, their wages are higher, their dwellings are good, their clothing as warm and their food certainly as substantial as that of the agricultural labourer. The Poor Law enquiry and successive Parliamentary committees have shown that the families of agricultural labourers subsist upon a minimum of animal food and an inadequate supply of bread and potatoes.' "[49, 50]

This was not by any means the only evidence that could be adduced to show that poverty was not the exclusive cause of the excess of infant deaths in Lancashire. On two distinct occasions when, because of fluctuations in trade, there was considerable distress in the cotton districts, evidence was collected which showed that there was a positive saving of infant life. As poverty on this scale could not be said actively to promote health, the fall of the infant death-rate was ascribed to the abatement of some other influence. What that influence was claimed to be we shall presently see.

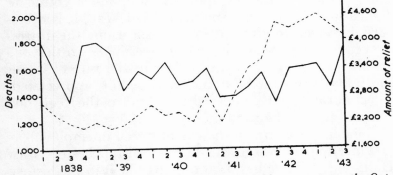

Graph 2, Chart of the rise and fall in amount paid per quarter to the Out-Door Poor of Manchester Union, and of the number of deaths in each quarter for the period 1838–43. Line of pauperism given by Mr. Royston––a clerk in the Manchester Union Office. Report of Health of Towns Commission, Part II, 1845, p. 69.

------- Amount of Relief
——— Number of Deaths

In the copy of the graph constructed by Lyon Playfair for the Health of Towns Commission[51] it will be noticed that in 1842, "a year of great outcry and distress" as compared with the year 1838, there was a decrease in the number of deaths in the Manchester Union, "notwithstanding the crowding of families into one tenement, due to poverty. Dr. Arnott, Mr. Chadwick, and others are of the opinion that the experience of the late distress indicates some *direct* connexion between the poverty of the country and its diminished mortality. . . . In years of distress, many mothers, unable to work at factories, remain at home, giving unusual care to their children. This circumstance, and the compulsory sobriety of the adults, will sufficiently account for the diminished mortality of such periods"[52]—a finding which agreed with the explanation given of the decrease of mortality in Paisley and Glasgow in similar circumstances a short time before.[53]

The evidence from the distress of 1842 was but slight in comparison with that collected during the years of the "Cotton Famine".[54]

This is not the place for a detailed history of the social consequences of the disruption of supplies of cotton to Lancashire during the American Civil War; it is necessary, however, to give a few facts concerning the distress it occasioned amongst the cotton operatives, so that the significance of the evident decline in the rate of infant mortality during the "Famine" may be fully appreciated, a decline to which Farr drew the attention of the Registrar-General in a memorandum.[55]

Cobden, speaking on the extent of the unemployment at a meeting on 29th April 1862 at the Manchester Town Hall, said: "There has been nothing like it in the history of the world for its suddenness, for the impossibility of dealing with it or managing it in the way of effective remedy."[56]

In 1863, the Registrar-General wrote that in Lancashire "the staple industry on which half a million persons is dependent is overthrown, and for a twelve-month, four-fifths of that number have subsisted, unless the pittance has been aided by previous earnings or sale of household stock, on less than 4d. a day per head".[57]

On this estimate, the operatives and their families were living on roughly 2s. per head per week; some were living on as little as 1s. per head per week. This was in many cases augmented by provision of fuel and blankets, and by tickets for the soup-kitchens opened by local philanthropists and relief committees.[58] Even so, the hardships sustained by a population which in normal times was accustomed to spend sometimes as much as 2s. 7½d. per head per week on food *alone* were obvious to all observers.[59]

Not only was meat eliminated from their diet almost entirely (except for such meat-soup as they were given or were able to purchase from the soup-kitchen),[60] many families were forced to move to cheaper dwellings in the more pestiferous quarters of the town, and there, crowded together, lived in extreme penury, "pinching and pining and nursing the flickering hope of better days which might enable them to flee from the foul harbour which strong necessity has driven them to".[61]

These facts made it all the more remarkable that in the years 1862 and 1864 there was a decrease in the number of deaths registered as compared with those of the previous year; and the increase in the deaths registered in the affected districts of Lancashire in 1863 was ascribed by the Registrar-General to "the unfavourable influences that were at work and pervaded the country generally, and Lancashire did not suffer more than most parts, but less than some".[62]

This was the subject of much comment at the time.[63] It was known that there was an increased migration from the stricken areas, but that this was not the cause of the fall in the number of deaths registered may be seen from the following comment by the Registrar-General:[64] "It might be presumed that emigration from the north-west counties during the continued depression of their staple industry has confined the registration of deaths in these parts within narrower limits than otherwise it would have attained. That cause has no doubt had its effect; but the fact that the registration of births, simultaneously conducted, was not inactive, proves that it did not operate to an important extent." The birth-rate in the affected areas in 1861 was 2·57 per 1,000 people living; in 1862, 2·68; in 1863, 2·66.[65]

As far as the present enquiry is concerned, however, the real significance in the number of deaths registered lay in the comparison of the general death-rate and the infant death-rate during the three years most affected by the distress, 1862, 1863, and 1864. While the general death-rate in 1861 was 34·55, in 1862, 40·79, in 1863, 31·08, in 1864, 40·19, the infant death-rates for the same years were 184, 166, 170, and 163. Moreover, as will be seen in the graph 5 on page 104, the fall in the infant death-rate in the districts most affected by the distress was more significant than for the county as a whole. Clearly, there was statistical evidence to support the view that the real saving of life during the "Famine" lay in the saving of infant life.[66] Nor was the evidence for this to be found only in the statistics. "Viewing the social and moral changes that may have resulted from the Lancashire distress, are there", asks Buchanan, "any exceptional material conditions that are likely to be related thereto? On few subjects was more singleness of opinion shown than on the mortality and diseases of young children. Medical men and registrars[67] were agreed that, apart from special epidemics, as in 1863–4,[68] the ordinary maladies of childhood had been very lightly felt up to the present time. This fact was imputed with almost equal unanimity to the greater care bestowed on infants by their unemployed mothers than by the hired nursery helpers."[69]

"The care of mothers has, it would seem, counteracted the effects of privation, so that the neglect of their homes by mothers at work in factories is apparently more fatal than starvation."[70]

Comparison between privation and maternal care on the one hand, and good cheer and maternal neglect on the other, to the advantage of the meaner diet and greater care must be kept within limits. "Nursing in straitened circumstances may be better for the children than fullness of good cheer without it; but when the bad times prolonged and the small stores that had been gathered in a day of full work are exhausted, the greatest amount of parental affection will not expel physical

decline, sickness, and death itself from the dwelling."[71]
But the obviousness of the limitation did not diminish
the significance of the facts, and of the official evidence
connected with them.[72, 73]

It was becoming increasingly clear that it was not only
true of the cotton mills that the employment of mothers
entailed the sacrifice of infant life. Data collected from
other sources showed that such was the price of the
employment of mothers away from home, whether in
factory or field.

An attempt was made to prove beyond doubt the
general relationship between the occupation of mothers
away from home and a high rate of infant mortality
by comparing the rate of infant mortality of districts
where married women were much employed away from
home with those where they were not.

In the anonymous pamphlet, *Public Nurseries*, published in 1851, which we have already quoted, tables
were given based on the Registrar-General's figures for
1838–44, which claimed to show that, in the first place,
towns with an equal general death-rate did not exhibit
an equal infant death-rate, and that, in the second place,
towns in which women were much employed away
from home tended to have a higher infant death-rate
than towns where they were not. However, the method
by which the authors of this pamphlet sought to prove
their case diminished the significance of their results. To
compare a crude general death-rate with a specific
death-rate, as was done in these tables, is not a valid
statistical procedure. Again, the infant death-rate in
these tables is expressed as a percentage of the total
number of deaths—a result obviously influenced by the
age structure of the population of these towns, of which
we are given no account.

Later investigations of the same type, but using valid
techniques, did appear to show, however, that such a
general relationship might be demonstrated. Particularly
interesting are the results of the investigations into the

causes of the high infant death-rate of Staffordshire by Dr. George Reid, County Medical Officer of Health. As Reid himself explained in a paper read to the Public Medicine Section at the Annual Meeting of the B.M.A. in 1892,[74] Staffordshire was an ideal area for such an investigation:

". . . The county is divided into two populous areas, each composed of abutting urban districts (central Staffordshire being mainly rural). As regards the general sanitary conditions, no apparent distinction can be drawn between the northern and southern towns, but in one respect—namely, occupation—the two populations differ considerably. In the south of the county the people are mostly engaged in coal-mines and iron works, in which the element of female labour may be disregarded, while in the north the chief industry is potting, in which large numbers of women are employed."

He then goes on: "Three years ago, when first it became my duty to collate the reports of the various medical officers of health, what impressed me most forcibly was the extraordinarily high infant death-rate in certain districts. Further than this . . . the broad fact was apparent that the rate was much higher in the north than in the south of the county, a circumstance which has since been proved by figures covering, in most cases, a period of ten years, and which show a rate of 182 as compared with 158.

"At first, I had not sufficient personal knowledge of the district to enable me to form an opinion with regard to the possible explanation of this, but I have since satisfied myself that it is not to be attributed to any appreciable difference in local conditions. This being the case, I determined, if possible, to institute an enquiry with a view to determining whether, and to what extent, female labour would account for the marked difference in the rates; this paper is the outcome of this enquiry."

The population included in Reid's investigation amounted to 529,501, and the mortality statistics were

collected for a period of ten years (1881–90). In dividing
the towns into groups for the purpose of comparison,
those which were distinctly rural, as regards population,
as well as others which were largely residential, were
excluded, the only towns included being "those having
distinctly artisan populations".

Of these there were twenty-six, with populations
varying from 32,121, to 2,454, their total population
being 438,712.

These towns he further subdivided into three groups
according to the relative proportion of married women
engaged in work. In addition to the blank forms for the
decennial returns of infant deaths, etc., a circular letter
was sent to each medical officer of health, explaining
the object of the enquiry and inviting qualifying
comments which each might consider necessary.

From this information, amplified in certain cases by
information from employers, the industrial towns were
subdivided into three broad classes as follows: towns
where women were largely employed; where they were
employed to a less extent; where few were employed. In
the first groups were placed those towns with one chief
industry in which the married women were largely
engaged; the second group comprised those towns
where different industries were carried on in some of
which married women were employed in considerable
numbers; in the third group were towns where the
industry or industries did not admit the employment of
married women.

The results obtained in this investigation were as
follows:

	Mean population	Infant death-rate per 1,000 births	General death-rate per 1,000 population
Class I . . .	112,078	195	22·6
Class II . .	161,560	166	19·4
Class III . .	165,074	152	18·1

It will be seen from this table that 28% more infants
died in the first group than in the third; the second

showed a decrease of 15% on the first and an increase of 9% on the third. Since the only dissimilarity known between the three groups was the employment of women who, through engagement in trade, were unable to suckle their children, it is impossible to disagree with Reid's conclusion: "to say the least, it is extremely probable that to this circumstance the unfavourable infant death-rate is attributable".

Thirteen years later Reid published in his Medical Officer's Report further statistics which confirmed the results of his earlier investigation:[75]

Percentage of married and widowed workers to female population aged 18–50 years	No. of towns	Population, 1901	Infant death-rates		
			1881–90	1891–1900	1900–5
12	5	132,299	195	212	183
−12 and +6	13	263,868	165	175	153
6	8	131,508	156	168	140

Lest it be protested that statistics relating to a particular area ought not to be offered as proof of a general thesis, we reproduce in Appendix II tables compiled by Sir George Newman in which the rates of infant mortality in a number of towns scattered over England and Wales are analysed. His conclusion is inevitable: "Broadly it is true that to whatever town or district we turn, the same general conclusion is inevitable—namely, that where there is much occupation of women away from home, there will be found, as a rule, a high infant death-rate, unless there are exceptional circumstances counteracting it."[76]

In the light of all the foregoing evidence, therefore, it becomes clear that, whatever the deficiencies in the statistical techniques of contemporary investigators, they did draw attention to the existence of a very urgent social problem—the manner in which mothers employed away from home provided for the care of their children during their daily absence at work.

CHAPTER IX

DAY NURSING AND ITS RESULTS

THE infant-welfare centre dispensing orange juice and advice; an abundant and cheap supply of clean milk; compulsory absence of women from employment for several weeks after their confinement, the State providing a maternity allowance; the day nursery of the local authority or factory: these are now accepted and familiar features of everyday life. They are in part a product of a conception of the functions and responsibilities of the State that was only just beginning to be accepted during the last two or three decades of the nineteenth century. Even in 1874, when it was already reasonably clear to any who studied the evidence that there was a preventable loss of infant life in certain districts due to the employment of mothers away from home, a public speaker could be sure of the support of the majority of his audience if he insisted that the State ought not to intervene, on the grounds that to do so would be an unwarranted interference with the freedom of the individual.[1]

At the same time, the ignorance on the subject of infant dietetics was, by the standards of our own day, appalling. Nor was ignorance confined to the layman. Only three years after the close of our period, the President of the Obstetrical Society of London and Professor of Midwifery at Birmingham University admitted that "in some cases, the want of knowledge of doctors themselves with regard to the most elementary principles of infant feeding is lamentable. . . . Infant dietetics might be better taught in medical schools", he observes; "it is a subject that is not taught properly. It is picked up by degrees and not taught so systematically as it should be."[2]

It is against this background of political conservatism and general ignorance in Victorian England that we have to examine the provision for their children made by working mothers.

To emphasize the significance of these arrangements, we might digress a little to consider a particular problem which caused pioneers in the field of infant welfare much concern.

In the early days of the infant-welfare movement, premature birth was prominent among the causes of infant mortality. It was at first attributed in large measure to the employment of married women in factories and workshops, being the result of their working too near the time of their confinement. "Like an Indian squaw", declares Gaskell, "she pursues her labour till the hour of her delivery."[3] Parliamentary debates,[4] reports of Government-sponsored investigations,[5] papers read before such societies as the National Association for the Promotion of Social Science,[6] and other contemporary accounts all contain evidence of a similar nature. "Instances of children actually born in the weaving sheds are numerous", claims Allen Clarke; "there was a report in one *Factory Times* not long ago: the woman was delivered in the midst of thundering looms. The child died while itself and the mother were being taken in a cab to the hospital."[7]

The allegation was not confined to the effect of the employment of married women in factories only: in Dr. Julian Hunter's Report, 1864, he claims that "There are numerous cases of labour coming on in the harvest field; and it may fairly be presumed that some of these premature births, succeeded by premature deaths, were the effect of field work."[8]

Precisely how much truth there was in these allegations is difficult to discern. In view of the wholehearted way in which such claims were made, curiously little comparison was made between the number of premature births among mothers employed away from home and those not so occupied: the only statistical evidence which appears to support the view we have outlined above was published some years after our period closed. Dr. Barker, Medical Officer of Health for Clitheroe, Lancashire, reported that the number of deaths due to premature births registered during the distress of 1908 in his district fell; this he attributed to the unemployment of women and the consequent inability of mothers to work too near to their confinement.[9] Dr. Miller, Medical Officer of Health for Bradford, in the course of his Annual Report for 1909, similarly claims of nineteen infant deaths in his district attributed to premature birth, congenital defect, and injury at birth, that the percentage of premature births among infants of non-working mothers was $1 \cdot 07\%$ and among working mothers, $3 \cdot 76\%$.[10]

Whatever significance is attached to such slight evidence as this, it is clear that it is insufficient to validate the particular view we are considering. Moreover, there is substantial evidence that this view was ill-founded.

Redgrave and Baker, when Joint Chiefs of the Factory Department, both gave evidence to this effect before the Factory and Workshops Acts Commission in 1875. "The working of women in factories up to the last moment is not so great as is generally believed", maintained Redgrave;[11] and Baker, though disagreeing that the working of married women near to their confinement was not common,[12] gave it as his opinion that, as a cause of infant mortality, "the time at which they leave before confinement was of less consequence than the time they returned after their confinement".[13]

Sir George Newman, reviewing all the available evidence relating to this problem in 1906, writes: "Prematurity is more a cause of death in districts where there are no factories than where there are. It is admitted that prematurity and immaturity is the chief cause of deaths in infants in the first trimester of their life. Is it not, then, a strange fact that only 47·6% of the deaths of infants in Lancashire occur within the first three months of life, whereas in the three counties where there is the least factory employment of women and the lowest infant mortality (Westmorland, Dorset, and Wiltshire) the percentage of deaths in the first three months is 61% (or 34% higher)?"[14] It should, of course, be remembered that in the time at which Newman wrote, fewer births and deaths escaped registration in rural areas than in the densely populated industrial districts. Even so, combined with that of Redgrave and Baker, his evidence casts serious doubt on the hypothesis that a high rate of infant mortality from premature births was the inevitable result of the employment of married women away from home: the case was non-proven. On the other hand, the evidence that the early return of the mother to work after her confinement endangered the life of her child was by no means so inconclusive.

All too frequently the records show that the married woman worker of our period, driven by necessity and the fear of losing her job, returned to work as soon as possible after the birth of her child.[15] In evidence given to the 1833 Factory Commission, it was stated of married cotton operatives that after their confinement "some go back after nine or ten days; some stay at home even three weeks or a month". On the whole, the shorter period was the most common. A Manchester midwife stated that "they go back at the end of fourteen days; three weeks they think a great bit"—a statement which is corroborated by the evidence of the married cotton operatives themselves.[16]

Nor in the following years did this practice show much sign of declining of its own accord. In the report on an investigation carried out in 1862 at the instruction of the Medical Officer of the Privy Council, "On the Circumstances under which there is an Excessive Mortality of Young Children in Certain Manufacturing Populations", the following passage occurs: "Factory women soon return to labour after their confinement. The longest mentioned time as the average period of their absence from work in consequence of child-bearing was five or six weeks . . . and it was stated by several medical men of great experience and by other witnesses in Coventry and Blackburn that the factory women sometimes return as early as eight or ten days or a fortnight."[17]

Some ten years later, Bridges and Holmes report on the information gained from a questionnaire sent to general practitioners in the northern textile districts:

"We have no medical practitioner in these parts who does not lament the short period that women in factories allow themselves for their confinement. . . . Out of those who answered this part of the question, seventy-one say they usually return to work in less than a month after delivery; and forty-seven more than a month. One of our correspondents instances a case, in his own experience, where a woman left her work at 6 p.m., was confined in the evening, and presented herself again at work next morning, but was sent home again. And although this is, of course, an extreme case, yet several say that they have known many cases of women returning within a week of their delivery, and being admitted to work."[18]

Statements made to the Select Committee on the Best Means of Protecting Infants put out to Nurse in 1871 and the 1876 Commission on the Working of the Factory and Workshops Acts showed that in the Staffordshire potteries, in the jute-manufacturing districts of Scotland, in Leicester—in fact, wherever women were employed— "it was common for them to return to work at the end of ten or twelve days, and most of them were back within the month".[19]

In 1891, by Section 17 of the Factory and Workshops Act of that year, it was made illegal for employers of labour in such premises "knowingly to employ" any woman within four weeks of her confinement. The weakness of this clause, as might have been expected, lay in the word "knowingly", for this placed the onus of proof in cases of prosecution under the Act on the factory inspector. As the inspectors were to find, it was in fact extremely difficult to prove that employers of large numbers of workpeople had full knowledge of all the circumstances relating to the withdrawal or reappearance at work of individual workers. Furthermore, the women most likely to be found back at work within the prohibited period were those forced back through poverty,[20] and were thus precisely those women who would conceal both from the employer and the inspector the real date of their confinement. Hence, although it was well known that evasion of the Act was persistent and widespread,[21] the first prosecution was not made till 1897; and year after year, whilst numbers of cases of evasion were brought to the notice of the factory inspectors, only a fraction of them were supported with sufficient evidence for prosecution.[22, 23]

In effect, there was little to prevent a mother resuming work within a month of her confinement, making what arrangements she could for the care of her child. And to leave a tiny baby to the care of others was a hazardous business till well into the twentieth century, for reasons we must now explain.

It will be simplest to discuss this problem first in terms of the Lancashire cotton districts, where arrangements for the care of employed mothers' children were more thoroughly investigated than elsewhere, and then see whether mothers employed away from home in other industries made any different provision.

After their mother's return to the mill, the care of these tiny babies was sometimes entrusted to elder sisters. "Young girls, aged seven or eight years, are frequently removed from school for the purpose of taking charge of young children while the mother is absent at work."[24] Where there was no elder sister, it was not uncommon to hire a nurse-girl, sometimes not more than eight or ten years of age,[25] who would often have the care of two or three infants and young children collected from neighbouring houses.[26]

It calls for little imagination to envisage the standard of "care" which these young nurses could give to their young charges. Too often such attention as they could give was distracted by the necessity of performing household drudgery for the absent mother.[27]

Commenting on this system of nursing, a contemporary pamphlet pronounces: "The unfortunates thus circumstanced are, almost without exception, injudiciously fed and injudiciously nursed, and from the neglect and improper treatment to which they are exposed frequently meet with accidents of a fatal character, or contract incipient diseases which undermine their constitution and produce premature death."[28]

The Rev. E. Canning, addressing the N.A.P.S.Sc., cites a case where a young girl was left in charge and "a fire broke out in the room from the children playing with the coals, the result being the death of two children"[29]—a case which, under the circumstances, can hardly have been unique.

Usually, the mother preferred to leave her infant in the care of some older person. Where there was a grandmother or elderly aunt living in the house, the child would naturally be left in her keeping.[30] According to our random sample of 1851 Census schedules, this could have been possible in only about one in three (33·93%) cases; but where this was not the case, some other woman had to be found, hence the practice, universal in the factory towns and villages of Lancashire, of "day-nursing".[31]

It should be clearly understood that this is a system to be distinguished from "baby-farming". This latter system, frequently criminal in character, was organized almost exclusively for illegitimate children. A "farm" would "take care" of numbers of such children for an indefinite period of time, on the payment by the mother or some other person of a lump sum.[32] That such a system could lead to abuse must be all too obvious.

There is no evidence that the married, nor indeed the unmarried, operatives put their infants out to nurse for a longer period than that of the working day.[33] The normal practice was for the mother to carry her baby to the nurse on her way to the mill at 5.30 in the morning, and to collect it or have it brought home by the nurse in the evening.

In some cases the nurse would live near to the operative's home, but often, particularly if the mother wished to leave it with a nurse near to the mill so that she could visit it during the dinner-hour, it would have to be carried some considerable distance.[34]

The *Morning Chronicle* gives two instances where the distance from the nurse's home was considerable. The first, relating to a woman who worked in a mill at Chorlton, describes how she "carried her own child to the nurse every morning, rising a full hour before she went to the mill for that purpose, because the nurse lived some way off. The nurse did not rise at the same time, but she [the mother] put the baby into bed to her, and left it there till evening." The second case is that of a Salford operative, who also "had to get up at four o'clock in the morning and carry her baby to the nurse's. The nurse brought it home at night."[35]

Some few of the nurses took the children in mainly as a personal kindness to a younger relative, friend, or neighbour.[36] "It does not amount to a trade; these old women are almost indifferent whether they take the child or not, the amount of benefit they get from it is so very slight. . . . There is a kindness existing between neighbours. . . ." Most of them, however, regarded day-nursing purely as a potential source of income. The Chorlton mill-worker, for instance, describes the woman who takes care of her baby in terms which imply that such nurses are the exception rather than the rule, as "a kind good nurse, a married woman, not one of those regular old nurses who made a trade of it".

These "regular old nurses" are variously described in the contemporary literature as "ignorant old beldams",[37] "old women who, from age and rheumatism, are unable to labour for themselves",[38] and "elderly old women who are unfit for any other employment".[39] They were usually of the same social class and standing as the mothers, "though perhaps rather more necessitous",[40] which led the more active of them to combine their role of child-nurse with that of local washerwoman.

This fact gives some idea of the degree of attention the nurses paid to their young charges. It was not uncommon for these women to depute some little girl to tend the infants, whilst they themselves were busy with their own affairs. "These persons, having their own household business to attend to, and, moreover, a certain and considerable amount of neighbourly visiting to perform, commonly depute some little girl to hold the baby in their absence; and such children may be seen any day, and at any hour, and almost anywhere in the town sitting on the doorstep of the house, exposing the infant to the cooling influence of the draught between the door and the fire."[41]

The number of infants a nurse would take for the day naturally depended on the amount of money the individual mothers were able or willing to pay. Most nurses had two or three infants, but the more active—or more avaricious—were known to take in four, and Dr. Thresh, referring in 1892 to his experience in Manchester, claimed that "he had seen as many as six children asleep in a large soap-box" in the house of one of these old crones.[42]

The amount paid for the services of such nurses varied, being largely a matter of bargaining between the mother and the nurse. Thus "a woman who earns good money might pay less than one earning less money".[43] It also depended on the type of food to be given to the child.[44] A Salford operative stated that he and his wife paid 5s.

per week to their nurse, but another operative, working at the same mill, says that they paid 3s. 6d. a week "and the weeks the nurse washes for it, 4s."[45] On the whole, in the 1870s 3s. to 3s. 6d. was as much as most operatives could afford to pay,[46] and there were large numbers paying less,[47] the normal range of payment at that time being from 2s. 6d. to 3s. 6d.[48] It was estimated, incidentally, that no infant could be adequately fed at a cost of less than 3s. 6d. a week.[49]

By the 1890s the cost of putting a child out to nurse in Lancashire had risen to about 5s. per week, but there were still numbers of women paying 2s.[50]

Such then were the nurses to whom the factory operative entrusted the care of her infant from a very few weeks old till about three years of age. "I have not found them over three years of age", says the Medical Officer of Health for Salford, "but as soon as they can run about a child can manage them, and they are kept at home."[51]

Such arrangements were by no means confined to the cotton districts. The children of married women employed in the Staffordshire potteries were cared for in the same way, the only difference being that here the nurses charged less.[52] A minister in the town of Hanley, for example, states: "There are numerous cases in this township of little infants being left in the care of old women, who have the care of their own household to attend to, besides attending to their little charges. I use the plural number, for in some cases such nurses have five or six to look after. . . ."[53]

In these districts also, child nurses were employed by some mothers:

"Is it the custom to employ very young children to look after the infants [while the mother is employed in the potteries]?"—"Yes; a very common custom."

"Does one little child take care of more than one infant?"—"Yes; they will at times."[54]

Similar evidence can be brought concerning mothers

employed in agriculture: although in early reports there are references to the mothers taking their babies with them into the fields,[55] it seems to have become more common to leave them in the custody of some other person:

"When a woman, the mother of children, works in the fields, what becomes of the children during her absence from home?"—"Sometimes there is a grandmother, but it depends on the circumstances: if the eldest daughter is old enough, she is left in charge of the others. In a few instances they are left alone, from which serious accidents have happened. I know of two or three cases of deaths . . . from burning of children since I have been in the neighbourhood."[56] Others left their babies with "an old woman" or "a professional nurse".[57]

Mothers working in the nail and chain-making "shops" of the Midlands, however, had rather more original arrangements. Either the babies were "minded" by a little girl at a charge of 2s. per week "or else they are perched on a warm heap of fuel or dangled in an egg-box from the shop ceiling. When they are old enough to walk, they play in the gutter and thrust their arms into the holes which ventilate the drains."[58]

The chances of survival of very young infants left in someone else's charge depended almost entirely on the success with which they could be fed artificially. In the Lancashire cotton districts, those mothers whose babies were left with a nurse within reasonable distance of the mill could feed the baby themselves during the break for dinner from twelve o'clock till one o'clock. The infants of these mothers were usually breast-fed four times a day—before being taken to the nurse, during the dinner-hour, once during the evening, and once again during the night.[59] In practice this meant an interval of at least six and a half hours between the first and second feed and an interval of at least four and a half hours between the second and third—allowing a quarter of an hour for travelling each way.[60] Very often, however, the infant's nurse lived too far from the mill for the mother to go to it during her dinner-hour; hence it would not be breast-fed from 5.30 a.m. or even earlier, as we have seen, till 6.30 or 7.0 p.m., when it was taken home for the night.[61]

Moreover, the majority of working mothers, to relieve themselves of the inconveniences of feeding their children themselves under such circumstances, weaned their babies as soon as possible,[62] in contrast to the general habit of working class mothers, who, whenever they were able, breast-fed their babies often for a very long time in the hope of preventing a recurrence of pregnancy.[63] It was stated by the Medical Officer of Health for Salford that "some mothers in the factory districts never nurse their children themselves; they want to what is called 'scale' their milk away; they are anxious to have no milk".[64]

Mothers who worked away from home all day were not, of course, alone in finding breast-feeding inconvenient. Women of the middle and upper classes had for some time employed wet-nurses to suckle their babies for them[65]—a practice which later in the century was superseded by the use of scientifically prepared baby foods.[66] Wet-nursing was, of course, a fairly expensive procedure, and thus only rarely adopted among the working classes. Only one reference has been found, among the material collected, to the factory women putting their children out to wet-nurse during the day; we therefore give this merely as an exception to the general practice of "dry" nursing:

"It also often occurs that infants are put out to nurse instead of hiring a servant to take care of them at home. A respectable woman who had considerable experience of this kind of nursing told me a short time ago that she had herself nursed and suckled as many as three children at a time, and that she had frequently been so exhausted by it as to be unable to walk across a room, and that the children had often been so helpless under such treatment as to be unable to move their hands and feet."[67]

In most cases, however, some alternative method to breast-feeding had to be found to rear the child. We have already mentioned that the middle and upper class woman gradually substituted patent foods for the milk of the wet-nurse. But if the services of the latter were too expensive to be utilized by the working classes, so also were patent foods beyond their means.

Familiar as we are today with advertisements for baby foods on the advertising hoardings, it is worth recalling that such foods are of very recent origin. They are, in fact the direct results of Liebig's researches into the chemistry of food. He himself devised and patented a "Food for infants: a complete substitute for that provided by Nature", which was commercialized in England by Liebig's Registered Concentrated Milk Co. of Titchborne Street, Regent's Quandrant, London, who had patents taken out with Liebig's approval by Baroness Liesner Ebersburg. This development, however, was not till 1867, and the cost of the food limited its sale to the prosperous.[68] Although during the next fifty years other baby foods gradually appeared on the market, such as Allenbury's, Nestlé's, Benger's, and Savory and Moore's, these too were hardly used by the working classes owing to their cost.[69] Thus other methods of hand-rearing had to be adopted by mothers of these classes who were out at work. It was the custom of some mothers to take milk to the nurse every day,[70] but the majority left it to the nurse to purchase milk for the child out of the money they paid her every week. The price of milk, however, was extremely high when related either to the earnings of the mother or the amount paid by the mother to the nurse. In the early 1870s, milk in Manchester and Bolton was 3d. a quart, at which price it was adulterated very extensively both with water and other ingredients.[71] "Babies' milk" cost 8d. a quart; this was milk which was all supposed to come from the same cow, and to be both creamier and purer than the cheaper variety.[72] It is hardly a matter for surprise, therefore, that Edwin Smith, referring to the normal diet of the cotton operatives and their families, reports: "in very few families can a proper amount of milk, even if any at all, be bought for the children". Elsewhere we read: "Cow's milk in large towns, even adulterated and diluted as it is so largely, is hardly tasted by the very poor."[73]

This remark was equally true of rural districts, where milk was equally dear and became increasingly scarce as improved transport facilities made it more profitable to despatch milk to the processing factories or to the towns. It was "no uncommon thing to see children literally starving for want of milk" in country districts.[74]

As the nurse had not only to feed the child out of the money given her, but also to make a profit, the amount of milk she could afford to buy for the child must have been small indeed. "A half-pennyworth or a penny-worth of milk ($\frac{1}{4}$ pint to a pint, according to the quality) *per diem* is considered a liberal allowance", states one observer.[75]

It is open to question, however, whether the health of the children would have been materially improved by drinking a greater quantity of milk. "The quality of the milk sold in the town and country alike was, till very late in the century, appallingly bad. It was for the most part heavily contaminated with germs, and a frequent source of infection and epidemics. Apart from serious outbreaks of typhus and dysentery caused by infected milk, the majority of tuberculous glands and joint affectations, which were very common in Victorian days, were caused by infection with a strain of the tubercular bacillus derived from cows (bovine tuberculosis) and conveyed in milk. An increased consumption of milk would have resulted in an increased incidence of the disease. It was not until the 1890s that people began to recognize that a measure of protection against infection by milk could be obtained by boiling it."[76]

From about 1870 an alternative supply of milk appeared on the market in the form of tinned condensed milk. The working classes were only able to buy the cheapest varieties of this, and although when the tin was opened it was certainly purer than the cow's milk they could purchase, it was devoid of vitamins A and D and of fats, and was made from evaporated skimmed milk; hence the prevalence of rickets amongst children to whom it was fed.[77] Further harm resulted from the opened tin being left about uncovered from one day to the next, and thus accumulating all the dirt and germs the freedom from which had at first made it in some ways preferable.[78]

With regard to cow's milk, it must be admitted that its qualities as a food for infants were not very well understood. It is in fact doubtful whether either nurse or mother would have given the children more milk even had it been far cheaper. "Spite of strenuous efforts of the intelligent and humane to indoctrinate the people with some elementary knowledge of dietetics, especially as relates to the nurture of infants", complains the *Lancet*, "cases are occurring every week in which injudicious feeding has been attended by fatal results."[79] A more specific complaint is voiced by Dr. Husband: "Some people seem to think that children can be brought up any way, and that bread steeped in water or anything else is all that is needed for their nourishment."[80] In the history of infant dietetics, these were still the "Dark Ages".

Through ignorance combined with poverty, therefore, the children of the working mothers were almost entirely spoonfed. "Pap made of bread and water sweetened with sugar and treacle is the sort of nourishment given during the mother's absence, even to infants of a very tender age, and in several instances little children, not more than six or seven years of age, were seen preparing and feeding the babies with this food, which in such cases consisted of lumps of bread floating on sweetened water; other farinaceous articles, such as arrowroot, oatmeal, and sago, are sometimes used, but less freely than bread. Milk is also occasionally but very rarely employed instead of water, partly no doubt on account of its expense, but also because of the prevalent belief that cow's milk disagrees with such infants as were partly suckled by their mother."[81]

It should not be assumed that, in the preparation of the food, these juvenile nurses were incomparably worse than the old nurses. Dr. Ballard goes to some trouble to describe how these old women prepared tempting repasts for their young charges: "The bread is sopped in warm water in a cup, which is left for hours upon the hob to keep warm and becomes sour. When about to be used, the bread is broken down with a spoon, and a little milk added. I saw one cup of sopped bread thus prepared for use. It was said to have been boiled, but it contained tough pieces which even boiling had not softened."[82, 83]

When we add to the total unsuitability of the diet the irregularity with which it was fed to them by their unqualified and too often uninterested nurses, who crammed their unfortunate charges with the food whenever they cried[84]—the poor things were probably only registering a feeble protest against the discomforts of chronic indigestion—we can but agree that "it is no matter for surprise that this system of management results in all the evils of malnutrition, and very often in the death of the infant".[85] The evidence of Dr. Strange of Ashton, to whose experience we have already referred above, supports the foregoing statement. "I am convinced", he declares, "of the great bearing of these facts upon the mortality of children from the circumstance that a greater proportional number of first and second children die before they attain five years than of children born after the mother has relinquished her employment."[86] Doctors in every other district where mothers were out at work were unanimous in their testimony to the disastrous consequences of this artificial feeding of infants.[87]

Moreover, Dr. Strange's private conviction is fully corroborated by evidence from other spheres. Contemporary examinations of the causes of mortality in foundling institutions, both in England and abroad, for instance, are particularly revealing with reference to the results of attempting to rear children by hand during the earlier years of our period.

The *Lancet* in 1838 reported on a French hospital for orphaned infants where "all those who are received are nourished by hand through a sucking-bottle", that of 382 infants fed in this manner 297 (78%) died before they were a year old. Apparently the French hospital found this encouraging.

Some years later, in the same journal, Dr. Routh contrasted the experience of French foundling hospitals where the orphans were put out to wet-nurse with that of hospitals where they were reared by hand: "In Lyons and Parthenay, when children were suckled at the breast, the mortality was respectively 33·7% and 36%, whereas in Paris, Rhiems, and Aix, where they were brought up by hand, it was respectively 50·3%, 63·9%, and 80%. . . ."[88]

In the subsequent discussion on Dr. Routh's article, it became clear that the experience of English foundling hospitals was identical with that of the French.[89]

Equally interesting are the results of an enquiry by Dr. Dolan, conducted at a later date into the fate of children born in the workhouse as compared with that of the infant of the factory operative. "I discovered", he says, "that infants confined in the workhouse at the end of a month were stronger and healthier than those of the operative class. Mothers who were admitted into the maternity ward of the workhouse had a full month's rest after their confinement, during which time they were able to give their infants their full care. Thus the recipient of Poor Law relief was in a better position than her hard-working sister.

"I was further able to test the mortality of infants in

the workhouse and the infants of the general factory population, and I found that, whilst taking into account the number of births, the infant mortality of the workhouse was proportionally lower."[90]

Later again, in the early years of the twentieth century, investigations made by medical officers of health all over the country yielded similar results.[91]

There can, in fact, be no doubt that throughout Victoria's reign, in so far as babies had to be artificially fed because of their mother's absence at work, their lives were imperilled.

CHAPTER X

INFANTS' PRESERVATIVES

It thus appears that if the perils surrounding the infant of the woman operative were merely those connected with its diet during her absence, these alone would be sufficiently serious to impair the health of the child or, worse, hasten it into an early grave. But there were yet others.

To soothe the distressed cries of the infants, who must have been in constant pain from their extraordinary diet, the nurses were in the habit of administering gin and peppermint and certain other nostrums, such as Godfrey's Cordial, Atkinson's Royal Infants' Preservative, and Mrs. Wilkinson's Soothing Syrup. Thus a vicious circle was established of feeding them on bread and water, "the consequence of the food being that they become fractious and cry; nearly the whole time they are in constant pain and difficult to nurse; then they give them cordial; then they sleep a certain time. When they rouse up again they feed them, and then they cry, and then they give them some more cordial, and this goes on all day."[1]

The composition of these soothing syrups varied from one chemist to another, but some narcotic—opium, laudanum, morphia—was an ingredient of all. "Generally, Godfrey's contains an ounce and half of pure laudanum to the quart. Infants' Cordial is much stronger, containing about two teaspoonsful to the quart, and occasionally paregoric, which is about one-quarter part as strong as laudanum, is used. The stronger it is, the faster it is used."[2] Indeed, it was stated by a druggist in the Manchester district that "laudanum is used in fact more than Godfrey's. There is no dread of laudanum now as there once was; so ten drops are given at a time; it is given neat or mixed with a little sugar and water. . . . On this account, Godfrey's is getting out of use. . . . 'Quietness' used to be bought a good deal, but laudanum, being cheaper and going further, is now substituted."[3]

One old woman describes how she made her particular brand of Godfrey's: "We took a penn'orth of aniseed, a quarter of a pound of treacle, and a penn'orth of laudanum [¼ oz.]; then we stewed down the aniseed with water and mixed up the whole in a quart bottle."[4]

The sale of these opiates in factory districts was enormous. In 1862 it was estimated that in Coventry 12,000 doses of Godfrey's were administered weekly, and even more, proportionately, in Nottingham. In fact, as a witness to the Select Committee on the Best Means of Protecting Infants put out to Nurse stated: "You will get evidence easily from the manufacturing districts that opiates are sold by the gallon by druggists there."[5] And this was still true at the end of the century.[6]

Some investigators were anxious to draw attention to the fact that the practice of dosing children was far from being confined to the more populous manufacturing towns. "The custom of administering opiates to children has extended to the small as well as the large towns of Lancashire", claims Playfair. "Thus in the small town of Clitheroe, the population of which amounted to 6,725, consisting partly of calico printers and partly of factory operatives, I found a weekly sale of four pints of Godfrey's Cordial and an annual sale of 4,000 poppy heads for making 'sleepy stuff' for the children. One druggist describes these drugs as being sold to an alarming extent among the factory population; not so much among the printers. Another describes the sale as 'decent for the size of the town', although it was larger than Colne, where I served my apprenticeship."[7, 8]

It is less easy, but still possible, to find evidence that

similar potions were administered when mothers were employed in the fields. "In other countries, where women work away from home, as in factory towns", writes Hunter,[9] "the children are drugged by nurses, and one need not be surprised to find the same plan adopted here. . . ."

Children were given these potions at a very early age. A druggist in Preston stated that "they generally begin to administer them when the child is only about three or four weeks old";[10] but amongst the evidence collected from fifteen druggists in Ashton-under-Lyne by the Health of Towns Commission will be found instructions as to the appropriate dose to give to infants "a few days old":

"The first dose given to a young child is about a teaspoonful a day, but it soon becomes accustomed to this quantity; thus the dose is increased gradually until it frequently amounts to three teaspoonfuls. Many give one pennyworth of Godfrey's, or $\frac{1}{2}$ oz., a day; this would mean, of this particular chemist's brew, that the child would be given at least fifty drops of laudanum daily."[11]

We have implied that the nurses dosed their charges out of sympathy for their obvious distress; but there can be no doubt that the nurses also used their cordials from less laudable motives. Sleeping babies, particularly when there were three or four to care for, were not only less trouble to their nurse; they consumed no food, and therefore made day-nursing a more profitable business.

Where the nurses were also washerwomen, it was often alleged that the women deliberately drugged the children so that they might, unhindered, attend to their wash-tubs.[12]

It would, however, be untrue to maintain that these children were never dosed by their own mothers. Sometimes when a mother left her baby in the care of a young girl, "the child is dosed with 'Quietness' to prevent its being troublesome. The child thus drugged sleeps, and may waken at dinner-time; so that when the mother goes out again, the child receives another dose. Well, the mother and father come home at night quite fatigued, and, as they must rise early to begin work for the day, they must have sleep undisturbed by the child; so again it is drugged."[13]

Time and again evidence is given that it was the practice for some parents to drug their baby at night when it had been brought home from the nurse and was still suffering from the effects of its treatment during the day, so that the family should not be disturbed by its cries.[14]

Although this is true, the evidence of the local druggists, chemists, and medical practitioners must inevitably lead to the conclusion that by far the greater proportion of the drugs administered to the children were given by the old women during the day, who were naturally more anxious to save their own time and thus more reckless in the use of narcotics.[15] In support of this view, there is no lack of material illustrative of the great suspicion evinced by the mothers of the use of narcotics by the nurses.

Mr. Robert Brown, a surgeon of Preston, affirms: "A child was brought to me for a little aperient medicine; the mother suspected that the nurse had been in the habit of giving it some narcotic. . . . I advised the mother to stay at home and attend it herself. The advice was followed, and the child recovered in a few days."[16]

Another "highly respectable chemist and druggist" writes: "A woman brought a bottle to me containing some medicine for examination, which was found to be an infusion of opium. She said a neighbour had given it to one of her children, upon the recommendation of some quack, who was in the habit of calling on poor families for the purpose of selling them medicine. Her child became stupefied in half an hour, and ultimately died."[17]

Yet another druggist in Manchester mentions that mothers often came to him in great trouble, asking what he thought could be the matter with their children and, though he knew very well, he dared not tell them, or they would have gone and charged the nurse with "sickening" the child, and the nurse would have made a disturbance, "daring him to prove what he could not prove legally".[18]

The *Morning Chronicle*, 4th January 1850, gives two cases where operatives put out their first child to be nursed while the mother returned to the mill; when they saw how the children were drugged by their respective nurses (as a result of which treatment one of the babies died), they neither of them put their children out to nurse again. We are not told whether this was achieved by the mother relinquishing her employment at the mill. As in both cases the amount paid to the nurse was well above the average, 5s. and 3s. 6d. to 4s. respectively, it is likely that this was the policy adopted, for these must have been operatives of the highest-paid class, who could thus afford to support a wife at home. In this they were extremely fortunate.

Deaths of young children from the persistent and reckless use of narcotics were all too frequent: Godfrey's, administered to calm children, in many cases established a calm that was but the prelude to a deeper quiet.[19]

Robert Baker, in one of his half-yearly reports as a factory inspector, quotes from a lecture given by Mr. Alexander Somers, "a lecturer in one of our largest provincial hospitals", in which he refers to the effects of the use of Godfrey's, etc., in the factory districts:

"Thousands of children so treated by those hired to care for them in the absence of their mothers lost flesh, colour, and appetite, their skin was sallow and wrinkled, their features pinched and shrivelled, and they gradually pined away and died; others perished from diseases of the brain; and some, after a larger dose than usual, fell into a profound sleep from which they never awoke."[20]

Scarcely twenty years before Somers delivered his lecture, Playfair, in his "Report on the State of the Large Towns of Lancashire", had noted: "Medical opinion holds that the real cause of many of the deaths registered as 'convulsions' are really the effects of Godfrey's, etc., which predispose children to tabes, mesenterica, marasmus, 'wasting' and consumption."[21, 22]

It is impossible to isolate the individual effects of the use of narcotics and its almost certain concomitant, bad feeding; deaths from convulsions, though commonly asserted in the reports we have quoted to be the results of drugging, can also reasonably be supposed to have resulted, in part at least, from unsuitable food. To whichever of these two causes we assign responsibility, however, it is significant that deaths of young children from convulsions were, on the whole, more frequent in districts where mothers were employed away from home than in districts where they were not.

"The mortality from nervous diseases of early life" (under which head he groups convulsions, teething, and hydrocephalus, but of which the first was by far the most important), wrote Dr. Greenhow in 1857, "is not only higher in towns than rural districts, but also higher in manufacturing than in other towns, and highest in places where female labour is in most request. Thus", he continued, "it is higher in Manchester, Leeds, Bradford, Halifax, and Wigan than in Bristol, Hull, and Newcastle. It is higher in districts where females work in factories than in their homes—higher, for example, in Macclesfield than Coventry. Although, doubtless, other circumstances influence the result, it is worthy of mention that the mortality from the cause in Manchester and Salford appears to have some relation to the proportion of females in each engaged in factory labour; in Salford, less than 15% are so employed. Out of each 100,000 males of all ages, 454 annually die from nervous diseases of children in Manchester: in Salford, the proportion is only 389. Even in rural communities, the influence of female occupation over mortality is apparent. The mortality caused by these diseases in the rural districts of Glendale, Haltwistle, Alston, Bootle,

Builth, and Halesworth—in which, with the insignificant
exception of glove-making in Halesworth, the females
follow no special industrial employment—is very much
less than the mortality these diseases produce in Towcester, Newport Pagnell, Leighton Buzzard, Hemel
Hempstead, and Berkhamstead, also rural districts, but
in which a proportion of women, varying from 21% to
nearly 40% of the adult population, are employed in
the manufacture of lace and straw plait."[23]

Lest it be objected that Greenhow's results might have
been invalidated by the age structure of the districts he
was examining—of which we are given no account—
the comments of the Registrar-General on the causes of
infant deaths in eighteen large towns of England, 1873–6,
are worth recording:

"In the factory towns of Oldham, Salford, and
Leicester, the proportional numbers who died from
convulsions were very much larger than the number who
died from this cause in London. It was not improbable
that this is partly owing to maternal neglect. Dr.
Tatham, Medical Officer of Health for Salford, suggests
some legislative enactment for the greater protection of
infant life in this class of town, so as to check the employment of mothers in factories within a certain period
after their confinement. Dr. Sutton, Medical Officer of
Health for Oldham, also states that the high rate of
mortality among infants was mainly due to the absence
of mothers, who were occupied at the mills. 'The
children suffer from indigestible food and are pacified
with soothing syrups containing narcotics, which en-
genders convulsions and, combined with other causes,
rapidly die off.' "[24]

A second investigation by Dr. Greenhow—"On the
Prevalence and Causes of Diarrhoea at Coventry,
Birmingham, Wolverhampton, Dudley, Merthyr, Not-
tingham, Leeds, and Manchester, with Chorlton and
Salford"—in 1859, revealed the not very surprising
fact that the artificial feeding of the babies of employed

mothers resulted in far more infant deaths from diarrhoea than would otherwise have been the case:

"A very large number of deaths were those of young
children, but the proportion varied in different places.
With the exception of Merthyr and Dudley, more than
half the deaths were those of infants in the first year after
birth. The deaths of infants have borne the highest
proportion to those of all ages in the manufacturing
districts—Coventry, Nottingham, and Manchester—in

The Proportion of Deaths at Each Period of Life in Each District[27]

Name of district	—1 year	From 2 years	—5 years	From 5–60 years	60 years upwards	All ages
Coventry . .	675·9	176·8	852·7	69·3	78·0	1,000
Birmingham .	549·0	267·0	816·0	87·0	97·0	1,000
Wolverhampton	522·2	310·1	832·3	94·0	73·7	1,000
Dudley . .	477·3	359·8	837·1	89·4	73·5	1,000
Merthyr Tydfil	385·4	370·3	755·7	128·5	115·8	1,000
Nottingham .	608·0	136·0	744·0	105·0	151·0	1,000
Leeds . . .	535·5	250·5	786·0	92·0	122·0	1,000
Manchester .	603·1	273·6	876·7	65·7	57·6	1,000
Chorlton . .	599·3	239·4	838·7	90·1	71·2	1,000
Salford . . .	578·8	277·4	856·2	72·2	72·2	1,000

each of which evidence has been adduced of the mis-
management of infants arising from the employment of
mothers in the factories. The different proportions in
each place would seem to countenance the opinion that
the assigned cause is not without effect, seeing that a
much larger proportion of married women at Coventry
were employed in the special manufactures of that city
in 1851 than in either Manchester or Nottingham. . . ."[25]

In this, as in Greenhow's previous investigation, no
account is given of the age structure of these populations;
but later investigations once more confirmed his conclusions. Dr. Reid, County Medical Officer of Health
for Staffordshire, in the course of the enquiry to which

we have already called attention,[26] noted the infant
death-rates from diarrhoea in each of his three classes
of towns—viz. towns where married women were largely
employed, where married women were employed to a
less extent, and towns where few women were employed. These he computed to be 28, 20, and 19 per
1,000 births respectively. It is important to note that
Reid maintained from his personal knowledge of the
towns involved that these results were not influenced by
differences of local sanitary conditions.

Stimulated by Reid's paper, the Parliamentary Bills
Committee of the British Medical Association decided to
institute an enquiry on similar lines throughout the urban
districts of England. This resulted in returns being
received from 283 towns, and in the case of 101 of them,
with a population of 3,368,568, the figures were sufficiently complete and reliable for the purposes of the
enquiry.

In collating returns, all towns with populations of
over 100,000 and under 10,000 were excluded—in the
former case because it was impossible, on account of the
large size of the towns, to arrive at an estimate of the
proportion of married women working in factories: and
in the latter case because, from the smallness of the
populations, in many cases the districts in all probability
were more rural than urban in character.

In the tabulated results of this enquiry, which were
published in the *British Medical Journal* in 1893, the
towns were grouped as artisan, mixed, and residential,
the first two being subdivided, as in the Staffordshire
enquiry, in accordance with the relative proportion of
married women workers in each. As, unfortunately, only
one town was returned under Sub-group I of the mixed
class, the figures, although they are given in the table,
can hardly be useful for comparative purposes.

This particular enquiry was extended so as to include
the returns of deaths among the children under five
years, in order to show whether the practice of mothers

150 WIVES AND MOTHERS IN VICTORIAN INDUSTRY

leaving home to work in factories affected injuriously the lives of children beyond the first year of life and whether, given a corresponding mortality among children under five years of age of the three sub-groups of towns, the general death-rate would approximate to the same figure in each sub-group.

Statistics of 101 Towns in England with Populations of 10,000 and under 100,000: Total Population, 3,368,568[28]

	Artisan class			Mixed class			Residential class
	I	II	III	I	II	III	
No. of towns	21	23	25	1	4	20	7
Population, 1891 . . .	556,986	829,509	945,099	25,933	119,805	693,958	197,278
General death-rate . .	21·5	20·2	19·2	18·4	18·5	17·8	16·6
*Hypothetical death-rate .	19·9	19·4	—	17·7	18·3	—	—
Zymotic death-rate . .	0·92	0·75	0·80	0·85	0·65	0·61	0·34
Infant mortality . . .	179	159	152	153	142	141	130
Percentage increase compared with Sub-group III	17·6	4·6	—	8·5	0·7	—	—
Death-rate, −5 years . .	73·3	67·3	61·0	60·0	56·0	54·5	46·6
Percentage increase compared with Sub-group III	20·2	10·3	—	10·1	2·8	—	—

* The hypothetical death-rate was calculated on the basis of a death-rate −5 years corresponding with Sub-group III.

The conclusions reached by the Parliamentary Bills Committee on this material are important, as they indicate the defects of their investigation compared with that of Reid:

"Although the increase of the infant death-rate in the case of similar groups of towns throughout England is shown by the returns to be only 17·8% in the first group and 4·6% in the second group, as compared with the third group (8·5% and 0·7% respectively in the mixed class) the difference, no doubt, is largely accounted for by less trouble having been taken by those who made the returns to arrive at facts concerning the number of married women engaged in work away from home, resulting in some towns being placed in the first or second sub-group, when, more accurately, they should have been returned under Sub-group III. As a matter of fact, the original enquiry in Staffordshire bears out this conjecture, for in that case it was found necessary to readjust the first classification on afterwards obtaining special information from manufacturers to the effect that, although in certain towns returned under Sub-group I many women were engaged in work, it was not the practice, for various reasons, to employ women after marriage.

"Although one would have expected to find in the high infant mortality towns a considerable increase in the death-rate from diarrhoea, the figures do not entirely bear this out; at the same time, in the case of both enquiries, this expectation is to some extent justified.

"Although in the cases of towns throughout England one cannot say, as one can in the case of Staffordshire, that the hygienic and other conditions of the population under each sub-group are practically identical, still, considering the number of artisan towns from which returns have been received, and remembering that the argument cuts both ways, it is reasonable to conclude that no great error has crept in from this source."

The results of these investigations not only confirm statistically the common-sense expectation as to the effects of drugging and artificial feeding; they also corroborate the general evidence presented in Chapter VIII. Human problems, however, are not always best appreciated when stated in terms of impersonal statistics. As a final comment on the management of infants directly attributable to the absence of mothers at work, we give below the experience of one mother, a cotton operative in Bolton:

"There was a baby aged eleven months in the infirmary with its mother. It was greatly emaciated, with a cough and diarrhoea. The woman said she was a 'card-room hand' at a factory and had had two children before, one of which had died at three months and the other at fourteen months of age. She resided in Gas Street, Bolton, and went to her work three months after her confinement. She used to take her baby at 5.30 in the morning to a woman in Spring Gardens and visited it at dinner-time. It was fed from the first with bread and milk out of a spoon. The neighbours told her that the woman used to give her baby 'sleepy-stuff' and she herself had noticed that the baby was always asleep when she visited it."

Dr. Ballard, from whose investigations this illustration was taken, continues: "I am informed on good authority that it is not an uncommon thing for persons of the operative class, like this last mentioned, to lose all their children one after another in this way."[29]

Small wonder then that Dr. Buchanan, in a report to the Medical Officer of the Privy Council during the "Cotton Famine", should write: "When the urgency of the present crisis has passed away, the power of the Lancashire manufacturers in solving difficult social problems cannot be directed to a better end than of organizing means of preventing the scandalous loss of life that prevails among the infants of the female operatives."[30, 31]

CHAPTER XI

THE STIRRING OF THE PUBLIC CONSCIENCE

"IT scarcely needs to observe", commented John Simon, "that against this state of things there is no resource in any present provision of the law. At the root of this evil is an influence with which English law has never professed to deal. Domestic obligation is out-bidden in the labour market; and the poor factory woman, who meant only to sell that honest industry of hers, gradually finds that she has sold almost everything which other women understand as happiness. But the root of the evil is perhaps out of the reach of the law—certainly out of reach of remedies which I am competent to advise. . . ."[1] Here was the problem to which those who sought to remedy the infant mortality attributable to the absence of mothers at the mill or factory had to find a solution. As the evidence of contemporary investigations accumulated, it became increasingly obvious that some remedial action should be taken. But to whom should the responsibility for action be assigned?

It was significant that until late in the century only a minority, even of the most enthusiastic reformers in the field called for legislative action. The current notion of the family as a unit whose peculiar sanctity should not be invaded by the State in any guise restrained all the rest from associating themselves with this radical group. "I desire to place it on record", proclaims Whately Cooke Taylor in 1874, "that I would far rather see even a higher rate of infant mortality prevailing than has ever yet been proved against the factory districts or elsewhere . . . than intrude one iota farther on the sanctity of the domestic hearth and the decent seclusion of private life. . . . That unit, the family", he continues, "is the unit upon which a constitutional Government has been raised which is the admiration and envy of mankind. Hitherto, whatever the laws have touched, they have not dared invade this sacred precinct; and the husband and wife, however poor, returning home from whatsoever occupation or harassing engagements, have *there* found *their* dominion, *their* repose, *their* compensation for many a care. . . ."[2] The chill wind of reality had yet to sweep through such minds as this.

For decades past, and for decades yet to come, the solution to many a social problem was either to ignore or deny its existence or—if this was impossible—to attempt to place the responsibility for action on the shoulders of some individual or group of individuals. Hence the moral responsibility for action in the matter which concerns us here was placed squarely on the shoulders of the manufacturers, who, after all, had taken it upon themselves to employ the women in the first place.[3]

J. Brendon Curgenven,[4] for example, in evidence before the Select Committee on the Best Means of Protecting Infants put out to Nurse (1871), urged that measures be taken to ensure the better care of the infants of married women operatives. He was challenged by a member of the Committee: "Are you not aware that there is a very great jealousy (and, I might add, in my opinion, a very legitimate jealousy) of interference with the domestic customs and habits of the people, and that more especially in Staffordshire and the manufacturing districts of the North, though it would be possible, no doubt, to carry out any scheme of kindness and charitable relief, or good advice and counsel, such as you have sketched forth, anything in the way of legal interference with the custom and habits of the people, or which would reduce their right to earn wages and lessen their responsibility to their children, would be extremely unpopular, that indeed it would be very difficult to carry out, because the legislature would not have the sympathy of the people in that matter?" To which query he hastens to reply: "I do not mention that as a thing to be carried out by the legislature, but as a philanthropic movement to be carried out by the manufacturers."[5]

In the light of this and many other similar appeals for action on the part of the manufacturers,[6] the manner and extent of their response is of some interest.

Of the sort of action required of them, the manufacturers were left in little doubt. It was clear from the reports of all investigations that the adverse effects of the mother's absence during the greater part of the day might be at least mitigated if the child was left in the care of a competent nurse and not, as was the prevailing custom, in charge of a child little older than itself or of a doddering old woman. Thus the manufacturers were advised to "establish within their factories under well-advised regulations, nursery-rooms, where working mothers might leave their children in some proper and kindly charge, and might as often as necessary have access to them".[7]

As with so many experiments relating to child welfare, the first day nursery had been established in France. In the early 1840s, M. Marbeau, *adjoint au maire du premier arrondissment de Paris*, had, from experience gained in the course of his duties, become convinced of the necessity for the provision of some sort of institution in which children under two years of age could be left during the day while their mothers were at work. (There were already in France charitable "infant asylums" where children of from two to six years of age were cared for.) This project he explained to the officers charged with the relief of the poor, and by them a committee was appointed to whom Marbeau represented that (*a*) such a scheme was necessary, (*b*) that it was practicable, (*c*) that the expenses should be as low as possible: that the mothers should pay wages to the nurses and that the other expenses incurred should be left to charity. The committee, although they were unwilling to finance the proposed crèche with money from public charities, were nevertheless persuaded of the truth of Marbeau's contentions and canvassed the financial support of private citizens. By no group was help more willingly given than by the religious orders, and it was in a house provided by the Superior of Les Sœurs de la Sagesse that the first crèche was opened in the Chaillot Quarter of Paris in 1844.[8]

The experiment was successful, and on its success other crèches were established, most of them by religious orders, but some of a semi-public and municipal character. By 1867 there were in France eighteen crèches in Paris, ten in the *banlieu*, and some 400 in the departments.[9]

The movement was by no means restricted to France: similar institutions were opened in Brussels and Vienna, and in several of the other large cities of Europe.

In March 1850, six years after the Chaillot crèche had been opened, a day nursery was established at 19 Nassau Street, St. Marylebone, by a group of women who had been inspired by Marbeau's own accounts of his work in Paris.[10] This institution was established "for the purpose of receiving the children of the married industrious poor during the working hours of the day— namely, from 6.30 a.m. to 7 o'clock p.m." states a pamphlet describing the work of the nursery. It was to be managed by "a committee of ladies who will attend on the first Tuesday of every month to inspect the books and transact all necessary business. And each member of the committee will take her turn as a visitor at the nursery."[11]

As this apparently was the first day nursery to be established in England, it is worth recording in some detail how it was organized and what sort of accommodation it offered.

The nursery consisted of two large first-floor rooms, to which water had been laid on, and it had eight cradles made from wire-work costing 16s. apiece. "Wood is not so well adapted for the purpose, as it holds allurement to other intrusive occupants, and the wirework, from its lightness, is found more convenient than iron bands. The bedding is stuffed with coconut fibre. There is a bath in the room and a piece of stuffed carpet on which children can be put down to crawl around."[12]

Six fundamental rules governed the work of this rather Spartan institution, the first of which owed nothing to Marbeau's influence whatsoever:

"1. Every mother applying for admission for her child must obtain a recommendation from the clergyman of the parish or a respectable householder of the district. Papers of the form required may be had at the nursery."[13]

The remaining five rules, however, were closely modelled on the regulations on which the Paris crèche was based:

"2. No child may be admitted unless it has been vaccinated and is in a state of health.

"3. Children will be received at any age between one month and three years.

"4. 3d. will be charged for the care and maintenance of each child, 4d. for two of the same family; and it is required that the money be brought with the child every day. Otherwise the Matron has strict orders to refuse admission.

"5. The child's clothing must be perfectly clean. All extra linen is provided by the nursery.

"6. Unweaned children may be nursed at the institution by the mothers during the day."[14]

But the really important characteristic of the Nassau Street nursery, and the one which, more than any rule, marks it as a copy of the Chaillot crèche, was that it was neither supposed nor expected to be self-supporting: it was in fact a charity. "Probably it would be impossible to establish self-supporting nurseries in London", we are told. "The class of matrons who go out to daily labour in factory towns is more numerous, more regularly employed, further removed from the bottom of society. Most London mothers who get good and regular employment work at home. Few of those who go out to work could afford 6*d.* a day for the care of a child."[15]

Herein lay the fundamental difference between this nursery—and also the nursery established shortly after in Kensington[16]—and those established at this time in the factory districts. For these last were quite definitely expected to be or become self-supporting. Failure to do so inevitably meant that the nursery would be closed.

In December 1850, for example, Mrs. Clements, the wife of the local Vicar, opened a day nursery at Halstead for the children aged one month to two years of mothers employed in the local silk mill. The charge was 4*d.* a week per child. But the nursery failed to pay its way, and was closed in September 1853.[17]

Also in December 1850, the first day nursery in Lancashire was opened in Ancoats Crescent, Manchester, next door to the Ancoats Dispensary, by the Association for the Establishment of Day Nurseries for the Infant Children of the Labouring Classes in Manchester and Salford, under the patronage of the Lord Bishop and the Mayors of both cities.[18] In the pamphlet issued to publicize the nursery, no direct reference is made to the earlier Continental experiments, but it was almost certainly influenced by them, for the fame of the French crèches was widespread.[19] Moreover, the rules of the Chaillot crèche seem to have been the pattern for those of the Ancoats nursery:

"Rules of Nurseries[20]

"1. Each nursery to be opened every day during the week at half-past five in the morning and closed at seven o'clock in the evening, except on Saturdays, when the institution will be closed at four o'clock. No children to be received on Sundays.

"2. The Committee of Management shall in all cases satisfy themselves that the parties applying for admission of the children are married and suitable persons to receive the benefits of the institution.[21] [Again the moral requirement unknown in Marbeau's crèche, and an illuminating comment on the social attitudes of the Victorian era.]

"3. No child who has not been vaccinated or who is affected with contagious disease to be admitted, and every child to be submitted to examination by the medical officer on the Saturday previous to admission.

"4. Children to be received at any age between one month and three years.

"5. The price to be charged, 2s. 6d. per week for each infant or, in the case of children requiring solid food during the day, 3s. per week.

"6. All payments to be made in advance: otherwise the Matron shall refuse admission to the child.

"7. The child's clothing must be sufficiently warm and perfectly clean when the child is brought in the morning. All extra linen to be provided by the nursery.

"8. Mothers to have access to their children for the purpose of nursing at any time during the day."[22]

In complete contrast to the French crèche, however, it was stated as a "fundamental principle" of this nursery that it was to be "as much as possible self-supporting, and not to be regarded as a charitable institution".[23]

The nursery was specifically established to provide for the care of the infants of the local women cotton operatives: so much is stated by the Association in its pamphlet, and it is obvious from the hours for which the nursery was to be open. But on the Gentlemen's Committee of the Association there were only two local cotton manufacturers of note, T. H. Birley, Jun., and Sir E. Armitage. Clearly, the manufacturers were not as sensible of their responsibilities as had been hoped. The most enthusiastic

supporters seem to have been the local medical practitioners: over one-third of the Gentlemen's Committee
were doctors.

Be this as it may, the venture was not successful. On
31st December a meeting was held in the Manchester
Town Hall of both the Ladies' and Gentlemen's
Committees. It was resolved to continue the nursery for
another twelve months, as there seemed to be some reason
to suppose that the past year had not really been a fair
test; but that if, during the further trial period, the
nursery failed to become self-supporting, it should be
closed. Presumably it continued to function till 1854, as
Alexander Redgrave, at that time the Factory Inspector
for the area, refers to a crèche existing in Manchester at
that time;[24] but eventually it was closed, and the failure
of this experiment seems to have discouraged others for
many years.[25]

If the local manufacturers had little connexion with
this first day nursery in Lancashire, they had even less
to do with later experiments. In evidence before the
Select Committee on the Best Means of Protecting
Infants put out to Nurse, it was stated that between
November 1869 and the middle of 1871 there had been
established three nurseries in Manchester and Salford,[26]
and with not one of these was any single local manufacturer connected. The first of these three nurseries,
in Charles Street, Manchester, was entirely under the
patronage of Mrs. Leigh Clare, wife of a local magistrate,
and the other two—one in Dickinson Street, Manchester,
and one by St. John's Church, Salford, this last being
supervised by two sisters, the Misses Sellon—were
supported by voluntary contributions.[27]

The statement that these nurseries were "supported"
by the generosity of one person or of many did not
imply that no charge was made to the mother for the
care of her child. The Charles Street nursery (sometimes referred to as the Greengate nursery) made a
charge of 2s. per week. The significance of the remark

was that the Charles Street nursery—and almost certainly the two other nurseries—unlike the earlier establishment in Ancoats Crescent, regarded itself as a "direct charity to the mother".[28] Thus the fact that the cost of running the nursery in 1870 (the first complete year of its existence) was £40 over the amount received from the parents[29] neither alarmed nor dismayed its patron and founder, for it was not expected to be self-supporting.

This particular nursery—the only one, unfortunately, of which complete details were recorded—was situated in the heart of a mill district. It was open from five o'clock in the morning till six or seven o'clock at night, when the mother would collect her child on her way home from the mill.[30]

Infants were taken in from two weeks of age till they were old enough to be sent to school for the day: in theory, this meant that they could be left in the care of the nursery till they were three or four years old, but Dr. Whitehead, the Honorary Medical Superintendent and a surgeon at St. Mary's Hospital, Manchester, records that there were some children left during the day at the nursery who were seven years old.[31]

Up to twenty children could be accepted, but admittance did not entirely depend on the parents' willingness or ability to pay the necessary fee. The first paragraph in the rules of the nursery stated that "the object of the nursery is to afford a place of safety where widows, widowers, and others who go out to work during the day and have no one suitable to take charge of their children may leave them during the waking hours".[32] Infants of married women were only accepted where it could be proved that it was financially imperative that the mother should be employed at the mill rather than tend her own baby.[33] "We believe", says Dr. Whitehead, "that the mother is the best, and ought to be the best, guardian of the child, and we encourage the mother to take charge of her child in preference to our doing it. . . . If we found that a mother wished to make use of the nursery simply as a matter of convenience, from laziness, and that it was not necessary for her to work, we should decline to receive the child."[34] . . . "Sometimes the mother is earning 12s. per week and the father £1 per week; they have no other child, and she wants to place this child in the nursery; we should consider there was no necessity for the mother to work."[35]

Nor was it merely the mother's financial background that was so carefully scrutinized: "everything connected with the mother is taken into consideration";[36] some infants were refused because the moral character of the mother "was not equal to our standard".[37]

Such children as were judged suitable to receive the benefits of the nursery were left in the charge of "a manager", whom Whitehead described as "the widow of a civil engineer; he was an engineer who went to Africa to erect an engine and was killed. She was left with two daughters, and she and one of the daughters manage the nursery."[38] Over the work of these two women the "lady superintendent"—who was in fact Mrs. Leigh Clare, the patron—exercised a general supervision.[39, 40]

The advantage of such day nurseries over the prevailing system of leaving infants with old women or young children were threefold. Instead of being crammed at irregular intervals with bread-and-water pap and their consequent cries of distress being hushed with narcotics, the children under one year of age were principally fed on milk; and every encouragement and facility was given to the mothers to feed the children themselves during the dinner-hour.[41] Scrupulous attention was paid to cleanliness, both of the nursery and the children: where children were left with day nurses, they were frequently not washed once during the whole day.[42] Lastly, and perhaps most important, the work of the nurses was closely and constantly supervised, both by the ladies responsible for the management of the nurseries and by the local doctors who took an interest in their venture.[43]

The beneficial results of these establishments were to be seen in the improved health and appearance of the children after a very short time.[44] In the Charles Street nursery there had not been a single death among the 5,016 children cared for from November 1869 to May 1871.[45] Despite this, the nurseries were not, to begin with, an overwhelming success. The Charles Street nursery, as we have noted, had room for twenty children, but from its opening in November 1869 to the middle of 1871 the average number left there each day was fifteen. Sometimes there were only as many as ten children left.[46] Without doubt, this was in part due to the suspicion of anything new and untried: the mothers had got into the habit of leaving their children with a near neighbour. But it was also due to the dislike of "charity" in any form. "The poor do not appear to take much pains to enquire into these institutions; they understand that they are charitable and do not ask questions because they have a preconceived prejudice. After a time they become better acquainted with them and more inclined to leave their children and sink their prejudices.[47] . . . The advantages have to be literally drummed into them."[48]

By 1871, however, the success was established of the Charles Street nursery, and the nursery of the Misses Sellon, with which Dr. Syson, the Medical Officer of Health for Salford, was connected. One mother walked three miles every morning to leave her baby at Charles Street; and when the Salford nursery closed down for a fortnight, its doors were said to have been besieged with mothers anxious for its reopening.[49]

The fame of this success drew visitors from all over the country: the third nursery in Dickinson Street was opened, and similar establishments were talked of in Eccles and round about.[50]

Indeed, during these years day nurseries seem to have been generally adopted by social workers as a panacea for the infant mortality attributable to the employment of mothers away from home.[51] A nursery was opened in Burslem, Staffordshire, for the children of mothers at work in the potteries there; in the ten years 1864–74 three were founded in Glasgow; and, in a leading article in the *British Medical Journal* on 27th September 1879, where the establishment of a day nursery in Leicester is recorded, there is also the comment: "It is eminently satisfactory to know that the remedial effect of crèches and day nurseries upon infant mortality is now engaging local attention and that their institution is already promising the best results."[52]

The *Lancet*, incidentally, appears to have had its own reasons for repeatedly noting the beneficial results of day nurseries, for it regarded their establishment as "a good occupation for those ladies of restless energy who now besiege the portals of our profession".[53]

Perhaps the most enterprising day nursery to be opened was that of one of the much-maligned factory-owners, Richard Stanway of Enderley Mills, Newcastle under Lyme. In addition to providing a works canteen, organizing a sick fund and a regular surgery for his employees, he also, in 1883, provided a crèche, under the supervision of a Matron. This consisted of a play-room and a cot-room, the latter being equipped with cradles which were gently rocked by steam machinery. "This, I imagine", observes the factory inspector, in whose report this unexpected and ingenious introduction of automation is recorded, "is a use of steam power never before contemplated, but which answers remarkably well."[54] Stanway also bought a perambulator, which he hired out to mothers at a moderate rate "to prevent the arm-aching and tiresome business of carrying their babies to and from the mill".[55]

The charge for the use of the nursery was purely nominal, 1*s*. per child per week, the greater part of the cost being met by this remarkable man, perhaps aided by subscriptions from some of his friends.

Not all day nurseries considered themselves a kind of

charity to the mother, however. The Bradford nursery certainly did not. But some at least, and possibly the majority, were in the Marbeau tradition.[56] Indeed, it is difficult to see how otherwise they were expected to be of much benefit to the women for whose children they were intended, since most nurseries only accepted children whose mothers were forced out to work through poverty and thus, of all working mothers, were able to pay least.[57]

This had been generally appreciated by the beginning of the present century, for Sir George Newman, in his book, *Infant Mortality: A Social Problem*, 1906, recorded that "almost without exception" the seventy-five nurseries then in existence were supported by private subscriptions,[58] the mothers being charged a nominal sum of between 2*d*. and 4*d*. a day per child, although the London School Board had established four day nurseries where no charge was made at all.[59]

Well-meant though all such efforts were, not all of them seem to have met with the success of the Manchester and Salford nurseries. And even the Charles Street nursery, it will be remembered, was never full; sometimes, in fact, it was half-empty. In the seventy-five nurseries of which Newman writes, attendance ranged from 50% to 90%.

The difficulty here, as in many another social welfare project, was to persuade those for whom it was intended to abandon the hazardous yet familiar for the potentially beneficial but still untried. Inability to solve this problem led to the failure of many nurseries. All the factory inspectresses, gathering evidence for the Interdepartmental Committee on Physical Deterioration, reported on efforts which had "more or less failed to establish crèches" because of local prejudice.

This prejudice was sometimes said to be rather more than the normal suspicion of the unknown. Women in the Potteries, for example, were alleged not to support such nurseries because to do so "would be to take the bread out of the old people's mouths":[60] would, that is to say, deprive women too old and frail to work in the local industry of their only source of income.

One might also hazard that the searching enquiries into the moral virtue and financial resources usually made on application for the use of a day nursery also did little to endear such institutions to the working mother.

But however successful these nurseries, gauged either by their popularity with the mothers or by the health of the children for whom they cared, it was clear to most of those concerned to remedy the infant mortality due to the employment of mothers away from home that they were only a palliative. The lives of children were still imperilled so long as, from a few weeks of age, they had to be artificially reared: the longer the period during which the infant could be fed naturally, the better its chances of survival. It was also clear, however, that the majority of mothers forced to return to the mill soon after their confinement were compelled by economic necessity. Something, therefore, had to be done to remedy this state of affairs, and the manufacturers were called upon to do it:

"The waste of infant life in the manufacturing districts might be greatly diminished", it was claimed, "did the manufacturers adopt the plan of instituting a maternity fund to which every married woman in their employ should be obliged to pay a small weekly sum, and which might be augmented by contributions from her employer. The lying-in woman should receive her weekly wages from this fund, and not be allowed to return to work for six weeks or two months, that she might be enabled to devote the necessary attention to her child."[61]

Unknown in England, such a scheme would not have been without precedent on the Continent. M. Jean Dollfus, a large cotton manufacturer at Mulhouse, instituted on 1st November 1862 a system whereby, on condition that all his female operatives above a certain age contributed 3 francs annually to the cost of the scheme, every mother was paid her full wage for the six weeks after the fortnight following her confinement. After three years, it was claimed, the effect of the mother's prolonged absence from work was a decrease in the mortality of infants from a mean of 36% or 38% to below 25%.

The success of this first experiment encouraged six other French mill-owners to establish similar schemes for their own women operatives.[62]

Unfortunately, the fact that French mill-owners had adopted such schemes and achieved such satisfactory results seems not to have moved English manufacturers to similar exploits. Curgenven complains bitterly:

"I think the manufacturers here in England are greatly to blame for not adopting something similar. That has been put before them by the Social Science Association years ago and by the Press and by other means, and yet I do not believe that they have ever *attempted* to establish such a system."[63]

CHAPTER XII

APPEALS FOR STATE ACTION

BOTH in the establishment of day nurseries and in the institution of maternity benefit schemes, the manufacturers had failed to shoulder their responsibilities, and a gradually increasing minority were beginning to turn elsewhere for a solution to the problem. Indeed, during the same year that Simon published his Fourth Report, in which he denied the possibility of legislative action in this matter, Kay-Shuttleworth, discussing the social problems created by the employment of mothers in textile factories, introduced the consideration, "in what cases *the law* should interfere".[1] Only two years later, in 1864, the results of Dr. Julian Hunter's investigations into "The Excessive Mortality of Infants in Some Rural Districts of England" led him to recommend the establishment "by Poor Law officials or by private benevolence of an infant nursery where a responsible nurse, liable to medical or other supervision, may receive and tend the infants in every village of more than 100 houses throughout the districts where women were much employed away from home in agricultural gangs".[2]

Similar suggestions emphasizing the need for public action were being made in contemporary magazines and periodicals. The *Lancet*, in a leading article in February 1867, stated: "We believe that in every parish there should be at least one large establishment jointly supported by Government and local government benevolence, and also, to a certain extent, self-supporting, where, for the payment of a nominal sum, a poor woman could leave her child where it could receive proper care, nourishment and support."[3] The *Public Health Magazine* went further, and demanded that "the Government should countenance and control day nurseries in factory districts".[4, 5]

There was some difference of opinion, however, amongst those who supported in principle some sort of governmental action in this field as to how far the nurseries established should be self-supporting. The Editor of the *Lancet* favoured charging only a nominal fee. The County Medical Officer of Health for Staffordshire, voicing the need for the provision of crèches by local adoptive Act, contended, on the contrary, that "they should be in nearly all cases self-supporting". This opinion, in which he was far from being alone, seems to have rested partly on the fear that the low charge that might otherwise be made would positively encourage mothers to abandon their children to the care of others in favour of the carefree life of the factory.[6]

The London School Board, as we have already seen,[7] did not apparently share this fear, for in none of the four nurseries it had opened by 1906 was any charge made at all.[8] But this School Board was clearly of "advanced" views, since, as far as one can tell, it was the only authority financed by public moneys which took any steps at all to establish nurseries during Victoria's reign.

In view of Cooke Taylor's declaration,[9] and of the many like it, the reason for this is not hard to seek. Whilst agreeing with Dr. Reid that crèches were needed in factory districts, Dr. Simpson of Manchester, for example, emphatically rejected the idea that they might be established by local authorities: "this was a matter for voluntary action rather than for State interference. The moral obligation rested upon the manufacturers who brought people together in such large numbers."[10] The provision of day nurseries aided by public funds was rather the plea of a number of isolated individuals than the sworn objective of an organized social movement.

There was, on the other hand, a growing and organized

body of opinion which demanded Government action in relation to the care of illegitimate children put out to nurse, the high infant death-rate among whom had been the cause of widespread concern for some years. In 1867, and again in 1869, the resolutions passed by the Health Section of the National Association for the Promotion of Social Science included several calling for the compulsory registration, as being of suitable character, of women who undertook the care of young children in the absence of their mothers. But while the earlier of these resolutions applied only to women who cared for illegitimate children, usually for periods much longer than a single day, the later resolutions applied to all nurses, including those who cared for the legitimate children of women employed in factories during the day.

Two years later, in 1871, the Infant Life Protection Society was formed by a number of people who, in the words of the prospectus, "had been for years endeavouring to arouse the Government and the Public to a knowledge of the great evils of Baby-Farming. This system has lately been brought prominently before the Public by the case of Margaret Waters and Mary Hall"[11] (two notorious baby-farmers). The primary object of this society was "to prevent the destruction of Infant Life and the moral and physical injury caused by the present system of Baby-Farming: and with this in view, to promote a Bill in Parliament requiring that any person taking charge of an infant or young child for gain shall be certified as of good character and registered: and that every child so placed out shall be the subject of proper supervision".[12]

On 21st February of this same year, the Infant Life Protection Bill was read in the House of Commons for the first time, being introduced by Mr. Charley, Member for Salford, and sponsored, *inter alia*, by Lyon Playfair, who sat for Edinburgh University. This Bill, although its primary intention was to protect the lives of illegitimate children put out to nurse,[13] contained a clause so framed that it would, if enacted, have enforced the registration and supervision of nurses in the manufacturing districts who took care of children during the day only. Of this the promoters of the Bill were perfectly aware, and, indeed, such had been their intention.[14] They can scarcely have expected the storm of protest which the clause aroused both within and without the House of Commons.

The National Society for Women's Suffrage published a "Memorial" in which they claimed that any restriction on the day nurses in the manufacturing districts "would interfere in the most mischievous and oppressive manner with domestic arrangements. It is very common", they maintained, "for women in non-domestic industries to put their babies out to be nursed while they are at work, and the poor women are enabled to earn honestly a few pence by the performance of this neighbourly office. But these women would be alarmed by the requirement to take out a magistrate's licence. They would not be aware that such a licence was necessary till a series of prosecutions and convictions had impressed on the female population of a district the fact that an act that had hitherto been a kind, neighbourly duty had suddenly been transformed into a legal crime for which they were liable to be summoned before the magistrate and condemned to imprisonment."[15]

To this allegation the Infant Life Protection Society retorted that "what is here referred to as a 'neighbourly office' is in fact a matter of business very largely carried on in manufacturing districts, often in a matter extremely fatal to the life of the children admitted into the crèches, and it is one which peculiarly requires supervision on behalf of the infants who are now the subjects of the business. It is well known that they are commonly neglected, half-starved, and continuously drugged with opiates, of which the sale for this purpose is incredibly extensive where the unregulated system exists."[16]

But the most damaging criticism levelled at the provisions of the Bill, and the one calculated to carry most weight in contemporary society, was that this was a violation of the liberty of the individual:

"It is not against the licensing of women as nurses that we protest—a Bill empowering suitable authorities to grant certificates of fitness to all nurses who desire to possess them, and can show they merit such distinction, would command our support—it is to the compulsion to be put on parents to employ none but those holding such licences that we object", claimed the Committee for amending the Law in Points where it is Injurious to Women. "The responsibility for the child in infancy, as in later life, lies with them, and we emphatically deny that the State has any right to dictate to them the way it shall be fulfilled. We hold that its functions ought to be confined to the imposing of penalties for the culpable neglect of this, as of any other department of parental duty. If, through indifference, ignorance, or wilful malice, parents place their infants in untrustworthy hands, and the child suffers in the consequence, the law should punish them equally with the nurse. Let self-interest and a wholesome fear of penalties be thrown, by all means, into the same scale with natural affection, but beyond such precautions against their exercising their right to choose a nurse, carelessly and wickedly, the State should forbear to limit in any way their perfect freedom of action in this, as in all matters connected with the rearing and maintaining of their families.

"What would the ladies of England say", demanded the Committee, "if some member of the House of Commons were to bring forward a measure for licensing nursemaids, and forbid them to employ any girl who could not produce such an official testimony to her competence? Yet in cases, and they are not rare, where the mother, absorbed in social duties or pleasures, leaves her child entirely in the care of servants, the need for such State interference may be absolutely the same. It is not alone the offspring of the poor who fall victims to ignorance or neglect, and unless Parliament is prepared to sanction the interference of the State in the selection of all persons to whom parental duties are deputed, it ought to content itself with imposing and inflicting punishment where such duties have been carelessly or culpably devolved upon incompetent substitutes, for it is the essence of just law that it shall be of so wide an application that none who violate its provisions shall escape its penalties."[17]

In the House of Commons, Jacob Bright, Member for Manchester, raised the same objection—that the provisions of the Bill, in so far as they would affect the manufacturing districts, constituted an unwarranted interference with the liberty of the subject.[18]

Because of this fundamental criticism of its provisions, the Bill was withdrawn on 19th July, its promoters agreeing that the whole issue of the licensing and inspection of nurses should be investigated by a Parliamentary Select Committee which was instructed to consider "the best means of protecting infants put out to nurse".

The bulk of evidence given before this Committee related to the care of illegitimate children put out to nurse for long periods of time; but evidence was given, most of it concerning the Lancashire textile districts, of the harmful effects of the day nursing of infants of mothers employed in factories. Opinion was divided among these witnesses, however, as to the advisability of enforcing the registration and inspection of this type of nurse.[19] In view of this, and of the outcry that had greeted the original proposal of such a measure, it was scarcely to be expected that the Committee would include such a policy in its recommendations. ". . . We are of the opinion", they reported, "that it would be reasonable and expedient to register persons who, for payment, take charge at the same time of two or more infants under one year of age for longer periods than one day (excluding relatives and institutions). Such limited registration would not interfere to an inconvenient extent with the habits of those persons in manufacturing districts who are accustomed to put their children under the charge of a caretaker for the day, or during the hours of work."[20]

These were the recommendations embodied in the Infant Life Protection Act (35 & 36 Vict., c. 38), which received the Royal Assent the following year, 1872.

Thus, although it had succeeded in bringing to the public notice the harmful effects of day nursing in manufacturing districts, this particular attempt to enforce by law the better care of infants of mothers employed away from home during the day failed. Nor did later modifications of the Act do anything to remedy this, although on more than one occasion the need to make the provisions of the Act relevant to conditions in factory districts was raised on a national level,[21] not only with reference to the welfare of babies left in the care of child-minders, young or old, but also of those left in the much-publicized day nurseries, which were also unaffected by the Act.[22]

On the other hand, an attempt of a very different nature to invoke Government assistance in protecting the lives of infants whose mothers went out to work met with rather more success.

"There can be no doubt", say Bridges and Holmes in their Report in 1873, "that if the abatement of the evil by legislation is as hopeless as Mr. Simon seems to think, some good might be done here and there by the benevolence of individual masters in establishing nurseries . . . or lying-in clubs, which would enable the mothers to give themselves a reasonable period of absence from labour. But it is obvious that no system which depends on individual good feeling can meet such an evil. And we cannot allow ourselves to despair of a practicable measure of legislation on this subject."[23]

These two investigators did not confine themselves to this general pronouncement. In Conclusion 5 to their Report they state categorically:

"It does not appear to us impracticable, and if practicable, it certainly appears to us desirable to make some arrangements by which mothers of young infants shall either be employed for half-time, or be excluded for a time from the factories altogether.

"A list of women who have borne children during the past month might be circulated by the various local registrars to the manufacturers of the district, who should then become responsible for avoiding to take into their employment any such women applying for work within the period that might be defined."[24]

The proposal that mothers of young infants should only be employed half-time for a certain period, though it had other supporters, among them the Commissioners on the 1873 Factory Amendment Bill and certain factory inspectors,[25] never seems to have aroused the same enthusiasm as the proposal that mothers should be excluded from the factory entirely for a period of time after their confinement. On going into Committee on this particular Factory Bill, a small batch of legislators were found to have tabled amendments. Dr. Lush advocated a period of exclusion of six weeks and a fine if they returned before that; Mr. Tennant, Member for Leeds, suggested an absence of six months, which he subsequently changed to six weeks, and sought to place responsibility on the owner of the factory; Mr. Assheton came forward with an heroic proposition of twelve months "right off".

Two years before this, in evidence to the Select Committee on the Best Means of Protecting Infants put out to Nurse, Dr. Whitehead of Manchester had advocated the prohibition of employment of "pregnant or suckling women", the period of the prohibition being unspecified.[26]

Factory inspectors, in evidence before the 1875

Commission on Factory and Workshops Acts, advocated similar legislative action. Baker, who by this date was Joint Chief of the Factory Department, having given it as his experience that "very considerable mischief arises with women going out to work, not only to the mother, but also to the child", was asked by the Chairman, Sir James Fergusson: "We may take it for granted that it is not theoretically desirable that women should go daily to work immediately after confinement, leaving the child to somebody else all day; but practically speaking, do you think from your experience of this matter that if Parliament interfered with it, it could be enforced with uniformity and without hardship?" To which Baker replied: "Yes. I think it might. I think that by the visitation of certifying surgeons it might be enforced decently and delicately, and sufficiently to make it useful."[27]

It will not come entirely as a surprise to the reader to learn that legislation to this end had already been passed on the Continent. Mundella, in evidence to the same Commission, explained how in Glarus, and some other Swiss cantons, a woman was obliged to remain at home for six weeks in all, fixing the time at her own discretion;[28] and that a similar provision was included in the factory law of Austria.[29]

In the 1870s, however, neither the precepts of their fellow countrymen nor the practice of Continental powers could persuade the majority of Englishmen by legislative action to invade the sacred hearth of the home. The Factory Commissioners of 1875 still voiced the prevailing opinion, when they denied the possibility and practicability of legislative action in this country, and recorded the pious hope that "the movement for organizing public nurseries in factory towns will continue to attract public notice and support".[30]

Inevitably, however, the truth of the contention that private action cannot be depended upon to remedy a national evil became increasingly clear. Not only did the day nurseries fail to prove popular with the mothers, but in some factory districts no voluntary attempt was made to provide them.[31] Furthermore, it became obvious that however successful or unsuccessful the provision of such institutions, the fundamental problem—namely, the premature return of the mother to work and her consequent inability to breast-feed her child, with all that that implied—remained untouched.[32] As Jevons expressed it: "We are on the horns of a dilemma: the infants die as it is, and they probably die if nurseries are established. We want some more radical remedy."[33] Such a remedy was forthcoming in the last decade of the century.

In 1891,[34] the Government, by now confident of support for such a measure, included in the Factory and Workshops Bill of that year a clause to make it illegal for any employer of labour at such premises "knowingly" to employ a woman within four weeks of her confinement.

In the course of the long debates on the whole Bill, this particular clause was scarcely discussed; and only once was it seriously challenged—by Lord Wemyss in the House of Lords. The peculiar interest of Lord Wemyss's speech lies in the fact that he acted as spokesman for the women's rights party, the leaders and prominent members of which he quoted at length as supporting his solitary opposition in Parliament.

Dr. Garrett Anderson, for example, urged that "many women who work hard all their lives are quite able to work in less than a month after their confinement, and whether they are or not, they ought to be left entirely to decide for themselves".[35]

The Secretary of the Women's Employment Association, Miss Ada Heather Bigg, saw in the clause yet another attempt on the part of male trade unionists to drive women out of the labour market.[36]

What was, in the event, to be the most pertinent criticism of the clause came from Mrs. Fawcett and Miss Lipton, the Secretary of the Laundry Women's Co-operative Association. "What", the latter demanded, "is to become of these women, who are mostly bread-winners, if they are prevented from working for a month, God alone knows. I don't know."[37] Mrs. Fawcett predicted that the proposed month's exclusion from work would press hard on widows, deserted wives and unmarried mothers, possibly encouraging them to look to the Poor Law for assistance or, as regards the unmarried mother, to yet further degradation.

No real answer was given to these last charges. In reply to Lord Wemyss, it was merely claimed that the inability of women to look after their own best interests had long been the basis of factory legislation, and that the country could no longer tolerate the evil effects of their employment so soon after confinement.

The clause was incorporated in the Act, which received the Royal Assent the same year.

As we have already seen, the failure of the Act to make it obligatory for the employer to obtain either the birth certificate or some medical certificate giving the date of birth of the child before engaging a woman after her confinement made it impossible for the factory inspec-tresses to prove in the majority of cases of evasion brought to their notice that a woman found back at work within the prohibited period had been "knowingly" employed. To the difficulty of their position in this respect the inspectresses repeatedly called attention in their annual reports and in evidence before official investigating bodies.[38]

More important in this present context, however, was the evidence they gave at the turn of the century, when it was being suggested that the period of absence should be extended to at least three months,[39] of the deliberate evasion of the existing law on the part of the women themselves. The reasons given for this evasion were to prompt further demands within our period for local, but later for statutory, action relating to the employ-ment of mothers away from home, for the evidence that was given on this point was overwhelming and irrefutable.

"Women know the advantages of at least one month off, if only they could live during the time. Unfortunately, it is just when she is least fit to work that she needs the money most."[40] "How some of the poor women live during their time of difficulty", declared one speaker to the 1906 Conference on Infantile Mortality, the Chief Lady Sanitary Inspectress for Leeds, "can only be explained by that charity of the poor towards the poor which is the result of a real and personal knowledge of privation and hunger and by taking into account a system of credit which means an accumulation of debt and the resulting need for further effort on the part of the woman as soon as it is possible for her to return to work."[41] One woman, asked by a factory inspectress why she had returned to work within four weeks of her confinement, retorted: "Well, we must live."[42]

Mrs. Fawcett had, in fact, underestimated the unfortunate consequences of this well-meant scheme, for it was not merely the mothers who were widowed, deserted or unmarried who, were they to observe the law, had to face privation. There were also the very large numbers of women who were out at work because the amount their husband could earn or his inability to earn at all made it imperative that they did so.[43] The position of such women was unenviable indeed. "The respectable married woman . . . can, with difficulty, take advantage of the free food, shelter and medical attendance provided at great expense by the destitution authorities for maternity cases", wrote the authors of the 1909 Report on the Poor Laws. "In Scotland she is, if living with her own husband, he being in good health, absolutely debarred from relief by law. In England and Wales she is, if possible, deterred."[44] For many women, therefore, to enforce the Act was to enforce starvation.[45]

"Disastrous as are the consequences in so many instances of the early return to work", writes the Chief Lady Factory Inspectress, "one can neither be surprised nor blame the mothers who take the risk of them rather than accept what seems to them the only alternative. Insurance of some kind against this recurring event", she concludes, "seems a necessary adjunct to the enforcement of the law."[46]

That this would be so might easily have been foreseen by the logic and consequent success of Dollfus's scheme nearly thirty years before, to which we have already drawn attention.[47] However, now that the need for some similar scheme in the country was only too clear, the employer or some local philanthropist was called upon to meet it—not the Government, for, as the Prime Minister had remarked, admittedly in another context, to an "admiring and applauding audience" in 1891: "There is a great tendency to come to the State for everything, but after all, with all the good-will in the world, there is little that the State could or ought to do."[48] Even those most anxious to establish some sort of maternity insurance scheme concurred in this. Thomas Oliver, for example, writing in 1902 of the fatal effects of the mother's early return to work, referred to the contemporary German practice of compulsory assurance under which the working mother drew half her normal weekly wage during the statutory four to six weeks' absence after her confinement. "This expedient", he claimed, not without a touch of insular pride, "could hardly be made applicable to this country."[49]

In the years which had elapsed since Dollfus's scheme had been made known to the English public there is no evidence that similar funds were established by any employer in this country. The investigators assembling evidence for the Physical Deterioration Committee were unable to find in this country any form of provident institution to which mothers could contribute whilst still earning.[50] Despite these facts, however, the Mulhouse scheme,[51] as well as the more recent one at Villiers-le-Duc,[52] were to be once more commended in 1904 as worthy models for private philanthropic endeavour, for, "whether by local trade or larger national efforts, provident societies of this kind might be expected in time to eliminate the present large number of cases where infant lives are lost to the State at birth".[53]

There is no doubt that maternity insurance was sound in principle; although how sound it could be financially at a time when many women were earning as little as 7s. a week is problematical. Lady MacLaren, commenting on the recommendation of the Physical Deterioration Committee that charitable efforts might be directed to endowing or maintaining insurance funds, to aid by voluntary subscription those of the women themselves, remarked that she was reminded of "a certain philanthropist who, in time of famine, would vote for nothing but a supply of toothpicks!"[54] Be that as it may, the practicability of such a fund was never put to the test in Victoria's reign, and the factory mothers were left to bear the full rigours of exclusion from work or the consequences of evading the law until the Insurance Act of 1911, when the first attempt was made in this country to institute some scheme of maternity benefits.

In the history of social insurance much has been claimed for the contribution made towards its general acceptance and inauguration by the work of early investigators. It is perhaps not sufficiently recognized how much the institution of social services connected with maternity owes to the work of investigators, public and private, whose reports we have embodied in these the last five chapters—reports which contain irrefutable evidence of the harmful, often fatal, results of the employment of mothers in mills and factories on the lives of their infants.

CHAPTER XIII

SOME UNSOLVED PROBLEMS

IT was not unreasonable, in view of the evidence concerning the causes of infant mortality in factory districts, that Victorians should deplore the employment of mothers of very young children away from home. Whether they were equally justified in condemning, as they did, the employment of married women in general is rather a different matter.

Before we make any comment on this last judgment, however, we should indicate some aspects of our subject concerning which little or no valid evidence is recorded. It would have been interesting, for example, to discover whether the husband of the married woman operative held the same position in his household as did the husband of the middle or upper class woman during our period: whether, that is to say, he was the lord and master of his home, the source of all authority and the fount of all wisdom. In Chapter VI we made passing reference to the opinion that, at least in the Lancashire mill-towns, the authority of a father over his unmarried daughters was diminished when they were economically independent of him. We might suppose that a married woman also capable of supporting herself might similarly assert her right to some degree of independent action, but whether this was so or not is rarely discussed by contemporaries. It need hardly be said that Lord Ashley was one of those who did do so:

"Listen to another fact, and one deserving of serious attention", he says in the course of the Ten Hours debates. "The females not only perform the labour, but occupy the places of men [in the mill towns]; they are forming various clubs and associations and gradually acquiring all those privileges which are held to be the proper portion of the male sex. These female clubs are thus described: 'Fifty or sixty females, married and single, form themselves into clubs, ostensibly for protection; but in fact they meet together to drink, sing and smoke; they use, it is stated, the lowest, most brutal, and most disgusting language imaginable.' Here is a dialogue in one of these clubs from an eyewitness: A man came into one of these clubrooms with a child in his arms. 'Come, lass,' said he, addressing one of the women. 'Come home, for I cannot keep this bairn quiet, and the other I have left crying at home.' 'I won't come home, idle devil,' she replied. 'I have thee to keep, and the bairns too, and if I can't get a pint of ale quietly, it is tiresome. This is but the second pint that me and Bess have had between us; thou may sup if thou likes, and sit thee down, but I won't go home yet.' Whence is it that this singular and unnatural change is taking place? Because that on the women are imposed the duty and the burden of supporting their husbands and families, a perversion as it were of nature, which has the inevitable effect of introducing into families disorder, insubordination and conflict. What is the ground on which a woman says she will pay no attention to her domestic duties? Nor give the obedience which is due to her husband? Because on her devolves the labour which ought to fall to his share, and she throws out the taunt, 'If I have the labour, I will also have the amusement.' "[1]

Interesting as this dramatic revelation may be, we have already seen that Ashley tended to err on the side of exaggeration in his accounts of the effects of the factory system on the home-life of the operatives. Disregarding for the moment the implication in his speech that the husbands of married women operatives were unemployed, the few descriptions of the home-life of operatives given by contemporary novelists fail to contain evidence that would support his main contention that the husband of the married woman operative was not the "head of the house"—that "a singular and unnatural change" had indeed taken place. This does not mean that Ashley's statement was necessarily entirely without foundation: the lack of corroborative evidence in the contemporary novel might well be because of the authors' unfamiliarity with working-class life and habits, and their consequent attributing to the working class husband the status and authority of the husband in the homes of the social strata to which they themselves belonged.

In our own day, the emphasis in discussions on the employment of married women is on the influence it does or might have on their children. This was equally true during Victoria's reign, but the Victorians were more concerned with the very youngest children. In the nineteenth century by far the most important aspect of married women's employment for its influence on public opinion and subsequent legislation was the problem of how the employed married woman provided for the care of her young baby during her absence at work. It is curious that although so much attention was paid to the welfare of these very young children, the fate of children only a few years older aroused little or no interest. Lack of attention to this particular problem is all the more notable in view of the fact that years before our period opened the necessity of some provision for the care of employed mothers' children aged two to six years, after which time it was theoretically possible for them to attend some day school, had aroused keen interest in some parts of the country. Robert Owen, it will be recalled, opened the first infant school in Great Britain in 1816 at his mills at New Lanark. In part, this was the outcome of his belief in the overwhelming influence of environment in the formation of character,[2] but it had the additional purpose of releasing mothers for work in Owen's mills:

"The institution has been devised to afford the means of receiving children at a very early age, as soon, almost, as they can walk. By this means many of you, mothers of families, will be enabled to earn a better maintenance or support for your children; you will have less care and anxiety about them, while the children will be prevented from acquiring bad habits and gradually prepared to learn the best."[3] Owen then describes how children would be taken to the school at two years of age, and remain there for two or three years, when they would be taken into the "superior school", which they were to leave when they were ten years of age: in his *Life*, however, there are references to children entering the infant school at as early an age as one year.[4]

Inspired by this experiment at New Lanark Mill, Brougham and Zachary Macaulay started a school on Owen's lines in Westminster in 1818; and a similar one in Spitalfields, in charge of which they appointed Samuel Wilderspin. It was because of the interest aroused by Wilderspin's treatise, *On the Importance of Educating the Infant Children of the Poor*, that the London Infant School Society was formed to provide schools for children aged from two to six years, Wilderspin himself acting as agent of the Society and travelling up and down the country to establish these "infants' asylums".

In his treatise, Wilderspin stresses the need for playgrounds as tending to good habits and also to "the acquisition of useful knowledge";[5] he saw the infant school as a possible check on "juvenile depravity",[6] but he also, like Owen before him, saw it as a means for releasing the mothers of young children for work.[7]

These philanthropic efforts, however, had their origin far from the factory districts of the North and Midlands, and such success as they met there seems to have been before our period opened.[8] It is true that the first free kindergarten to be opened in Great Britain was opened in Salford in 1883 by Sir William Mather on the site of a cleared slum, and presided over by a *Kindergärtnerin* from Berlin. It provided baths, meals, training, rest and play for children aged from two to six or seven years. But this seems to have been rather an experiment in Froebel methods for the benefit of the poor than a charitable institution for the convenience of employed mothers.[9]

Any institution whose avowed purpose was to release mothers for work was scarcely calculated to appeal to Victorians interested in the problems of the married woman worker, believing as they did that women's work "lays the axe to the root of social confederacy, paves the way for the break-up of the bonds of society which are the basis of national and domestic happiness".[10] But the comparative absence of comment on the fate of the older children of the married women workers, in sharp contrast to the concern shown in the fate of their babes in arms, was probably also occasioned by a rather different factor. Our contemporary observers were neither dispassionate nor objective: almost without exception, they were concerned to show that the employment of married women was accompanied by the worst possible consequences. They could argue—and produce evidence to support their contention—that, however bad contemporary standards of infant welfare might be,[11] the neglect of infants whose mothers were absent at the factory gave rise to more fatal consequences than would otherwise have been the case. With the older children of the working mothers it was more difficult, during our period, to exhibit the consequences of neglect as equally dramatic.

The pamphlet, *Public Nurseries* (1851), for example, contains information from the police report for Manchester, 1848, to the effect that "a great number of children are constantly lost in Manchester. During the last four years, ending 1848, rather more than 4,000 children have been lost each year, and of these nearly half have been returned to their friends by the police, the remainder having been found by means of a hue and cry raised by the parents themselves."[12] The majority of these children, it is inferred, were the children of operatives—of mothers employed in the mills and elsewhere. But for this inference no evidence is adduced. Nor, in all probability, would it have been an easy task to do so. In a paper read to the N.A.P.S.Sc. in 1867 "On Compulsory Education", the Rev. James McCosh revealed that "in 1865, the means of education were wanting in the diocese of London for between 150,000 and 200,000 children. Everyone has heard of the active society which aims at providing education for the poor in Manchester and Salford. The Committee of the Council on Education thus sums up its doings: 'Certain defined districts of Manchester and Salford are being visited one after another from house to house. The results for several districts were published in November 1865, and they showed that in every fifteen children between the ages of three and twelve, one was at work, six were at school, and the other eight were neglected. It is probable that a majority of the neglected eight-fifteenths do pick up some schooling between three and twelve years of age at irregular intervals; but there is no doubt that the general result is that there are many thousands of children in towns like Manchester growing up and going to work without any education. . . . Coming to Glasgow, we find that in the rich district of Blythswood, there is 1 in 7·1 at school; but then in the poorer district, we have in Hutchensontown 1 in 12·3; in Tradeston, 1 in 13·2; in Bridgeton 1 in 14·5; and the whole of Glasgow, 1 in 11·1. Messrs. Harvey and Greig report: 'The voluntary system has hitherto proved utterly inadequate to effect the education of the masses of the population congregated in our large towns.' Referring to the Clyde district, two out of three of the children of school age are attending no school. 'And what are these neglected children doing if they are not at school? They are idling in the streets and wynds; tumbling about in the gutters; selling matches; running errands; working in tobacco shops, cared for by no man, and with parents or guardians over them who would resent as an impertinent interference any care or sympathy that expresses itself in any other way than a gift of money, of clothes or of bread.' "[13] Nor were conditions any better in this respect in rural districts;[14] the bands of "street Arabs" were notorious merely because they were less easily ignored than children roaming about the country villages.

Education was not universally compulsory in England till 1881, and then not below the age of five years: in our Bibliography we list the titles and authors of papers read before the Education Section of the N.A.P.S.Sc., which indicate the concern at the lack of education of young children of the "industrious and perishing classes" during our period and which contain a vast amount of evidence of the general neglect of these children throughout the country. In view of this prevailing neglect, it would indeed have been difficult for our observers to maintain that the older children of the married operative would have been better cared for and supervised had she not been employed away from home.

CHAPTER XIV

PROFIT OR LOSS?

THE insistence of contemporary writers on the disadvantage of the employment of married women away from home makes it extremely difficult to reach any definite conclusion as to whether, after all, any benefit was derived by the families of wives and mothers so employed.

Even though we allow for the exaggeration of contemporary accounts, it is simple enough to list the disadvantages from the point of view of routine housekeeping. Either she was too exhausted after the day's toil to clean the house in the evenings—in which case her home became dirty and neglected—or she had either to devote her few hours of leisure both during the week and at the week-end to cleaning—a practice more common than was credited by contemporary observers—or employ someone else to perform her tasks for her, which was expensive, and, judging from the type of person generally employed, probably not always justified by results. It is simple enough to demonstrate how uneconomical both in energy and money this system of housekeeping was. Beyond doubt, the employment of mothers was a threat to the health and well-being of their babies, not only in the Lancashire cotton districts, but in any district where married women were employed away from home. Yet the problem still remains as to whether these disadvantages were not counterbalanced by other factors.

At the root of our dilemma in solving this problem is the fact that the Victorians were so anxious to get the married women out of the mills and factories that they gave scant attention to the reasons for the women being there at all. We have drawn attention several times to the commonly accepted notion that one of the chief reasons for married women's employment in Lancashire was that their husbands preferred to remain at home idle, supported by their wives.[1] Other detractors of the factory system held the view that it displaced adult men and imposed on women "the duty and burden of supporting their husbands and families".[2] Statistically these views should rest on the same evidence: both parties should be able to produce figures showing that the majority of married women employed in the Lancashire cotton industry were in fact supporting their husbands and families unaided. On examination, however, neither of these assumptions proves to have any statistical foundation whatsoever. Engels, in 1844, quoted figures showing that of the husbands of 10,721 married women employed in 412 factories, 5,314 were also employed in factories, 3,927 were otherwise engaged, information was not forthcoming for 659, and only 821 were unemployed and presumably supported by their wives.[3]

Two surveys by the Manchester Statistical Society, the first during the year 1864-5 in Deansgate, and the second during the following year in Ancoats, also failed to substantiate the views we have outlined above. This result is especially interesting in view of the fact that in both these districts of Manchester the employment of mothers in the local cotton mills was so extensive as to move local philanthropists to establish day nurseries there.[4] The survey of Deansgate showed that of the whole number of families in the district, whereas 44·31% were supported entirely by the head of the family and a further 15·84% by the father and children, only 1·99% were supported by the wife alone where there was a husband, and only 0·85% by the mother and children alone where there was a father. The corresponding figures for Ancoats were 39·29% and 22·43%, as against 1·01% and 1·25%.[5]

It had been hoped that an analysis of our random

sample of 1851 and 1871 Census household schedules would throw further light on this problem, but as no single return showed the husband as not occupied,[6] it must be assumed that in some cases the employment which the husband is recorded as pursuing should be qualified by the phrase, "when in employment".

The allegation was sometimes made that "many women in the North of England continued to work in factories after they were married without the actual compulsion of work".[7] Observers claimed indignantly that "the going out of women to work seemed to have arisen out of necessity, but there was now an extended taste for it".[8] Allen Clarke, after describing the effect on the home when the wife and mother was employed in the mill as "simply awful", remarks: "I must admit, however, that many women like the mill . . . some women prefer the crowded factory to the quiet home because they have a hatred of the solitary housework. I have often heard married females say they would rather be in a factory than in the home, because the comparative isolation gave them the dumps after being in the company of hundreds of workmates."[9] Or, again, George Reid, reflecting on his experience in manufacturing districts, states that "in many cases the wife . . . goes out to work while at the same time the husband is earning ample wages. In Lancashire it is common for a man to receive 25s. a week while his wife earns from 15s. to 20s.; and in Staffordshire, where the potting trade is ordinarily prosperous, the weekly wages of a man and his wife amount to 30s. and 12s. respectively. These figures", he remarks, "represent a fair average, but many of the men receive much higher wages."[10] This argument, even if we accept these estimates as correct, passes over the fact that married women cotton operatives were not necessarily the wives of men also engaged in cotton manufacture; an analysis of our random sample of 1851 and 1871 Census household schedules shows that a very considerable proportion of these women—36.56%

and 37·78%—were either married to men in other occupations or were returned as not living with their husbands. The possibility that not a few of the married women were compelled to work in the mills because their husband's wage was insufficient to keep the home going was virtually ignored by contemporary investigators. In so far as the possibility was considered at all, it was claimed that the husbands were habitual drunkards who spent all their wages in the numerous beer-houses[11]—an allegation incapable of disproof, but which appears a trifle exaggerated, to say no more.

Not till the last ten years of the nineteenth century, when some local authorities followed Manchester's example of appointing women health visitors and sanitary inspectresses, largely in connexion with infant-welfare education schemes and when the Government appointed women factory inspectresses "to be always ready to receive and attend to any complaints received from or relating to the employment of women in any part of the United Kingdom", were there any serious attempts made to analyse and assess the relative import-ance of the reasons for married women going out to work. But when the attempt was made, it became apparent immediately that although it was true that "in some cases, married women whose husbands are well able to support them prefer to work in factories, not only for the sake of the additional money, but because they miss otherwise the sociable factory life to which they were accustomed and find home duties dull and purpose-less,[12] such women were in the minority. The Principal Lady Factory Inspectress in 1904 placed actual prefer-ence for going out to work as the last and least on her list of reasons for married women's employment, which were as follows:

"1. Death of father or lack of employment or in-sufficiency of father's wage.

"2. Desertion by father.

"3. Preference for factory over domestic work.

"In the great majority of cases", she reports, "the reason for married women's employment is one of those mentioned in Category I."[13]

Her inspectresses found that only in 18% of cases investigated in the Potteries was there no financial necessity for the wife to work.[14] Indeed, since well-paid men's employment was scarce in this area, it was claimed that "a woman is looked upon as lazy unless she takes her share in contributing to the family income. In Staffordshire, the men and boys appear to be willing to do their part in the domestic work of the home, and it is no uncommon sight to find a man cleaning and sweeping, caring for the children and even putting them to bed on the evening when the women were engaged in the family washing."[15]

This attitude was also said to prevail in the northern textile towns, where, in Preston as in Dundee, scarcity of employment for men in the major local industry often made the wife the chief wage-earner of the family.[16] It is interesting to note, incidentally, in view of our own calculations and of Reid's assertions, that although witnesses to the Royal Commission on Labour in 1893 admitted that there was perhaps less need for wives of men cotton operatives to go out to work, only about half the married women cotton operatives were said to be wives of men also employed in the mills. The remainder were married men in less well-paid and more uncertain jobs, as in Oldham, for example, where it was found that they were wives of "outdoor workmen, such as masons, navvies, bricklayers, labourers and suchlike persons who were unable to find work for more than thirty weeks in the year; thus the woman has to go out".[17]

In either case, however, it was maintained that wives were not out at work merely for the personal pleasures it might bring. "While no doubt young girls and young women often spend a good deal on clothes, the married woman who works for 'spending money' for herself, apart from her family, is at present so rare as to be negligible."[18]

Even supposing for the moment that the husband's wage was in fact adequate to maintain his wife at home, had it been so desired, the possibility that her wages procured extra comforts for the home cannot be overlooked in balancing this profit and loss account. Robert Baker, one of the severest critics of married women's employment, went so far as to admit that: "In all the families of the working classes, the wages of the women and children add, if I may use the expression, the luxuries of their condition to the mere necessities earned by the men, since all their wants are now greater than when, to paraphrase the quotation, 'man delved and woman span'. "[19] Whately Cooke Taylor, one of the few who did not share the current view that all the consequences of married women's employment were for the bad, also draws attention to "the greater comforts that are to be procured by the earning of good wages by the wife".[20] These advantages were often overlooked by observers to whom it was an article of faith that the woman's place was in the home, but which we here cannot disregard.[21]

In the reports of the Royal Commission on Labour, one of the lady Assistant Commissioners reported that: "The advocates of restriction [of married women's employment] say that the loss to the home consequent on the absence of the mother is much greater than the gain obtained by her wages. This is sometimes the case when the calculation is made in actual money when the amount earned in the mill is paid weekly to someone else for the cleaning and care of the home. Mr. Egerton, the Manager of Messrs. John Brooke & Sons' mill, quoted in support of this argument a case in which a woman drew 10s. a week in wages and paid 12s. for the care of her home. In such cases, of course, the husbands are also employed."[22] Until, however, evidence is forthcoming that such cases were the rule, and not the exception, we have no right to assume it.

Indeed, the necessity for caution in accepting contemporary statements as valid descriptions of the effects of married women's employment away from home is more than obvious in the foregoing pages. It would certainly be a dramatic conclusion to this study were we able to proclaim with Mrs. Bayley that "the wife and mother going abroad for work was, with few exceptions, a waste of time, a waste of property, a waste of morals, and a waste of health and life and ought in every way to be prevented",[23] but our evidence does not yield convincing proof of this. There is not sufficient data to substantiate the first two of these points: as for the third, the whole of Chapter IV is devoted to showing that there is no reason to suppose this to be true. Where the married operative was the mother of a young baby and not compelled by financial necessity to go out to work in the mill, no advantage could counterbalance the disadvantages of her employment: health and life are not balanced, still less outweighed, by "added luxuries". But where this was not the case, the question is much more open. In view of this, we have scant justification for concluding that married women's employment away from home in Victorian England was "in every respect . . . an individual mistake, a social tragedy, a communal blunder. . . ."[24]

NOTES AND REFERENCES

CHAPTER I

1. "The Employment of Women", *N.A.P.S.Sc. Transactions*, 1861, p. 532.
2. H. Hamilton, *History of the Homeland* (Allen and Unwin, 1947), p. 317.
3. Ibid., p. 319.
4. Alice Clarke, *The Working Life of Women in the Seventeenth Century* (Routledge, 1919), p. 93.
5. I. Pinchbeck, *Women Workers and the Industrial Revolution* (Routledge, 1930), p. 122.
6. H. Hamilton, *History of the Homeland* (Allen and Unwin, 1947), p. 320.
7. Ibid., p. 319.
8. Ibid., p. 320.
9. *Women in Modern Industry* (Bell & Sons, 1915), p. 28.
10. Quoted by M. Dorothy George, *London Life and Labour in the Eighteenth Century* (London, 1925), pp. 168–9.
11. "Our Unemployed Females—What may Best be done about Them?", *Manchester Statistical Society Transactions*, 1862–3, pp. 37–8.
12. Wanda F. Neff, *Victorian Working Women* (Columbia University Press, 1929), pp. 85–6.
13. Ibid., p. 86.

CHAPTER II

1. *B.P.P.*, 1893–4, XXXVII, p. 507.
2. Op. cit., 1904, XXXII, p. 63, 1,432, 1,433.
3. Hodder, "Answer to an Address of the Central Short-Time Committee", *Life of the Seventh Earl of Shaftesbury*, Popular Edition, p. 234.
4. *Hansard*, 1844, vol. LXXIII, col. 676.
5. Ibid., col. 1,091.
6. Ibid., 1844, vol. LXXV, cols. 144–5. Cf. also Lord John Manners, vol. LXXII, col. 1,418.
7. Ibid., 1844, vol. LXXIV, cols. 665–6.
8. Ibid., vol. LXXIII, col. 1,428.
9. Ibid, col. 1,145.
10. Medical Evidence to the Commission on the Employment of Children in Factories, Dr. Mitchell's Report, *B.P.P.*, 1834, XIX, p. 38.
11. Ibid., 1833, XX, p. 63.
12. *Hansard*, 1847, vol. LXXIII, col. 630.

13. Manchester, 1850.
14. Ibid., pp. 1–2.
15. *B.P.P.*, 1864, XXII, p. 709.
16. *Hansard*, 1873, vol. CCXVII, col. 1,301.
17. Ibid., vol. CCXVI, col. 825.
18. Cf. reference 16.
19. 1911 Census (General Report), *B.P.P.*, 1917–18, p. 133.
20. Ibid.
21. Wanda Neff, op. cit., p. 100.
22. Ibid., p. 126.

CHAPTER III

1. Cf. *Leeds Mercury*, 16th and 30th October 1830. Also *Leeds Intelligencer*, 11th November, 1830. Oastler's first letter to the *Leeds Mercury* is reproduced in full by Cecil Driver on pp. 42–4 of his book, *Tory Radical* (O.U.P., 1946). Driver also gives extracts in subsequent pages from the correspondence which ensued in the columns of both papers.
2. Horner was factory inspector for a large area of the north-west.
3. *Hansard*, 1847, vol. LXXIII, col. 1,379.
4. Quoted by Ashley, *Hansard*, 1844, vol. LXXIII, col. 1,379.
5. Ibid., col. 1,092.
6. Letter from Lord Ashley to Mr. Mark Crabtree, Secretary of the Yorkshire Central Short-Time Committee, quoted by Hodder, *Life of the Seventh Earl of Shaftesbury*, vol. I, p. 359.
7. B. L. Hutchins and A. Harrison, *History of Factory Legislation* (3rd edition; London, 1926), p. 65.
8. *Manchester and Salford Advertiser*, 15th January 1842.
9. Appendix to Horner's Report, *B.P.P.*, 1849, XXIII, p. 188.
10. *B.P.P.*, 1847–8, XXVI, p. 159.
11. Cf. factory inspectors' reports, *B.P.P.*, 1847, XV, p. 133.
12. *B.P.P.*, 1849, XXIII, p. 287.
13. Quoted by Mr. Howell, Factory Inspector, *B.P.P.*, 1847–8, XXVI, p. 171. Cf. also Saunders, *B.P.P.*, 1849, XXII, p. 139.
14. Cf. Ashley, *Hansard*, 1850, vol. CIC, col. 884.
15. Cf. Mr. Howell, *B.P.P.*, 1849, XXII, p. 225.
16. Ryder *v.* Mills, *B.P.P.*, 1850, LXVII, p. 3.
17. *Hansard*, 1850, vol. CIX, col. 834.
18. This, in fact, added two and a half hours a week to the total number of hours worked, but the addition was accepted to achieve the greater advantage of a "normal working day".
19. *B.P.P.*, 1851, XXIII, p. 29.
20. Horner, *B.P.P.*, 1856, XVIII, p. 349.
21. *B.P.P.*, 1873, LV, p. 60.
22. Report of the Commissioners on the Factory and Workshops Acts, *B.P.P.*, 1876, XXIX, pp. xxix and xxxv. Cf. also ibid., evidence of Colonel Wilkinson, 9,855. Cf. also ibid., evidence of Alex. Redgrave (Factory Inspector), 52. This very early start of the working day for women was a peculiar feature of the cotton industry; cf. ibid., Baker (Factory Inspector), 699 and 710.

23. See M. Hewitt, *The Effect of Married Women's Employment in the Cotton Textile Districts* (Ph.D., University of London, 1953), Appendix I, Table 2.

24. Cf. *B.P.P.*, 1840, XXIV, p. 9—Report of Mr. Hickson on the Condition of Hand-loom Weavers in Lancashire.

25. See M. Hewitt, op. cit., Appendix I, Table 4.

26. See relevant Census reports.

27. See Census reports for 1911.

28. See M. Hewitt, op. cit., Appendix I, Table 3.

29. Factory inspectresses reports, *B.P.P.*, 1902, XII, p. 158.

30. *Hansard*, 1844, vol. LXXIII, col. 1,092.

CHAPTER IV

1. J. R. Coulthart, "Report on the Sanitary Condition of Ashton-under-Lyne", *B.P.P.*, 1844, XVII, Appendix, p. 77.

2. Ibid.; cf. also *B.P.P.*, 1845, XVIII, Appendix, pp. 66–7.

3. Fanny Herz, "Mechanics' Institutes for Working Women", *N.A.P.S.Sc. Transactions*, 1859, p. 351. Cf. also Rev. J. P. Norris, "On Girls' Industrial Training", ibid., p. 375.

4. Reports of factory inspectors, *B.P.P.*, 1864, XXII, p. 709.

5. Fanny Herz, op. cit., p. 351.

6. *B.P.P.*, 1864, XXII, p. 709.

7. R. Smith Baker, "The Social Results of the Employment of Girls and Women", *N.A.P.S.Sc. Transactions*, 1868, p. 543.

8. Evidence of John Butcher, Overseer, *B.P.P.*, 1833, XX, D.2, p. 62.

9. Report of Health of Towns Commission (II), *B.P.P.*, 1845, XVIII, Appendix, p. 66. Cf. also First Report of the Commission, *B.P.P.*, 1844, XVII, Appendix, p. 77.

10. R. Arthur Arnold, "The Cotton Famine", *N.A.P.S.Sc. Transactions*, 1864, p. 612.

11. "Infant Mortality", ibid., p. 505.

12. *B.P.P.*, 1864, XXII, p. 708.

13. Cf. M. Hewitt, op. cit., Appendix II.

14. *B.P.P.*, 1834, XXXVII, p. 125.

15. Cf. Evidence to Royal Commission on Employment of Children in Factories, *B.P.P.*, 1833, XX, D.2, p. 49: evidence of Rev. Will, Huntingdon; and also p. 62: evidence of John Butcher, Overseer.

16. Evidence of Thos. Southwood Smith to Health of Towns Commission, *B.P.P.*, 1844, XVII, p. 71. Cf. also ibid., p. 342: evidence of Joseph Toynbee, surgeon, who, for the same classes, gives the age at marriage of women as twenty-one and of men as twenty-five.

17. Registrar-General, Annual Report, *B.P.P.*, 1842, XIX, p. 6. It should be noted, however, that this is only a rough estimate, as a large proportion of the returns of marriages failed to give the age of both parties. Cf. Registrar-General, Annual Report, *B.P.P.*, 1876, XVIII, p. 13.

18. Cf. G. Talbot Griffith, *Population Problems of the Age of Malthus* (Cambridge University Press, 1926), p. 112.

19. Registrar-General, Annual Report. *B.P.P.*, 1886. XVII. p. viii.

20. *B.P.P.*, 1834, XIX, p. 302.

21. Ibid., p. 304.

22. Cf. pp. 44, 45.
23. *B.P.P.*, 1887, XXIII, p. viii.
24. Fertility Census, 1911, p. lxxxix.
25. *B.P.P.*, 1840, XXIV, p. 682.

CHAPTER V

1. *Hansard*, 1847, vol. LXXIII, col. 1,100.
2. Evidence of Simeon Cundy, *B.P.P.*, 1833, XX, D.1, p. 667.
3. Evidence of Jane A.B., ibid., p. 648.
4. Charlotte Tonna, *Collected Works*, vol. I, p. 531.
5. Robert Baker, Reports of factory inspectors, *B.P.P.*, 1863, XVIII, p. 495.
6. Evidence of W.W., Royal Commission on Employment of Children in Factories, *B.P.P.*, 1833, XX, D.1, p. 687.
7. *The Manufacturing Population of England* (London, 1833), p. 147.
8. *The Effects of the Factory System* (3rd edition, London, 1913), p. 17.
9. Reports of Royal Commission on Labour: Reports on the Employment of Women by the Lady Assistant Commissioners, *B.P.P.*, 1893–4, XXXVII, p. 537.
10. Evidence to Select Committee on the Best Means of Protecting Infants put out to Nurse, *B.P.P.*, 1871, VII, 3,605, 1907–08.
11. *Hansard*, 1844, vol. LXXIV, col. 1,033.
12. Cf. Scriven's report, Second Report of Commissioners on Employment and Conditions of Children, *B.P.P.*, 1843, XIV, C.6.
13. Evidence of Rev. Thos. Askley Maberly, Report of Special Assistant Poor Law Commissioners on Employment of Women and Children in Agriculture, *B.P.P.*, 1843, XII, p. 201.
14. Sixth Report of Medical Officer of Privy Council, *B.P.P.*, 1864, XXVIII, Appendix 14, p. 461.
15. Sixth Report of Children's Employment Commission, *B.P.P.*, 1867, XVI, p. 87.
16. W. Cooke Taylor, *Factories and the Factory System* (London, 1844), p. 41.
17. *The Manufacturing Population of England* (London, 1833), p. 29.
18. *The Effects of the Factory System* (3rd edition, London, 1913), p. 18.
19. *Infant Mortality—Its Causes and Remedies* (Manchester, 1871), p. 20 (footnote).
20. Evidence of a curate in Burslem, Second Commission on Employment of Children, *B.P.P.*, 1843, XIV, C.65, No. 233.
21. W. Cooke Taylor, op. cit., p. 41.
22. Report of Special Assistant Poor Law Commissioners, *B.P.P.*, 1843, XII, Appendix IV, pp. 62–3.
23. Sixth Report of Children's Employment Commission, *B.P.P.*, 1867, XVI, p. 15.
24. Evidence of the deleterious effect of overcrowding on morals is not restricted to southern England. It was stated that the unchastity of women in Northumberland was partly due to the one-room cottages in the county, and that the superior morals of the women in rural Yorkshire were to be explained by better housing conditions: Doyle's report, *B.P.P.*, 1843, XII, pp. 249, 295.

25. *B.P.P.*, 1833, XX, p. 36. Gaskell, op. cit., p. 102 (footnote), quotes the Poor Law Commissioners, 1834, as saying: "It may safely be affirmed that the virtue of female chastity does not exist among the lower orders of England, except to a certain extent among the domestic female servants, who know that they hold their position by that tenure and are more prudent in consequence."

26. *B.P.P.*, 1843, XIV, p. 733.

27. Ibid., C.68, No. 237.

28. *B.P.P.*, 1867–8, XVII, p. 346.

29. *B.P.P.*, 1871, VII, 2,390–4.

30. Op. cit. (Reports on Employment of Women, by Lady Assistant Commissioners), p. 537, section 759.

31. Ibid., p. 536, section 759.

32. Loc. cit., *Improvements in the Textile Trades*, p. 147.

33. *Hansard*, 1844, vol. LXXIII, col. 1,182.

34. "Victorian Ideas of Sex", *Ideas and Beliefs of the Victorians* (Sylvan Press, 1949), p. 354. Mr. Beales also quotes (ibid., p. 355): "Prostitution is a transitory state through which untold numbers of British women are for ever passing" (Acton).

35. *B.P.P.*, 1833, XXI, p. 133.

36. W. Cooke Taylor, *Factories and the Factory System* (London, 1844), p. 45.

37. *B.P.P.*, 1871, VII, 1929–36, 2,095.

38. Ibid., 3,310–15.

39. See Chapter IX.

40. W. Cooke Taylor, op. cit., p. 44.

41. Ibid., p. 45.

42. Evidence to Interdepartmental Committee on Physical Deterioration, *B.P.P.*, 1904, XXXII, 9,115.

43. Evidence of the Incumbent of Tunstall, Royal Commission on Employment of Children, *B.P.P.*, 1843, XIV, C.64, No. 229.

44. Printed as supplement to Dr. Farr's Annual Letter to the Registrar-General, *B.P.P.*, 1873, XX, p. 344.

CHAPTER VI

1. *B.P.P.*, 1840, XXIV, p. 44.

2. *Women Workers and the Industrial Revolution* (Routledge, 1930), p. 307.

3. *B.P.P.*, 1833, XXI, D.3, p.3.

4. Robert Baker, *B.P.P.*, 1861, XXII, p. 698.

5. Charlotte Tonna, *Wrongs of Women* (London, 1844), Part II, p. 1.

6. Op. cit., p. 25.

7. *Manufacturing Population* (London, 1833), p. 108.

8. *B.P.P.*, 1840, XXIV, p. 609. Cf. also Gaskell, *Manufacturing Population* (London, 1833), p. 277.

9. *B.P.P.*, 1840, XXIV, p. 689.

10. *Hansard*, 1844, vol. LXXIV, col. 1,052.

11. *B.P.P.*, 1849, XXII, p. 203, No. 166.

12. *Hansard*, 1844, vol. LXXXIII, cols. 1,383–4.

13. Ellen Barlee, op. cit., p. 27.

14. *Wrongs of Women* (London, 1844), Part II, p. 49.

15. *Manufacturing Population* (London, 1833), pp. 106–9.

16. *Effects of the Factory System* (3rd edition, London, 1913), p. 111.

17. *Mary Barton* (1848), Chapter X.

18. Evidence to Interdepartmental Committee on Physical Deterioration, *B.P.P.*, 1904, XXXII, p. 125, section 16.

19. Royal Commission on Labour: Reports on Employment of Women, *B.P.P.*, 1893–4, XXXVII, p. 509.

20. Evidence to Interdepartmental Committee on Physical Deterioration, *B.P.P.*, 1904, XXXII, p. 124, section 32.

21. Cf., *inter alia*, ibid., and also *B.P.P.*, 1867, XVI, pp. 84.5.

22. Evidence of Rev. W. T. Beckett, Report of Mr. White, *B.P.P.*, 1867, XVI, p. 85. See also earlier evidence of Mr. Austin, *B.P.P.*, 1843, XII, p. 47.

23. First Report on Children, Young People, and Women Employed in Agriculture, *B.P.P.*, 1867–8, XVII, p. xiv.

24. Report of Mr. Denison on Suffolk, Norfolk, and Lincoln, *B.P.P.*, 1843, XII, p. 242.

25. Ashley, *Hansard*, 1844, vol. LXXXIII, cols. 1,093–4.

26. Op. cit., Era I.

27. Robert Baker, *B.P.P.*, 1860, XXXIV, p. 468.

28. *Hansard*, 1844, vol. LXXV, col. 144.

29. Ibid., vol. LXXIV, cols. 676–7.

30. Mrs. Gaskell, op. cit., Chapter X.

31. Evidence of Thos. Jones, *B.P.P.*, 1833, XXI, D.1, p. 877.

32. Evidence of Mr. Mayne, ibid., D.1, p. 707.

33. Ibid., D.2, p. 211.

34. Published in the *Transactions* of the Society, 1865–6.

35. *B.P.P.*, 1843, XIV, C.48, No. 172.

36. *B.P.P.*, 1843, XII, p. 213.

37. *B.P.P.*, 1867, XVI, p. 93.

38. "Remarks on the Industrial Employment of Women", *N.A.P.S.Sc. Transactions*, 1857, p. 536.

39. *Women Workers and the Industrial Revolution* (Routledge, 1930), p. 310.

40. G. Greaves, M.R.C.S., "On Homes for the Working Classes", *Manchester Statistical Society Transactions*, 1860–1, p. 84.

41. W. O. Henderson, *The Lancashire Cotton Famine* (Manchester University Press, 1930), pp. 3–4.

42. Evidence to Interdepartmental Committee on Physical Deterioration, *B.P.P.*, 1904, XXXII, 5,614 (Horsfall).

43. Evidence to Royal Commission on Labour, *B.P.P.*, 1894, XXXV, 9,057 and 9,087.

44. Seventh Report of Medical Officer of Privy Council, *B.P.P.*, 1865, XXVI, p. 13.

45. Quoted by Drummond and Wilbraham, *The Englishman's Food* (Cape, 1939), p. 389.

46. Ibid.

47. *Journal of Society of Arts*, 1864, vol. 13.

48. Evidence to Interdepartmental Committee on Physical Deterioration, *B.P.P.*, 1904, XXXII, 7,472 (Bostock) and 7,982–3 (Drouble).

49. Ibid., 4,554 (Bagot) and main report, section 290.

50. Anna Martin, "The Married Working Women", *Nineteenth Century*, December 1910, pp. 1, 114–15. Also evidence to Interdepartmental Committee on Physical Deterioration, *B.P.P.*, 1904, XXXII, 4,992 (Rowntree) and 7,544 (Eves).

51. *B.P.P.*, 1843, XVI, pp. 25–6.

52. *B.P.P.*, 1867–8, XVII, p. 359.

53. Evidence to Interdepartmental Committee on Physical Deterioration, *B.P.P.*, 1904, XXXII, 6,669–70 (Fosbroke).

54. "On a Progressive Physical Degeneracy of the Race in Town Populations of Great Britain", *N.A.P.S.Sc. Transactions*, 1871, p. 466.

55. Memorial of the School Board of Wolverhampton to the Education Department, 17th June 1877, *B.P.P.*, 1877, LXVII, p. 559. Cf. also Mr. Cornish's Report on Board Schools in Salford District, ibid., 1870, XXIII, p. 544.

56. *B.P.P.*, 1878–9, XXIII, p. 764.

57. Ibid., p. 632.

58. *B.P.P.*, 1860, LIV, p. 98.

59. "Domestic Subjects in Elementary and Industrial Schools", *The Englishwoman*, 1912, pp. 8–16.

60. Ibid.

61. *Household Words*, 20th March 1952, p. 84.

62. *B.P.P.*, 1861, XLIX, p. 100; *B.P.P.*, 1862, XLII, p. 76. Cf. also Reports of Factory Inspectors, *B.P.P.*. 1861, XXII, p. 383.

63. *B.P.P.*. 1864, XXII, p. 683.

64. Clapham, *The Early Railway Age* (Cambridge University Press, 2nd edition, 1930), p. 158.

65. *B.P.P.*, 1843, XII, pp. 143–4.

66. Ibid., pp. 316, 321, 364.

67. Op. cit., p. 140.

68. Ibid.

69. "English Cookery", ibid., 26th January 1856, p. 116.

70. *Penny Scrap Book*, 1st April 1871.

CHAPTER VII

1. *Hansard*, 1844, vol. LXII, col. 1,092.

2. *B.P.P.*, 1833, XX.

3. *B.P.P.*, 1834, XIX.

4. Medical evidence to Factory Commissioners, *B.P.P.*, 1834, XIX, p. 533. Cf. also *B.P.P.*, 1833, XX, D.2, p. 143 (main report), evidence of Joseph Hutton, surgeon, Stayley Bridge: "Are the wives of factory operatives equally prolific as those of other classes?"—"They are."

5. Cf. ibid., Table XXII, p. xcii.

6. Fertility Commission Report, 1911, p. xcii.

7. Ibid., Table XLVIII.

8. Ibid., p. cxiii.

9. Ibid., p. cxi.

10. Cf. op. cit., pp. 80 *et seq.*, Table 32.

11. Cf. ibid., pp. 144 *et seq.*, Table 36.

12. Op. cit., p. cxii.

13. Ibid., p. cxiii.

14. Ibid.

15. Ibid.

16. Ibid., p. cxvii.

17. *B.P.P.*, 1833, XX, D.2, p. 108.

18. Evidence to Royal Commission on Labour, *B.P.P.*, 1894, XXXV, C.1, 606 and 610 (President of Card and Blowing Room Operatives' Association).

19. N. E. Himes, *Medical History of Contraception* (Allen and Unwin 1936), p. 213.

20. Ibid., p. 233.

21. Cf. W. F. Neff, op. cit., pp. 54–5.

22. Op. cit., p. 13.

23. Cf., *inter alia*, ibid., letters Nos. 33, 47. See also A. N. Chew, "All in a Day's Work", *The Englishwoman*, July 1912.

24. Op. cit., Appendix V, p. 127.

25. Evidence of Joseph Hatton, *B.P.P.*, 1833, XX, D.1, p. 75.

26. Evidence to Interdepartmental Committee on Physical Deterioration, *B.P.P.*, 1904, XXXII, Appendix V, p. 127.

27. *B.P.P.*, 1914, XXXIX, p. 69.

28. Op. cit., p. 87.

29. Ibid., p. 100.

CHAPTER VIII

1. Quoted by Rev. J. Elder Canning, "On the Neglect of Infants in Large Towns", *N.A.P.S.Sc. Transactions*, 1874, p. 723.

2. *Hansard*, 1847, vol. LXXXIX, cols. 489–90.

3. R. Smith Baker, "The Social Results of the Employment of Girls and Women in Factories and Workshops", *N.A.P.S.Sc. Transactions*, 1844, p. 544.

4. Some idea of the great attention paid to the problem may be gathered from glancing down the titles of papers delivered to the Annual Congresses of the N.A.P.S.Sc., some of which are listed in the Bibliography.

5. Cf. Presidential Address to the First National Conference on Infant Mortality, 13th June 1906, by Rt. Hon. John Burns, M.P., President of Local Government Board. Also three reports of Medical Officer of Local Government Board: *B.P.P.*, 1910, XXXIX; 1913, XXXII; 1914, XXXIX.

6. See Chapter II.

7. Pamphlet circulated by Association for the Establishment of Day Nurseries in Manchester and Salford, Manchester, 1850.

8. Evidence to Select Committee on the Best Means of Protecting Infants put out to Nurse. *B.P.P.*, 1871, VII, p. 99, 2,056.

9. *B.P.P.*, 1863, LIII, parts 1 and 2.

10. *Hansard*, 1873, vol. CCXVI, cols. 822–3.

11. Cf. Fawcett's remarks on this, *Hansard*, 1873, vol. CCXVI, col. 1,301. Also R. W. Cooke Taylor, "The Employment of Married Women in Manufactures", *N.A.P.S.Sc. Transactions*, 1873, p. 612.

12. Cf. *B.P.P.*, 1852, LXXXVIII, part II.

13. Ibid., 1852–3, LXXXVIII, part I, p. lxxxix. This is not the first time that the Registrar-General had made this comment with particular reference to the death-rate of infants in Lancashire. Cf. *Hansard*, 1847, vol. LXXXIX, col. 488.

14. Fourth Report of Medical Evidence of Privy Council, *B.P.P.*, 1862, XXXI, p. 494. Cf. also *B.P.P.*, 1865, XIII.

15. *B.P.P.*, 1864, XXII, p. 698.

16. Discussion on "Infant Mortality and Female Labour in Relation to Factory Legislation", read by G. Reid, M.D., *Journal of the Sanitary Institute*, vol. XV, 1895, p. 503.

17. Cf. *Lancet*, vol. 1, 1874, p. 849. Dr. Dudley, Medical Officer of Health, Staleybridge, in his Annual Report, calls attention to the excessive infant mortality of the district. This he attributes to the employment of married women.

18. J. H. Bridges, M.D., and T. Holmes, Report to the Local Government Board on the Proposed Changes in the Hours and Ages of Employment in Textile Factories, *B.P.P.*, 1873, LV, pp. 41–2.

19. Cf. Appendix I.

20. Farr was Head of the Statistical Department of the Registrar-General's Office during the whole of the period for which the graphs are appended. Note particularly his Annual Letter for 1864, *B.P.P.*, 1866, XIX.

21. This Act affects the data for the period of our graphs; compulsory registration of births and deaths was only introduced in England in 1874.

22. English registration law was different in this respect from Irish and Scottish.

23. Registrar-General's Annual Report for 1873, *B.P.P.*, 1874, XVIII, part I, p. 6: "The precise extent of the deficiency cannot be determined: but I am inclined to believe . . . that the probable annual deficiency in the ten years 1841–50 was 38,036; in the next ten years, 19,323; and in the last ten years . . . 13,614. The deficiency thus rapidly declined: calculated on 1,000 births, it was, in the three decades, 65 in the first, 29 in the second and 18 in the third."

24. Farr's evidence to the Select Committee on the Best Means of Protecting Infants put out to Nurse, *B.P.P.*, 1871, VII, 3,611. Farr calculated that in England and Wales there were between 30,000 and 40,000 children stillborn: ibid., 3,612.

25. Dr. Chas. Drysdale in the discussion on "What Influence has the Employment of Women on Infant Mortality?", *N.A.P.S.Sc. Transactions*, 1882, p. 387. But cf. *B.P.P.*, 1865, XIII: Farr's Supplement to Twenty-seventh Annual Report of the Registrar-General, p. v.

26. *B.P.P.*, 1871, VII, 3,635.

27. Ibid., 3,636.

28. Farr's letter to the Registrar-General on the causes of death, *B.P.P.*, 1866, XIX, p. 178.

29. Ibid., p. 182.

30. *B.P.P.*, 1871, VII, 3,639.

31. Evidence of Syson, Medical Officer of Health for Salford, ibid., 2,417: "We caught a woman the other day going and obtaining [from the

Registrar] a certificate of a child that had never died and using it for begging, and the enquiries led to prove that such had been the woman's way of getting her living."

32. Cf., for instance, *Hansard*, 1844, vol. LXXXIII, col. 1,094, vol. LXXXIX, col. 488; also ibid., col. 493. Also cf. Lyon Playfair, Report on the Sanitary Condition of the Large Towns of Lancashire, printed as Appendix to Second Report of the Health of Towns Commission, *B.P.P.*, 1845, XVIII, p. 689. Note that, after London, Lancashire was the most densely populated registration division in the entire country—more than three times as dense as the rest of England: Registrar-General's Annual Report, *B.P.P.*, 1875, XVIII, part II, p. 50.

33. *B.P.P.*, 1866, XIX, p. 51. He is quoting from the report of Robert Rawlinson to the President of the Poor Law Board, April 1864.

34. Introduction to "Papers Relating to the Sanitary State of the People of England", *B.P.P.*, 1857–8, XXII, p. 331.

35. Appendix to First Report of Health of Towns Commission, *B.P.P.*, 1844, XVII, p. 46.

36. Ibid., p. 47.

37. Quoted by Lord John Manners in the Ten Hours debates, *Hansard*, 1844, vol. LXXXIX, cols. 1,117–74. It is necessary to assume in this argument that the majority of married women employed in Bury were employed in the textile industry of the town. In the 1851 Census, 21·03% of women over twenty years of age were employed in the cotton industry in Bury: this proportion is only slightly less than the proportion in Haslingden, 23·71%, and Oldham, 25·73%. As our random-sample analysis shows that in these last two districts the majority of the occupied married women were employed in the textile industries, of which the cotton industry was the most important, this assumption seems valid.

38. *B.P.P.*, 1873, LV, p. 57.

39. "Papers Relating to the Sanitary State of England", *B.P.P.*, 1857–8, XXIII, p. 484.

40. Published as Appendix V to the Fourth Report of Medical Officer of Privy Council, *B.P.P.*, 1862, XXII.

41. Cf. Appendix IV to Sixth Report of Medical Officer of Privy Council, *B.P.P.*, 1864, XXVIII.

42. These figures are for 1851–60, and are extracted from the Registrar-General's Supplementary Report, *B.P.P.*, 1865, XIII.

43. Hunter, op. cit., pp. 449–50.

44. Health of Towns Commission, *B.P.P.*, 1844, XVII, Appendix, pp. 165–74.

45. *The Statistics of Families in the Upper and Professional Classes* (London, 1874).

46. Similar calculations were made for various districts in Lancashire, e.g. Ashton-under-Lyne: Health of Towns Commission Report, *B.P.P.*, 1845, XVIII (II), Appendix, p. 76.

47. Simon, Introduction to "Papers Relating to . . .", *B.P.P.*, 1857–8, XXIII, p. 332.

48. Ibid., pp. 68–9.

49. Cf. Eighth Report of Poor Law Commissioners, p. 751.

50. Similarly it was argued that it was not poverty *per se* which produced a high infant death-rate, otherwise Ireland would have shown a much higher rate than England and Wales, instead of the reverse, which, in fact, it did.

51. Health of Towns Commission, *B.P.P.*, 1845, XVIII (II), p. 69.

52. Ibid.

53. Ibid.

54. Strictly speaking, the "Famine" dated from 1861–5, but its full effect was not felt till 1862; and by the first quarter of 1864 the employment situation was easing: cf. W. O. Henderson, op. cit.; also Bridges and Holmes, op. cit., p. 54; also Registrar-General's Report for 1864, *B.P.P.*, 1866, XIX, p. 49.

55. Curgenven's evidence to the Select Committee on the Best Means of Protecting Infants put out to Nurse, *B.P.P.*, 1871, VII, p. 68, 1,380.

56. Quoted by Edwin Waugh, *Home Life of the Lancashire Factory Folk during the Cotton Famine* (London, 1867), p. 223.

57. *B.P.P.*, 1865, XIV, p. 27. For corroboration of these figures of unemployment, cf. Dr. Buchanan's report on the "Health of Operatives as affected by the Distress", *B.P.P.*, 1863, XXV, p. 303.

58. Buchanan, op. cit., p. 310. This includes all sources of monetary relief —charitable and parish. Cf. also Waugh, op. cit., p. 103.

59. Dr. Edwin Smith's Report on "The Nourishment of the Distressed Operatives", *B.P.P.*, 1863, XXV, Appendix III, p. 330.

60. Cf. Buchanan, op. cit., p. 313; also comments of Alex Redgrave, Factory Inspector, *B.P.P.*, 1862, XXII, p. 233.

61. Edwin Waugh, op. cit., p. 109.

62. *B.P.P.*, 1865, XIV, p. 35. The number of deaths registered in the districts affected by the "Famine" were: 1861, 46,838; 1862, 45,168; 1863, 47,208; 1864, 47,057.

63. Cf. Reports of Registrar-General for 1862 and 1864, *B.P.P.*, 1864, XVII, and *B.P.P.*, 1866, XIX. Also Buchanan, op. cit., and reports of factory inspectors, particularly Redgrave, *B.P.P.*, 1862, XXII.

64. *B.P.P.*, 1866, XIX, p. 58.

65. The districts affected by the "Famine" were Ashton, Barton-on-Irwell, Blackburn, Bolton, Bury, Chorley, Chorlton, Clitheroe, Fylde, Garstang, Oldham, Preston, Rochdale, Haslingden, Lancaster, Leigh, Manchester, Salford, Warrington, and Wigan.

66. This was anticipated by John Simon. See Fifth Report of Medical Officer of Privy Council, *B.P.P.*, 1863, XXV, p. 20.

67. The Registrar of Wigan, referring to the decrease in the number of deaths, refers to "better nursing"; so also do the Registrars of Little Bolton, Hulme, Preston, and Knott, Lancs (Ashton); see Registrar-General's Reports, e.g. *B.P.P.*, 1864, XVIII, pp. 36–7. See also reports of Baker and Redgrave, *B.P.P.*. 1864, XXII. Also R. Arthur Arnold, "The Cotton Famine", *N.A.P.S.Sc. Transactions*, 1864, p. 615.

68. The higher infant mortality of 1863–4 was ascribed to epidemics of whooping-cough, measles, smallpox, and scarlet fever which prevailed all over the country.

69. Buchanan, op. cit., p. 308.

70. Report for 1862, *B.P.P.*, 1864, XVII, p. 28.

71. Ibid.

72. Note particularly that in the graph of the infant mortality of Lancashire when the infant death-rate of the districts affected by the "Famine" is shown separately, the fall during the years 1862-3-4 is more significant than the fall for the county generally.

73. Cf. also the report of Dr. Barker, M.O.H., Clitheroe, quoted by Dr. Newsholme, p. 108; cf. his "First Report on Infantile Mortality", *B.P.P.*, 1910, XXXIX: "I am pretty confident that two factors have been at work during the past twelve months which have influenced favourably the infant mortality of Clitheroe, and I shall be much surprised if the truth of this surmise is not reflected in a diminished rate of mortality throughout the whole of the manufacturing districts of Lancashire. I allude to the cool, wet summer and the scarcity of employment, affecting the employment of mothers." This view was, in fact, corroborated by Dr. Holt of Burnley.

74. *Infant Mortality and the Employment of Married Women in Factories* (Stafford, 1892).

75. Quoted by Newman, op. cit., p. 106.

76. Ibid., p. 109.

CHAPTER IX

1. Cf. R. W. Cooke Taylor, "What Influence has the Employment of Mothers in Manufactures on Infant Mortality?", *N.A.P.S.Sc. Transactions*, 1874, p. 576.

2. Evidence to Interdepartmental Committee on Physical Deterioration, *B.P.P.*, 1904, XXXII, 3,195 (Malins).

3. *Manufacturing Population* (1833), p. 167.

4. Cf. *Hansard*, 1844, vol. LXXIII, col. 10,891; also 1847, vol. LXL, col. 144.

5. Cf. Bridges and Holmes, op. cit., p. 20.

6. Cf. *N.A.P.S.Sc. Transactions*, 1882, p. 360.

7. *The Effects of the Factory System—Effects on Women and Children* (3rd edition, 1913), p. 19.

8. Hunter, op. cit., pp. 460-1.

9. *B.P.P.*, 1910, XXXIX, p. 54.

10. *B.P.P.*, 1913, XXXII, p. 64.

11. Redgrave, *B.P.P.*, 1876, XXX, 553.

12. Baker, ibid., 1,304.

13. Baker, ibid., 1,305.

14. Newman, op. cit., p. 136. Cf. also G. F. McCleary, *The Early History of the Infant Welfare Movement* (London, 1933).

15. In Salford in 1871 it was estimated that "a good two-thirds came under this category". The remainder were those operatives whose husbands earned sufficient to support their wives during a somewhat longer period of unemployment. See evidence of E. J. Syson, M.O.H., Salford, to the Select Committee as the Best Means of Protecting Infants put out to Nurse, *B.P.P.*, 1871, VII, 2,267, 2,268, 2,269.

16. Evidence of May Woodhouse, Report of Royal Commission on the Employment of Children in Factories, *B.P.P.*, 1833, XX, D.3, p. 11;

evidence of Mary Royston and Betty Hulme, ibid., D.2, p. 110; medical evidence: evidence of Elizabeth Taylor, midwife, ibid., 1833, XXI, D.3, p. 13.

17. *B.P.P.*, 1862, XXII, p. 649.

18. Op. cit., p. 38.

19. *B.P.P.*, 1873, LV, p. 55. See also evidence of Mr. Whitehead, surgeon at St. Mary's Hospital, Manchester, *B.P.P.*, 1871, VII, 3,554, and evidence to Commission on Factory and Workshops Acts, ibid., 1876, XXX, 11,167.

20. Haslam, "The Burden of the Factory Mother", *The Englishwoman*, October 1909, p. 306.

21. Hutchins and Harrison, op. cit., p. 211.

22. See Annual Reports of Principal Lady Factory Inspectress, *B.P.P.*, 1905, X, pp. 273-4; *B.P.P.*, 1907, X, p. 233.

23. Evidence to Interdepartmental Committee on Physical Deterioration, *B.P.P.*, 1904, XXXII, Appendix V, p. 116.

24. Fourth Report of Medical Officer of Privy Council, Appendix V, *B.P.P.*, 1862, XXII; pp. 653-4.

25. Ibid., p. 653.

26. P. Kay-Shuttleworth, *Four Periods of Public Education* (London, 1862), p. 43.

27. Ibid., p. 43.

28. Published by Association for the Establishment of Day Nurseries in Manchester and Salford (Manchester, 1850).

29. "On the Neglect of Infants in Large Towns", *N.A.P.S.Sc. Transactions*, 1874, p. 724.

30. W. Cooke Taylor, *Notes on a Tour in the Manufacturing Districts of Lancashire* (London, 1842), p. 179. See also evidence to Select Committee on the Best Means of Protecting Infants put out to Nurse, *B.P.P.*, 1871, VII, 2,046-7.

31. Whitehead, ibid., 3,484.

32. Main report, ibid., p. iii.

33. It is worth noting that such criminal baby-farms were virtually unknown even in the large towns of Lancashire. In evidence to the Select Committee on Infant Life Protection, "the Coroner for Manchester, who has been officially connected with that city for many years, has distinctly stated that, since the year 1838, only one case of a criminal character has been brought under his notice", op. cit., p. iii. The "children of servants and persons of that class" were usually boarded out with women, who took care of one or two such children. In this case, the mother paid the nurse weekly or monthly, visiting her for that purpose, and thus keeping up a connexion with the child. The illegitimate children of mill-hands were cared for in the same way as legitimate, op. cit., 2,198, 2,022.

34. Evidence of Herford, ibid., 20,471. See also Bridges and Holmes, op. cit., p. 55.

35. *Morning Chronicle*, 4th January 1850.

36. Evidence to Interdepartmental Committee on Physical Deterioration, *B.P.P.*, 1904, XXXII, Appendix V, p. 128, section 55. See also evidence of W. Whitehead, 2,537, to Select Committee on the Best Means of Protecting Infants put out to Nurse.

37. Fifth Report of Medical Officer of Privy Council, *B.P.P.*, 1863, XXV, Appendix V, p. 301, footnote.

38. Rev. J. Elder Canning, op. cit., p. 724.

39. Evidence to Select Committee on the Best Means of Protecting Infants put out to Nurse, *B.P.P.*, 1871, VII, 3,278.

40. Ibid., 2,004.

41. Dr. Ballard, Report on the Sanitary Condition of Bolton, *B.P.P.*, 1873, LV, p. 56. See also evidence to Select Committee on the Best Means of Protecting Infants put out to Nurse, *B.P.P.*, 1871, VII, 2,005.

42. *B.M.J.*, 1892, vol. II, p. 277.

43. Evidence to Select Committee on the Best Means of Protecting Infants put out to Nurse, *B.P.P.*, 1871, VII, 2,336 (Syson).

44. Ibid., 3,534 (Whitehead).

45. *Morning Chronicle*, 4th January 1850.

46. Evidence to Select Committee on the Best Means of Protecting Infants put out to Nurse, *B.P.P.*, 1871, VII, 3,382 (Whitehead).

47. Ibid., 2,332 (Syson).

48. Ibid., 3,256 (Whitehead).

49. Ibid., 2,329 (Syson).

50. Evidence to Interdepartmental Committee on Physical Deterioration, *B.P.P.*, 1904, XXXII, Appendix V, p. 128. Also *B.P.P.*, 1893-4 XXXVII, C.1, 610.

51. Evidence to Select Committee on the Best Means of Protecting Infants put out to Nurse, *B.P.P.*, 1871, VII, 2,259.

52. Evidence to Interdepartmental Committee on Physical Deterioration, *B.P.P.*, 1904, XXXII, 9,026–30, and Appendix V, p. 128.

53. Evidence of Rev. John J. Braine, Minister of Brunswick Chapel, Hanley, Second Report of Children's Employment Commission, *B.P.P.*, 1843, XIV, C.33, p. 120.

54. Evidence of Dr. J. T. Arlidge, Stoke, to Commission on the Working of Factory and Workshop Acts, *B.P.P.*, 1876, XXX, 1,395–6.

55. Second Report of Poor Law Commissioners, *B.P.P.*, 1836, XXXIX, p. 221; cf. also *B.P.P.*, 1843, XII, Appendix VII, p. 66.

56. Evidence of Mr. Henry Phelps, Bramhill, Wilts, Report of Special Assistant Poor Law Commissioners on the Employment of Women and Children in Agriculture, *B.P.P.*, 1843, XII, Appendix 3, p. 101.

57. Sixth Report of Medical Officer of Privy Council, Appendix C.4, p. 101; cf. also *B.P.P.*, 1843, XII, Appendix 33, p. 101.

58. Reports of Lady Assistant Commissioners, Reports of Royal Commission on Labour, *B.P.P.*, 1893–4, XXXVII, p. 509.

59. Evidence to Select Committee on the Best Means of Protecting Infants put out to Nurse, *B.P.P.*, 1871, VII, 3,254; cf. also Bridges and Holmes, op. cit., p. 55.

60. Cf. May Tennant, "The Incompatibility of Breast Feeding and the Employment of Mothers", *Women in Industry from Several Points of View*, p. 118.

61. *Morning Chronicle*, 4th January 1850.

62. Evidence to Select Committee on the Best Means of Protecting Infants put out to Nurse, *B.P.P.*, 1871, VII, 2,015; cf. also Dr. Robert Dudley, M.O.H. for Staleybridge, *Lancet*, 13th June 1874, p. 849, "Note".

63. Report of the Infant Mortality Committee of the Obstetrical Society of London, 1870, published as a supplement to Dr. Farr's Annual Letter to the Registrar-General, *B.P.P.*, 1873, XX, p. 342.

64. Evidence to Select Committee on the Best Means of Protecting Infants put out to Nurse, *B.P.P.*, 1871, VII, 2,263 (Syson).

65. Drummond and Wilbraham, *The Englishman's Food* (Cape, 1939), p. 444.

66. Ibid.

67. Report of Health of Towns Commission (I), *B.P.P.*, 1844, XVII, Appendix, p. 77.

68. Drummond and Wilbraham, op. cit., p. 446.

69. Main Report of Interdepartmental Committee on Physical Deterioration, *B.P.P.*, 1904, XXXII, para. 270

70. Cf. Ballard, "Report on the Sanitary Condition of Bolton", contained in Bridges and Holmes, op. cit., p. 55.

71. Ibid., p. 56. See also evidence to Select Committee on the Best Means of Protecting Infants put out to Nurse, *B.P.P.*, 1871, VII, 3,257 (Whitehead).

72. Ibid., 3,461 and 3,462 (Whitehead).

73. Fifth Report of Medical Officer of Privy Council, Appendix V, "Report on the Nourishment of the Distressed Operatives", *B.P.P.*, 1863, XXV, p. 313. See also H. W. Rumsey, M.D., "On the Progressive Degeneracy of the Race in Towns' Populations", *N.A.P.S.Sc. Transactions*, 1871, p. 468.

74. Evidence to Interdepartmental Committee on Physical Deterioration, *B.P.P.*, 1904, XXXII, 5,371 (Lyttleton). Also "The Supply of Milk for Village Infants", *Lancet*, 5th December 1885, p. 1,073.

75. Ballard, op. cit., p. 56.

76. Drummond and Wilbraham, op. cit., pp. 373–4.

77. Ibid., pp. 446–7.

78. Evidence to Interdepartmental Committee on Physical Deterioration, *B.P.P.*, 1904, XXXII, 10,754–5 (Eccles).

79. *Lancet*, 6th May 1876, p. 694, "Annotation".

80. W. D. Husband, F.R.C.S., "Infant Mortality", *N.A.P.S.Sc. Transactions*, 1864, p. 504.

81. Fourth Report of Medical Officer of Privy Council, Appendix V, report of T. Headlam Greenhow: "On the Circumstances under which there is Excessive Mortality of Young Children . . .", *B.P.P.*, 1862, XXII, p. 656.

82. Ballard, op. cit., p. 56.

83. To save themselves the trouble that the preparation of such food involved, the nurse would often give the baby "a little of what she was having herself". From Dr. Strange of Ashton-under-Lyne we learn that "it was no uncommon thing to be consulted about emaciated children with extreme mesenteric disease, and on enquiry to find that the food consists in great part of bacon, fried meat and salt potatoes, when the child has not perhaps two teeth in its jaws to masticate it": Second Report of Health of Towns Commission, *B.P.P.*, 1845, XVIII, Appendix, p. 66.

84. W. D. Husband, op. cit., p. 504.

85. Ballard, op. cit., p. 57.

86. Ibid., p. 67. It was, as we have already noted, the usual custom of mothers to cease work at the mill after the birth of their third children.

87. Cf., *inter alia*, evidence to Factory and Workshops Acts Commission, *B.P.P.*, 1876, XXX, 1,387; (Arlidge)—11,167 and 11,171 (Folkes). For medical opinion in agricultural districts, see Hunter, op. cit.

88. Dr. Routh, "On the Mortality of Infants in Foundling Institutions", *Lancet*, 24th October 1857.

89. See remarks of Dr. Chowne: "The mortality in the London Foundling Hospital had much decreased of late years in consequence of breast-milk having been substituted for artificial diet", ibid.

90. "What Influence has the Employment of Mothers . . . on Infant Mortality?", *N.A.P.S.Sc. Transactions*, 1882, p. 360.

91. For later evidence, which corroborated these findings, see Appendix III; also Newsholme, Second Report on Infant Mortality, *B.P.P.*, 1913, p. 83.

CHAPTER X

1. Evidence to Select Committee on the Best Means of Protecting Infants put out to Nurse, *B.P.P.*, 1871, VII, 3,345 (Whitehead).

2. *Public Nurseries* (pamphlet; London, 1850), p. 11.

3. Report of Health of Towns Commission (II), *B.P.P.*, 1845, XVIII, Appendix: Report on the State of the Large Towns of Lancashire, p. 62. In Appendix V of the Fourth Report of Medical Officer of Privy Council (1862) it is stated that "there is less laudanum used than formerly in Godfrey's". This, however, appears misleading in the light of other, and later, evidence. Cf. *inter alia*, remarks of Mr. Poole, Coroner for Furness, Lancs, who states that "the use of laudanum is on the increase", *B.M.F.*, 28th October 1876, p. 561.

4. *Morning Chronicle*, 4th January 1850.

5. Op. cit., 2,116 (Herford).

6. Cf. "The Massacre of Innocents", *Lancet*, 18th September 1886, p. 547. Also *Records of Second National Conference on Infant Mortality* (1908). p. 178.

7. Playfair, op. cit., p. 63.

8. See Appendix III.

9. Hunter, op. cit., p. 65.

10. Playfair, op. cit., p. 65.

11. Ibid.

12. *Morning Chronicle*, 4th January 1850.

13. Playfair, op. cit., p. 62.

14. Cf., *inter alia*, Fourth Report of Medical Officer of Privy Council, *B.P.P.*, 1862, XXII, Appendix V, p. 657.

15. Cf., for example, evidence to Select Committee on the Best Means of Protecting Infants put out to Nurse, *B.P.P.*, 1871, VII, 2,007 (Herford).

16. Quoted by Rev. Clay, "Report on the Sanitary Conditions of Preston", p. 46, published as Appendix to Health of Towns Commission Report (I), *B.P.P.*, XVII.

17. Ibid., p. 46.

18. *Public Nurseries* (pamphlet; London, 1850).

19. Cf. comments of Lyon Playfair, Health of Towns Commission Report (II), *B.P.P.*, 1845, XVIII, Appendix, p. 63.

20. *B.P.P.*, 1864, XXII, p. 630.

21. Printed as Appendix to Health of Towns Commission Report (II), *B.P.P.*, 1845, XVIII, p. 166.

22. For evidence relating to the later years of our period, cf., *inter alia*, evidence to Select Committee on the Best Means of Protecting Infants put out to Nurse, *B.P.P.*, 1871, VII, 2,105 and 2,112 (Herford).

23. Thos. Headlam Greenhow, "Illustrations of the Necessity for a more Analytical Study of the Statistics of Public Health", *N.A.P.S.Sc. Transactions*, 1857, p. 380. The mortality statistics are based on the Registrar-General's figures for 1847–54.

24. Registrar-General's Annual Report for 1876, *B.P.P.*, 1877, XXV, pp. 22–3.

25. First Report of Medical Officer of Privy Council, *B.P.P.*, 1859, XXIX, pp. 359–60.

26. See Chapter IX.

27. First Report of Medical Officer of Privy Council, *B.P.P.*, 1859, XXIX, p. 360, based on Registrar-General's figures for 1848–58.

28. Based on the tables published in *B.M.J.*, 1893, vol. I, p. 900.

29. Ballard, op. cit., pp. 56–7.

30. Op. cit., p. 308 (footnote).

31. In addition to the factors we have already mentioned above which tended to inflate the local infant death-rate in areas where mothers were employed away from home, it was alleged—particularly towards the end of the nineteenth century—that the lead poisoning sustained by mothers employed in the potteries and other industries where white lead was used not only injured the mother, but her unborn child. Thus it was claimed that the high rate of miscarriage, abortion and premature death of the infants of such mothers was attributable in part to the peculiar circumstances of their employment. Whether, and how far, this was true is difficult to assess for our period, since the evidence on which such assertions was based related either to small numbers of such mothers or to records of dubious validity; cf. Burns, Presidential Address to National Conference on Infantile Mortality, 1906, *Papers in the 1906 National Conference on Infantile Mortality*, p. 16, also *Dangerous Trades*, ed. Oliver (London, 1902), pp. 226-7, 301-2.

CHAPTER XI

1. Fourth Report of Medical Officer of the Privy Council, *B.P.P.*, 1862, XXII, p. 111.

2. R. W. Cooke Taylor, "What Influence has the Employment of Mothers . . . on Infant Mortality?", *N.A.P.S.Sc. Transactions*, 1874, pp. 574–5.

3. Cf. Dr. Simpson's views recorded in *B.M.J.*, 1892, vol. II. p. 277.

4. *Inter alia*, Hon. Sec. of Harveian Medical Society and Hon. Sec. of Infant Life Protection Society.

5. Evidence to Select Committee on the Best Means of Protecting Infants put out to Nurse, *B.P.P.*, 1871, VII, 1,344.

6. John Simon's recommendations, *B.P.P.*, 1862, XXII, p. 497.

7. Cf. *Sessional Papers of Social Science Association*, March 1874, p. 260: "*Resolution:* That every encouragement should be given to the establishment of infant day nurseries where the young children of female operatives and other working women could be properly cared for in the absence of their mother at work." Cf. also R. W. Cooke Taylor, op. cit., *N.A.P.S.Sc. Transactions*, 1874, p. 576. In the same paper in which he denies any connexion between the employment of mothers and the mortality of infants, he advises the establishment of day nurseries to cure the evil!

8. The full history of the crèche can most easily be found in an anonymous pamphlet, *Public Nurseries* (London, 1851).

9. J. Brendon Curgenven, "The Waste of Infant Life", *Sessional Papers of Social Science Association*, March 1867, p. 228.

10. *Public Nurseries* (pamphlet; London, 1850), p. 1.

11. Ibid., p. 32.

12. Ibid., p. 32.

13. This requirement of moral virtue was to become familiar in the regulations of day nurseries in England.

14. Op. cit., pp. 32–3.

15. Ibid., p. 29.

16. Ibid.

17. Mary Merryweather, *Factory Life* (London, 1852).

18. *The Establishment of Day Nurseries in Manchester and Salford* (pamphlet; Manchester, 1851).

19. Cf., *inter alia*, Half-yearly Report of Alexander Redgrave, Factory Inspector in the north-west for second half of 1853, *B.P.P.*, 1858, XVIII, p. 305.

20. It was the Association's intention, if the Ancoats nursery proved successful, to establish similar nurseries in other districts of the two cities.

21. This should be contrasted with the regulations in Marbeau's nurseries, to be found in pamphlet, *Public Nurseries*, referred to above.

22. Pamphlet issued by Association (Manchester, 1851).

23. Ibid.

24. *B.P.P.*, 1865, XVIII, p. 305.

25. Evidence to Select Committee on the Best Means of Protecting Infants put out to Nurse, *B.P.P.*, 1871, VII, 2,309 (Syson).

26. Ibid., 2,308 and 2,388 (Syson).

27. Ibid., 3,249 (Whitehead).

28. Ibid., 3,338 (Whitehead).

29. Ibid., 3,322–5 (Whitehead). In 1870 the actual receipts from parents was £43 10s. 4d. Thus 50% of the expenditure was charitable. It should be remembered that the services of Dr. Whitehead and those of the lady supervisor, Mrs. Leigh Clare, were gratuitous.

30. Ibid., 3,270 (Whitehead).

31. Ibid., 3,273 (Whitehead).

32. Ibid., 3,500 (Whitehead).

33. Ibid., 3,510 (Whitehead).

34. Ibid., 3,511 and 3,338 (Whitehead).

35. Ibid., 3,345 (Whitehead).

36. Ibid., 3,337 (Whitehead).

37. Ibid., 3,336 (Whitehead).

38. Ibid., 3,268 (Whitehead).

39. Ibid., 3,268 (Whitehead).

40. Ibid., 3,564 (Whitehead).

41. Ibid., 3,259 (Whitehead) and 2,410 (Syson).

42. Ibid., 3,332 (Whitehead).

43. Whitehead was asked: "If the supervision of both the lady superintendent and yourself was withdrawn, do you think the children would derive the same advantages?"—"I think they would degenerate into the same condition as those of ordinary nurseries": op. cit., 3,580. Whitehead visited the Charles Street nursery whenever sent for or when he happened to be in the vicinity. Syson visited the Salford nursery every week: ibid., 2,322.

44. Ibid., 3,348 (Whitehead).

45. Ibid., 3,263 (Whitehead).

46. Ibid., 3,269 (Whitehead).

47. Ibid., 3,365 (Whitehead).

48. Ibid., 3,528 (Whitehead).

49. Ibid., 3,376 (Whitehead) and 2,319 (Syson).

50. Ibid., 2,318 (Syson). There is no evidence whether these were regarded as charitable or as self-supporting ventures.

51. Cf., inter alia, B.P.P., 1876, XXX (Folkes), 11,170.

52. Op. cit., p. 509. Lancet, 2nd February 1867, p. 151, also records the fact that in the Peabody Homes special arrangements were made for the care of the children of mothers who were employed away from home during the day.

53. Lancet, 20th June 1874, p. 889.

54. Report of Mr. Cramp, B.P.P., 1884, XVIII, pp. 47–8.

55. Ibid.

56. Cf. Lancet, 20th June 1874, p. 889; 23rd October 1875, p. 605; and "The Crèche System", by Rev. J. Elder Canning, N.A.P.S.Sc. Transactions, 1874, p. 727.

57. Cf. Annual Report of Principal Lady Factory Inspectress, B.P.P., 1906, XV, p. 320.

58. Op. cit., p. 271.

59. Ibid.

60. Evidence to Interdepartmental Committee on Physical Deterioration, B.P.P., 1904, XXXII, 9,031–4 (Garnett).

61. J. Brendon Curgenven, "The Waste of Infant Life", N.A.P.S.Sc. Transactions, 1867, p. 222.

62. Ibid., p. 225. A very full account of this experiment is to be found in the factory inspectors' reports for 1863: B.P.P., 1864, XXII, p. 702. See also Thos. M. Dolan, F.R.C.S., "How does the Employment of Mothers . . . influence Infant Mortality?", N.A.P.S.Sc. Transactions, 1882, p. 363.

63. Evidence to Select Committee on the Best Means of Protecting Infants put out to Nurse, B.P.P., 1871, VII, 1,342 (Curgenven). Cf. Resolution of Social Sciences Association: "That it is desirable for the checking

of excessive infant mortality in manufacturing towns where women are employed that a maternity fund be established in connexion with each factory, out of which a lying-in woman should receive a sum equal to her weekly wages, and in lieu thereof, for a period of two months from the birth of the child, provided it lives, to enable her to devote the necessary maternal care to it", *Sessional Papers of Social Science Association*, March 1867, p. 259.

CHAPTER XII

1. P. Kay-Shuttleworth, *Four Periods of Public Education* (London, 1862), p. 141.

2. Sixth Report of Medical Officer of Privy Council, *B.P.P.*, 1864, XXVIII, Appendix 14, p. 465.

3. *Lancet*, 2nd February 1867, p. 151.

4. Quoted by Mrs. Baines, "On the Prevention of Infantile Mortality", *Manchester Statistical Society Transactions*, 1868, p. 8.

5. Evidence to Interdepartmental Committee on Physical Deterioration, *B.P.P.*, 1904, XXXII, 7,544 *et seq.* (Eves).

6. "Infant Mortality and Female Labour", *Journal of the Sanitary Institute*, 1894, vol. CV, p. 502.

7. See Chapter XI, p. 165.

8. Newman, *Infant Mortality: A Social Problem* (London, 1906), p. 271.

9. See Chapter XI, p. 153.

10. Dr. Simpson, M.O.H., Manchester, *B.M.J.*, 1892, vol. II, p. 277.

11. Prospectus (London, 1871).

12. Ibid.

13. Cf. Playfair, *Hansard*, 1873, vol. CCIX, cols. 1,872 and 1,495.

14. Charley, ibid., cols. 1,487–8.

15. Quoted in *Reply of the Infant Life Protection Society to a Memorial of the National Society for Women's Suffrage objecting to the Proposed Measures* (London, 1871).

16. Ibid.

17. *Infant Mortality—Its Causes and Remedies* (Manchester, 1871).

18. *Hansard*, 1873, vol. CCIX, cols. 1,872 and 1,487–8.

19. Cf. evidence to the Select Committee on the Best Means of Protecting Infants put out to Nurse, *B.P.P.*, 1871, VII, 2,285, 2,297 (Syson); also 2,040 (Herford), 2,823 (Whitehead), 1,106–52 (Curgenven).

20. Op. cit., p. vii.

21. Cf. "Baby-farming", *B.M.J.*, 30th September 1876, p. 435, and "Cases of Baby Farming", ibid., 1st May 1880, p. 670.

22. W. S. Jevons, "Married Women in Factories"—a chapter in *Methods of Social Reform* (1883), pp. 158–66.

23. Op. cit., p. 41 (footnote).

24. Ibid., p. 61.

25. *Hansard*, 1873, vol. CCXVII, col. 1,547.

26. Cf. evidence of Whitehead, Select Committee on the Best Means of Protecting Infants put out to Nurse, *B.P.P.*, 1871, VII, 3,526.

27. Evidence of Baker, *B.P.P.*, 1876, XXX, 1,303; also ibid., Appendix C, p. 30.

28. Legislation was being considered by the Swiss Federal Assembly to make this provision in all Swiss cantons.

29. Main report of Commissioners, *B.P.P.*, 1876, XXX, p. lxxvii; also evidence of Mundella, ibid., 20,660–73.

30. Ibid., p. lxviii.

31. Reports of Royal Commission on Labour: Reports on the Employment of Women by the Assistant Lady Commissioners, *B.P.P.*, 1893–4, XXXVII, p. 509.

32. Chapter XI, p. 166.

33. Op. cit., p. 166.

34. The Government had in fact publicly committed themselves to bring in such a measure at the Berlin Conference, 1890; cf. *B.P.P.*, 1890, LXXXI, pp. 531, 613.

35. *Hansard*, 1891, vol. CCCLVI, col. 80.

36. Ibid., col. 81.

37. Ibid., col. 77.

38. See Chapter IX, references 20, 21, 22 and 23.

39. E.g. Reports of Royal Commission on Labour: Reports on the Employment of Women by the Assistant Lady Commissioners, *B.P.P.*, 1893–4, XXXVI, p. 508, section 78.

40. Haslam, "The Burden of the Factory Mother", *The Englishwoman*, 1909, p. 307.

41. *Papers of 1906 Conference on Infantile Mortality*, p. 231.

42. Quoted in ibid., p. 231.

43. Cf. Reports of Royal Commission on Labour: Reports on the Employment of Women by the Assistant Lady Commissioners, *B.P.P.*, 1893–4, XXXVII, p. 507, section 726.

44. Quoted by Lady MacLaren, "Wage-earning Mothers", *The Englishwoman*, November 1909, p. 49.

45. Miss Squires, Factory Inspectress, quoted by Principal Lady Factory Inspectress in her Annual Report, *B.P.P.*, 1906, XV, p. 320.

46. Ibid., p. 320.

47. Chapter XI, pp. 166 and 167.

48. Quoted by Lord Wemyss, *Hansard*, 1891, vol. CCCLVL, col. 82.

49. Op. cit., p. 89.

50. Evidence of Miss Squires, Report of Interdepartmental Committee on Physical Deterioration, *B.P.P.*, 1904, XXXII, Appendix V, p. 128, section 55.

51. Ibid.

52. This is well described by the Hon. Mrs. A. Russell, "The Ghent School for Mothers", *The Nineteenth Century*, December 1901, pp. 970–6.

53. Report of Interdepartmental Committee on Physical Deterioration, *B.P.P.*, 1904, XXXII, Appendix V, p. 128, section 55 (Miss Squires).

54. Op. cit., p. 50.

CHAPTER XIII

1. *Hansard*, 1844, vol. LXXIII, col. 1,096.

2. *A New View of Society* (Everyman Edition), p. 62.

3. Ibid., p. 68.

4. Op. cit., pp. 186, 191, 241.
5. Op. cit. (London, 1825), p. 7.
6. Ibid., p. 4.
7. Ibid., p. 49. Rule 3 of these nurseries ran: "Parents may send their children's dinner with them in the morning, so that children may be taken care of the whole day to enable the mother to go out to work."
8. Cf. P. Kay-Shuttleworth, *Four Periods of Public Education* (London, 1862), pp. 132–3. Also Gaskell, *Manufacturing Population* (London, 1833), p. 276.
9. Cf. Phoebe Curden, *The English Nursery School* (London, 1938), p. 5.
10. Gaskell, *Manufacturing Population* (London, 1833), p. 185.
11. Dr. Syson, M.O.H. for Salford, brought evidence to show that the mortality of infants put out to day nurses was such as to justify their regular visiting by an inspector—but by a doctor, not "a band of women": "You do not think there is a class of women in Manchester and Salford sufficiently informed and intelligent upon those things?"—"I have not met them. I may supplement that remark by saying that even in a better class of life, about the food, for instance, I find that a great deal of ignorance prevails." Evidence to Select Committee on the Best Means of Protecting Infants put out to Nurse, *B.P.P.*, 1871, VII, 2,366–7.
12. Op. cit., p. 5.
13. *N.A.P.S.Sc. Transactions*, 1867, pp. 381–2.
14. For evidence of this, see Edward Brotherton, "The State of Popular Education", *N.A.P.S.Sc. Transactions*, 1865, pp. 332 *et seq.*

CHAPTER XIV

1. See Chapter IV.
2. Ashley, *Hansard*, 1844, LXXIII, col. 1,096.
3. *Conditions of the Working Classes* (1844), p. 147 (footnote).
4. See Chapter XI.
5. "Inquiry into the Condition of a District in Deansgate", *Manchester Statistical Society Transactions*, 1864–5, p. 11. See also "Inquiry into Ancoats", *Transactions* for 1865–6, p. 15.
6. See M. Hewitt, op. cit., Appendix I, Tables 5, 6, 7 and 8.
7. Letter from Isabella M. S. Todd, *Lancet*, 21st November 1874, p. 750.
8. Mrs. Bayley, "The Employment of Women", *N.A.P.S.Sc. Transactions*, 1861, p. 532.
9. *The Effects of the Factory System* (3rd edition, London, 1913), p. 19.
10. "Infant Mortality and Factory Labour", published in *Dangerous Trades*, edited by Thos. Oliver (London, 1902).
11. E.g. Robert Baker (Factory Inspector), *B.P.P.*, 1864, XXII, pp. 699 *et seq.*
12. Final Report of Royal Commission on Labour, *B.P.P.*, 1894, XXXV, p. 93, section 277.
13. Report of Interdepartmental Committee on Physical Deterioration, *B.P.P.*, 1904, XXXII, Appendix V, p. 125, section 37.
14. Ibid., section 50.
15. Ibid., section 51.

16. Ibid., sections 37 and 52.

17. Reports of Commission on Labour: Reports on the Employment of Women by the Lady Assistant Commissioners, *B.P.P.*, 1893–4, XXXVII, p. 507, section 726.

18. Report of the Interdepartmental Committee on Physical Deterioration, *B.P.P.*, 1904, XXXII, Appendix V, p. 127.

19. Annual Reports of the Factory Inspectors, *B.P.P.*, 1860, XXXIV, p. 540.

20. "What Influence has the Employment of Mothers . . . on Infant Mortality?", *N.A.P.S.Sc. Transactions*, 1872, p. 377.

21. The importance of the financial contribution of married women to their homes in agricultural districts was pointed out by a Commissioner in 1843: *B.P.P.*, 1843, XII, pp. 27–8.

22. *B.P.P.*, 1893–4, XXXVII, part I, p. 102.

23. "The Employment of Women", *N.A.P.S.Sc. Transactions*, 1861, p. 532.

24. Presidential Address to 1906 National Conference on Infantile Mortality, recorded on p. 18 of *Papers of the 1906 Conference on Infantile Mortality*.

APPENDIX I

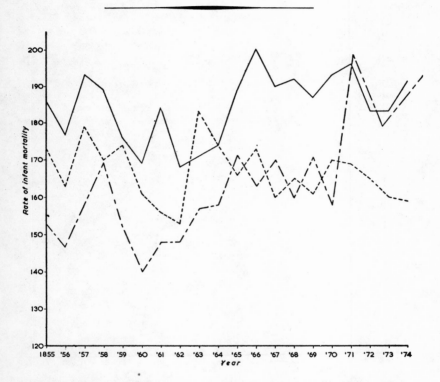

Graph 3 illustrating the mortality of infants, of −1 year per 1,000 births, in the County of Lancaster, in the County of Stafford and in the County of Durham, 1855–87.

———— Lancashire.

-------- Staffordshire.

— — — Durham.

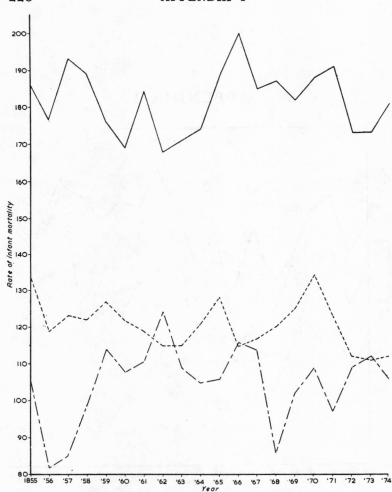

Graph 4 illustrating the mortality of infants −1 year per 1,000 births in the County of Lancaster, in the Counties of Berkshire, Hampshire and Surrey, and in the County of Westmorland, 1855–74.

———————— Lancashire.

- - - - - - - - Berkshire, Hampshire and Surrey.

— — — — Westmorland.

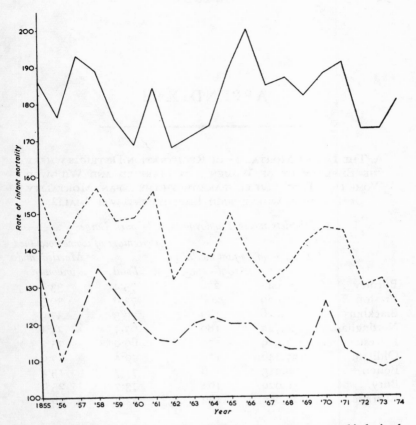

Graph 5 illustrating the mortality of infants —1 year per 1,000 births in the County of Lancaster, in the Counties of Essex, Suffolk and Norfolk, and in the Counties of Wiltshire, Dorset and Somerset, 1855–74.

——————— Lancashire.

- - - - - - - - Essex, Suffolk and Norfolk.

— · — · — · — Wiltshire, Dorset and Somerset.

APPENDIX II

A. The Infant Mortality of Registration Districts where the Employment of Women and Married and Widowed Women was Extensive compared with the Infant Mortality of Districts where such Employment was Small[1]

I. Districts where Employment of Women Large

	Population, 1901	Infant mortality, 1896–1905	Percentage of women occupied	
			Total	Married and widowed
Burnley . .	94,043	208	75·4	33·8
Preston . .	112,989	208	73·8	30·5
Blackburn .	127,626	183	76·5	37·9
Nottingham .	239,743	180	67·7	24·1
Leicester . .	211,579	175	69·8	25·2
Oldham . .	137,246	170	70·4	20·0
Bolton . .	168,215	166	71·7	15·1
Bury . .	58,029	164	73·7	25·6
Average . .	128,052	182	72·3	26·5

II. Districts where Employment of Women Small

	Infant mortality, 1896–1905	Percentage of women occupied	
		Total	Married and widowed
Sunderland . . .	166	38·2	7·7
Swansea	160	42·1	8·7
Lincoln	157	47·2	7·8
South Shields . .	155	34·9	7·4
Newport	153	44·4	7·0
Cardiff	147	43·6	8·4
Barrow-in-Furness .	144	40·7	5·8
Burton	119	41·8	6·9
Average	150	41·6	7·4

[1] George Newman, *Infant Mortality—A Social Problem* (Methuen, 1906), pp. 103–10.

B. The Same Tables reproduced, but noting the Percentage of Women, Married Women and Widows employed
between the ages of 15 and 35 Years[1]

I

	Infant mortality, 1896–1905	Percentage of women employed 15–35 years	
		Total	Married and widowed
Burnley	208	90·9	59·7
Preston	208	89·4	50·5
Blackburn	183	91·8	63·9
Nottingham . . .	180	84·6	27·5
Leicester	175	87·6	41·6
Oldham	170	87·3	33·4
Bolton	166	87·4	24·7
Bury	164	88.9	44·8
Average . . .	182	88·4	43·2

II

	Infant mortality, 1896–1905	Percentage of women employed 15–35 years	
		Total	Married and widowed
Sunderland . . .	166	55·1	2·8
, Swansea . . .	160	59·4	5·0
Lincoln	157	63·3	3·2
South Shields . .	155	53·8	3·0
Newport	153	63·6	2·6
Cardiff	147	62·6	3·8
Barrow	144	57·9	2·9
Burton	119	60·5	3·0
Average . . .	150	59·5	3·1

[1] This Newman took to be the main child-bearing period.

APPENDIX III

COMPARATIVE MORTALITY OF BREAST- AND HAND-FED INFANTS[1]

(1) *Salford*

Subject of Inquiry: Death-rate of infants per 1,000 births.

Infants breast-fed	128·6
Infants having breast milk and other food. . .	190·4
Infants having cow's milk only	263·9
Infants having other food (condensed milk, etc.) .	439·0

Annual Report on Health of Salford, 1904.

(2) *Birmingham*

Infants breast-fed	7·8
Infants breast-fed and otherwise.	26·5
Infants having no breast milk	252·3

Annual Report on Health of Birmingham, 1904.

(3) *Stockport*

Subject of Inquiry A: Deaths of 116 infants from diarrhoea; 95% fed wholly or partially by hand.

Subject of Inquiry B: Feeding of 977 infants. The infants were breast-fed and only 2% were in "delicate health".

Subject of Inquiry C: Feeding of 363 children. The children were artificially fed, and over 68% were delicate.

(4) *St. Pancras*

"The third or summer quarter of the year is the crucial period of infant mortality in relation to ... feeding, and the following tables show the remarkable diminution during the past two years on the infantile mortality rates of St. Pancras as compared with London and 76 great towns of England and Wales."

[1] May Tennant, "Infant Mortality", *Women in Industry from Several Points of View* (London, 1908), Appendix II, p. 111.

INFANT MORTALITY RATES PER 1,000 BIRTHS IN THE THIRD
QUARTERS OF 1904, 1905, 1906: ST. PANCRAS COMPARED TO
OTHER LOCALITIES

Third Quarter of:	1904	1905	1906	Per 1,000 fall in St. Pancras First period	Second period	Both
St. Pancras compared with London . .	−24	−4	−28	20	32	52
St. Pancras compared with 76 large towns	−3	−11	−46	14	35	49
St. Pancras compared with England and Wales	−42	−20	−13	22	33	55

"The measures pursued in St. Pancras have been the discouragement of the artificial feeding of infants of suckling age and the encouragement of natural and breast feeding by prompt advice and the personal influence of women inspectors and women voluntary visitors. The efforts tentatively commenced in 1904 were pursued with greater confidence and thoroughness during 1905, and have been extended and elaborated in 1906. . . .

"The interesting point to bear in mind is that the lowering of the infantile mortality has been accomplished without the municipal distribution of milk, the Borough Council not having established a milk depot, and no such milk depot existing in the Borough, and the fall in the mortality rates must be mainly attributed to the diminished use of cow's milk for infants and the increase of breast-feeding."

Report of M.O.H. upon Infant Mortality Rates of St. Pancras, 1906.

BIBLIOGRAPHY

OFFICIAL REPORTS AND PUBLICATIONS

1. Population (Number, Age, Occupation, Fertility and Mortality)

(*a*) Census Reports, England and Wales
1851: *B.P.P.*, 1852–3, LXXXVIII, parts 1 and 2.
1861: *B.P.P.*, 1863, LIII, parts 1 and 2.
1871: *B.P.P.*, 1873, LXXI, parts 1 and 2.
1881: *B.P.P.*, 1883, LIII, LXXX.
1891: *B.P.P.*, 1893–4, CVI.
1901: *B.i`.P.*, 1902, CXIX and CXXI.
1911: *B.P.P.*, 1917–18, XXXV.

(*b*) Fertility Census, England and Wales, 1911

(*c*) Scottish Census Reports, 1911, *B.P.P.*, 1911, XIV, part 3.

(*d*) Annual Reports of Registrar-General
1842, XIX; 1843, XXI; 1844, XIX; 1846, XIX; 1847–8, XXV; 1849, XXI, 1850, XX; 1851, XXII; 1852, XVIII; 1852–3, XL; 1854, XIX; 1854–5, XV; 1856, XVIII; 1857 (Session I), XVIII; 1857 (Session II), XII; 1860, XXIX; 1861, XVIII; 1862, XVIII; 1863, XIV; 1864, XVII; Supplement, 1865, XIII; 1865, XIV; 1866, XIX; 1867, XVII; 1867–8, XIX; 1868–9, XVI; 1870, XVI; 1871, XV; Summary for 1861–70, 1872, XVII; 1873, XX; 1875, XVIII, parts 1 and 2; 1876, XXVIII; 1877, XXV; 1878, XXII; 1878–9, XIX; 1880, XVI; 1881, XXVII; 1882, XIX; 1883, XX; 1884, XX; Supplement, 1884–5, XVII; 1886, XVII; 1887, XXIII; 1888, XXX; 1889, XXV; 1890, XXIV.

2. Industry

(*a*) Report of Commissioners appointed to Collect Information in the Manufacturing Districts relative to the Employment of Children in Factories:
First Report: 1883, XX.
Second Report: 1883, XXI.
Supplementary Reports: 1834, XIX and XX.

(*b*) Memorial of Short-time Committee of Manchester:
1837, L.
1837–8, XLV.

(*c*) Reports from the Commissioners on Hand-loom Weavers:
1841, X.

Assistant Commissioner's Reports:
  1839, XLII.
  1840, XXIII and XXIV.
Report of Mr. Hickson on the condition of Hand-loom Weavers:
  1840, XXIV.
(d) Second Report of Commissioners for inquiring into the Employment
  and Conditions of Children (Trades and Manufactures), 1843, XIV.
(e) Memorial of Manufacturers, 1847, XLVI.
(f) The Number of Persons employed in Cotton, Woollen, Flax and Silk
  Factories respectively in the United Kingdom, 1847, XLVI.
(g) Report to the Local Government Board on Proposed Changes in
  Hours and Ages of Employment in Textile Factories, by J. H. Bridges,
  M.D., and T. Holmes, Esq., 1873, LV.
(h) Report of Commissioners on the Working of the Factory and Workshops Acts with a View to Their Consolidation and Amendment, 1876,
  XXIX and XXX.
(i) Royal Commission on Labour, 1893: Reports of the Lady Assistant
  Commissioners, 1893–4, XXXVII, part 1.
(j) Half-yearly Reports of Factory Inspectors:
    1836, XLV; 1840, XXIII; 1841, X; 1841 (Session II), VI; 1842,
    XXII; 1843, XXVII; 1844, XXVIII; 1845, XXV; 1846, XX; 1847,
    XV; 1847–8, XXVI; 1849, XXII; 1850, XXIII; 1851, XXIII;
    1852–3, XL; 1854, XIX; 1854–5, XV; 1856, XVIII; 1857 (Session I),
    III; 1857 (Session II), XVI; 1857–8, XXIV; 1859 (Session I), XII;
    1859 (Session II), XIV; 1860, XXXIV; 1861, XXII; 1862, XXII;
    1863, XVIII; 1864, XXII; 1865, XX; 1866, XXIV; 1867, XVI;
    1867–8, XVIII; 1868–9, XIV; 1870, XV; 1871, XIV; 1872, XVI;
    1873, XIX; 1874, XIII; 1875, XVI; 1876, XVI; 1877, XXIII;
    1878, XX; 1878–9, XVI; 1882, XVIII; 1883, XVIII; 1884,
    XVIII; 1884–5, XV; 1886, XIV; 1887, XVI; 1888, XXVI; 1889,
    XVIII; 1890, XX; 1890–1, XIX; 1892, XX; 1895, XIX; 1896,
    XIX; 1897, XVII; 1898, XIV; 1899, XII.

3. Agriculture

(a) Second Report of Poor Law Commissioners, 1836, XXIX.
(b) Report of Special Assistant Poor Law Commissioners on the Employment of Women and Children in Agriculture, 1843, XII.
(c) Fifth Report of the Children's Employment Commission, 1866, XXIV.
(d) Sixth Report of the Children's Employment Commission, 1867, XVI.
(e) Reports of Commission on the Employment of Women and Children
  in Agriculture, 1867–8, XVII; 1868–9, XIII.

4. Child Care and Infant Mortality

(a) Reports of Commissioners for Inquiring into the State of Large Towns
  and Populous Districts:
    First Report: 1844, XVII.
    Second Report: 1845, XVIII.
(b) Papers Relating to the Sanitary State of England, with an introduction
  by John Simon, 1857–8, XXIII.

(c) Reports of Medical Officer of Privy Council:
    First Report: 1859, XXIX.
    Third Report: 1861, XVI.
    Fourth Report: 1862, XXII.
    Fifth Report: 1863, XXV.
    Sixth Report: 1864, XXVIII.
(d) Appendices to Reports of Medical Officer of Privy Council:
    (i) First Report: Dr. Greenhow's Report on the Prevalence and Causes
    of Diarrhoea at Coventry, Birmingham, Wolverhampton, Dudley,
    Merthyr Tydfil, Nottingham, Leeds and Manchester, with Chorlton
    and Salford, p. 359.
    (ii) Third Report: Dr. Greenhow's Report on Districts with Excessive
    Mortality from Lung Diseases, Appendix VI, p. 442.
    (iii) Fourth Report: Dr. Greenhow's Report on High Local Death-
    rates from Particular Kinds of Diseases, Appendix IV, p. 653.
    (iv) Fourth Report: Dr. Greenhow's Report on the Circumstances
    under which there is Excessive Mortality of Young Children among
    Certain Manufacturing Populations, Appendix V, p. 649.
    (v) Fifth Report: Dr. Buchanan's Report, 30th December 1862, on the
    Health of Operatives as affected by the Prevailing Distress, Appendix
    V, p. 303.
    (vi) Fifth Report: Dr. Edwin Smith's Report on the Nourishment of
    the Distressed Operatives, Appendix V*b*, p. 313.
    (vii) Sixth Report: Dr. Julian Hunter's Report on the Excessive
    Mortality of Infants in Some Rural Districts of England, Appendix
    XIV, p. 458.
(e) Report of the Select Committee on the Best Means of Protecting
    Infants put out to Nurse, 1871, VII.
(f) Report of the Interdepartmental Committee on Physical Deterioration,
    1904, XXXII.
(g) Report by Medical Officer of Local Government Board on Infant and
    Child Mortality during the First Five Years of Life; dealing with the
    Statistics of Sanitary Areas (Grouped) and of the Administrative Counties
    of England and Wales, 1910, XXXIV.
(h) Report of Medical Officer of the Local Government Board on Infant
    and Child Mortality, dealing with the Statistics of 212 Towns and 29
    Metropolitan Boroughs during the Four years 1907–10 (Grouped) and
    1911–13, XXXII.
(i) Third Report of Medical Officer of Local Government Board on
    Infant and Child Mortality, dealing with Infant Mortality in Lancashire,
    1914, XXXIX.

5. Education

(a) Annual Reports of Committee of Council:
    1859, XXI; 1860, LIV; 1861, XLIX; 1862, XLII; 1863, XLVII;
    1864, XLV; 1865, XLII; 1866, XXVII; 1867, XXII; 1867–8, XXV;
    1868–9, XX; 1870, XXII; 1871, XXII; 1872, XXII; 1873, XXIV;
    1874, XVIII; 1875, XXIV; 1876, XXIII; 1877, XXX; 1878,
    XXVIII; 1878–9, XXIII; 1880, XXII.

(b) Memorial of School Board of Wolverhampton to the Education Department, 17th June 1877, LXVII.

6. Juvenile Delinquency

(a) First Report of Select Committee of the House of Lords, appointed to enquire into the Execution of the Criminal Law especially relating to Juvenile Offenders and Transportation, 1847, VII.
(b) Report of Select Committee on Criminal and Destitute Juveniles, 1852, VII.

7. Hansard Debates

1844, vol. LXXIII, cols. 1,406–69, 1,078–1,124, 1,141–7, 1,182–1,251, 1,379–84.
1844, vol. LXXIV, cols. 630–1,090.
1844, vol. LXXV, cols. 140–5.
1847, vol. LXXXIX, cols. 488–93, 1,091–1,139.
1847, vol. XC, col. 797.
1867, vol. CLXXXV, col. 1,081.
1867, vol. CLXXXVIII, col. 1,663.
1873, vol. CCXVI, cols. 822, 824, 825.
1873, vol. CCXVII, cols. 1,301, 1,304, 1,549.
1891, vol. CCCLVI, cols. 77, 80, 81.

CONTEMPORARY JOURNALS AND PUBLICATIONS OF SOCIETIES AND PROFESSIONAL BODIES

1. National Association for the Promotion of Social Science

(a) Transactions

1857 p. 51   Lord Stanley's Address on Public Health.
      p. 257 "On Crime and Density of Population", Jelinger Symons.
      p. 380 "Illustrations of the Necessity for the More Analytical Study of the Statistics of Public Health", E. Headlam Greenhow.
      p. 545 "The Industrial Employment of Women", Chas. Bray.
1858 p. xxxii Introduction.
      p. 267 "On the Principles on which Educational Legislative Measures should be based", Rev. Nash Stephenson.
      p. 278 "Compulsory Education", Rev. W. Frazer.
1859 p. 47   Address on Public Health, Rt. Hon. W. Cowper, M.P.
      p. 526 "The Establishment and Progress of the Manchester Certified Ragged and Industrial Schools Act", Joseph Adshead.
1860 p. 635 "On Infantile Death-rates in Their Bearing on Sanitary and Social Science", W. T. Gairdner, M.D., F.R.C.P.
      p. 649 "On the Excessive Mortality occurring in Cities and Large Towns", James Frazer, M.D.
1864 p. 500 "Infant Mortality", W. D. Husband, F.R.C.S.
      p. 509 "On the Undue Mortality of Infants and Children in Connection with the Questions of Early Marriages, Drugging Children, Bad Nursing, Death Clubs and Certificates of Death, etc.", J. I. Ikin, F.R.C.S.

1864	p. 578	Discussion on above.
	p. 616	"The Cotton Famine", F. Arthur Arnold.
	p. 621	"Co-operation during the Cotton Scarcity", G. J. Holyoake.
1865	p. 319	"Our Neglected and Destitute Children—are They to be Educated?", Mary Carpenter.
	p. 322	"The State of Popular Education", Edward Brotherton.
	p. 458	"Causes of the Differences existing between the Death-rates of Urban and Rural Districts and, incidentally, of Sheffield", G. L. Saunders.
1866	p. 62	Address on Education, Rt. Hon. H. A. Bruce, M.P.
	p. 307	"By what Means can the Impediments to the Education of Children of the Manual-labour Class, arising from the Apathy and Poverty of the Parents, and the Claims of the Market for Labour be most effectively removed?", J. A. Brenner.
	p. 387	On the same, R. S. Bartlett.
	p. 395	Discussion on above.
1867	p. 381	"On Compulsory Education", Rev. James McCosh.
1868	p. 330	"What are the Principal Causes of Crime considered from a Social Point of View?", Rev. H. Lettsom Elliot.
	p. 395	Discussion on "Primary Education".
1869	p. 244	Discussion on "Reformatory and Industrial Schools".
	p. 303	"How may the State best promote the Education of the Destitute and Neglected Portion of the Population?", Mary Carpenter.
	p. 313	"Education of Neglected Children", de Bunsen.
1870	p. 346	"Education in the Mining Districts of Durham and Northumberland", Rev. W. A. Scott.
1871	p. 335	"The State of Popular Education and Suggestions for Its Advancement", E. Brotherton.
	p. 341	Discussion on neglected children.
	p. 345	"Education of Neglected Children", Rev. Brooke Lambert.
	p. 468	"On the Progressive Degeneracy of the Race in Town Populations", H. W. Rumsey, M.D.
	p. 479	"Diseases Prevalent among Potters", J. T. Arlidge, F.R.C.P.
1872	p. 119	"Is it desirable that Industrial Day Schools should be established?", Mary Carpenter.
	p. 204	Discussion on above.
1873	p. 341	Discussion on industrial feeding schools.
	p. 612	"The Employment of Married Women in Manufactures", R. W. Cooke Taylor.
1874	p. 267	"How Far is it Desirable that the Industrial Schools Act should be extended to Day Schools?", Mary Carpenter.
	p. 401	"How Far can Children of the Wage-earning Classes be best brought under Elementary Instruction by Means of the Factory, Workshops and Other Acts, and by the Action of School Boards?", Rev. J. Page Hopps.
	p. 437	Discussion on above.

1874 p. 445   "The History, Principle and Progress of Education in Scotland on the Working of the Scottish Education Act", Rev. Jas. Taylor.

p. 573   "What Influence has the Employment of Mothers in Manufactures on Infant Mortality; and ought any, and what, Restrictions be placed on Such Employment?", R. W. Cooke Taylor.

p. 585   Discussion on above.

p. 723   "On the Neglect of Infants in Large Towns, with Some Remarks on the Crèche System", Rev. J. Elder Canning, D.D.

1875 p. 53   Address on health, Edwin Chadwick.

p. 246   "Should the Labour of Women in Factories be regulated by Legislation?", Miss Mary Burton.

p. 374   "What Influence has the Employment of Mothers in Mills and Factories on Infant Mortality?", R. W. Cooke Taylor.

p. 423   "Primary School Attendance", Wm. Mitchell.

p. 428   On the same, George Leith.

p. 436   Discussion on above.

1880 p. 391   Discussion on juvenile delinquency.

1882 p. 358   "How does the Employment of Mothers in Mills and Manufactures influence Infant Mortality?", Thos. M. Dolan, F.R.C.S.

p. 381   On the same, Dr. Martin.

p. 384   Discussion on above.

(b) Sessional Papers

1865 p. 565   Third Annual Report of the Coroner for Central Middlesex.

1867 p. 222   "The Waste of Infant Life", J. Brendon Curgenven.

1868 p. 573   Sixth Report of the Coroner for Central Middlesex.

1868 p. 562   Seventh Report of the Coroner for Central Middlesex.

2. *Manchester Statistical Society: Transactions*

1835   (manuscript copy) "On Immoral and Irreligious Works Sold in Manchester."

1860–1 p. 84   "On Homes for the Working Classes", Mr. George Greaves.

1861–2 p. 47   "On Social and Educational Statistics of Manchester and Salford", David Chadwick.

1862–3 p. 16   "On Infanticide", Mr. George Greaves.

p. 37   "Our Unemployed Females and what may Best be done for Them", Rev. Alex. Munro.

1864–5 p. 11   "Inquiry into the Condition of a District in Deansgate".

p. 83   "The Duty of England to provide a Gratuitous Compulsory Education for the Children of the Poorer Classes", Mr. John Robertson.

1865–6 p. 1   "Report of the Committee of Inquiry into the Educational and other Conditions of a District in Ancoats".

1867–8 p. 57   "Report on the Educational and other Conditions of a District at Gaythorne and Knott Hill, Manchester".

1868–9 p. 8   "On the Prevention of Infant Mortality", Mrs. Baines.

3. British Medical Journal

1860	vol. II	p. 785	6th October, "Infantile Death Rates", W. T. Gairdner.
1862	vol. II	p. 374	4th October, "Opiates for Children".
1864	vol. I	p. 46	14th January, "The Causes and Prevention of Infant Mortality", Isaac Pidduck.
		p. 83	28th January, "Infant Baptism".
		p. 131	5th August, "Infanticide".
	vol. II	p. 380	1st October, Sir Charles Hastings' Address to the N.A.P.S.Sc. at York.
1876	vol. I	p. 388	25th March, "Repression of Baby-farming".
	vol. II	p. 435	30th September, "Baby-farming".
		p. 506	14th October, "Report of the Hygienic Congress at Brussels".
		p. 561	28th October, "The Administration of Sedatives to Young Children".
1877	vol. I	p. 365	24th March, "Factory Legislation".
1878	vol. I	p. 938	29th June, "Causes of Infant Mortality".
	vol. II	p. 226	10th August, "Baby-farming".
		p. 330	31st August, "Infant Mortality in Leicester".
1879	vol. II	p. 509	7th September, "Infant Mortality in Leicester".
		p. 920	6th December, "Poisoning by Opiates".
1880	vol. I	p. 635	24th August, "Infant Mortality in Worcester".
		p. 670	1st May, "Cases of Baby-farming".
1881	vol. I	p. 365	5th March, "Infant Mortality in Nottingham".
1882	vol. I	p. 482	1st April, "Infant Mortality at Keighley".
1884	vol. I	p. 71	12th January, "Infant Mortality at Leicester".
		p. 1,104	7th June, "Infant Mortality at Leicester".
	vol. II	p. 974	5th November, "Infant Mortality at Nottingham".
		p. 1,027	22nd November, "Infant Mortality in Oldham".
		p. 1,051	22nd November, "Infant Mortality".
1885	vol. II	p. 1,073	5th December, "The Supply of Milk for Village Infants".
1893	vol. I	p. 1,124	27th May, "Infant Mortality and Factory Labour".
1894	vol. II	p. 1,384	15th December, "Infant Mortality and Factory Labour".
1901	vol. II	p. 627	7th August, "Infant Mortality and the Employment of Married Women in Factories".
		p. 1,146	7th September, "Infant Mortality and the Occupation of Married Women".

4. Lancet

1857	vol. II	p. 420	24th October, "On the Mortality of Infants in Foundling Institutions and Generally as Influenced by the Absence of Breast Milk", Dr. Routh.
1858	vol. I	p. 345	3rd April, "The Murder of Innocents".
1861	vol. II	p. 256	14th September, "Infant Mortality".

1861		p. 299	28th September, "Premium for Infanticide".
		p. 334	5th October, "Infant Mortality".
1867	vol. I	p. 61	12th January, Report of the Harveian Society on Infanticide.
		p. 151	2nd February, "Infant Mortality".
		p. 619	18th May, "Infant Food Society".
1874	vol. I	p. 26	3rd January, "Infant Mortality".
		p. 423	21st March, "Infant Mortality in Bradford".
		p. 849	13th June, "Infant Mortality in Stalybridge".
		p. 889	20th June, "Infant Mortality".
	vol. II	p. 563	17th October, "Infant Mortality".
		p. 750	21st November, Letter from Isabella M. S. Todd.
1875	vol. II	p. 605	23rd October, "Infant Mortality in Manufacturing Districts".
		p. 680	6th November "Infant Mortality".
1876	vol. I	p. 644	29th April, "Non-certified Deaths and Infant Mortality".
		p. 694	6th May, "Infant Mortality".
1882	vol. I	p. 923	3rd June, "Dosing Infants with Drugs".
1884	vol. II	p. 270	16th August, "Rearing of Hand-fed Infants".
1886	vol. II	p. 547	18th September, "The Massacre of Innocents".
1888	vol. II	p. 274	11th August, "Opium Poisoning in Infants".
		p. 877	3rd November, "Infant Feeding in Cities".
1894	vol. I	p. 748	6th March, "Infants' Foods".
1897	vol. II	p. 824	2nd October, "Unrestricted Sale of Opium by Druggists".
1898	vol. I	p. 878	26th March, "Industrial Occupation of Women and Infant Mortality".
1901	vol. I	p. 763	1st June, "Infant Mortality and the Occupation of Married Women".
1902	vol. I	p. 259	25th January, "The Influence of Maternal Factory Labour on Infant Mortality".
	vol. II	p. 302	2nd August, "Municipal Depots for Hand-fed Infants".
1904	vol. II	p. 1,309	5th November, "The Drugging of Infants".
1906	vol. I	p. 778	17th March, "The Drugging of Infants".

CONTEMPORARY PERIODICALS AND NEWSPAPERS

People's and Howitt's Journal (London, 1849; 2 vols.).

Morning Chronicle, 4th January 1850.

Household Words (London, 1850).

The People's Illustrated Journal of Arts, Manufactures, Practical Science and Social Economy (London, 1852).

The People's Miscellany (London, 1853).

The Household, London, 1866.

Manchester Guardian, May–July 1870.

The Penny Scrap Book (London, 1871; 2 vols.).

House and Home (London, 1879–82; 3 vols.).

The Economic Journal, 1894, pp. 51–8.

The Journal of Hygiene, vol. IV, 1904.
The Practitioners, October 1905.
The Nineteenth Century, December 1906, April 1910, December 1910.
The Englishwoman, August 1909, September 1909, October 1909, November 1909, January 1910, July 1911, August 1911, November 1911, July 1912, October 1912, November 1912.

EARLIER LITERATURE

Samuel Wilderspin, *Infant Education—or Remarks on the Importance of Educating the Infant Poor from the Age of Eighteen Months to Seven Years* (London, 1825).

CONTEMPORARY LITERATURE

P. Gaskell, *The Manufacturing Population of England* (London, 1833).
G. Head, *A Home Tour through the Manufacturing Districts* (London, 1835).
John Fielden, *The Curse of the Factory System* (Halifax, 1836).
R. W. Cooke Taylor, *Notes on a Tour in the Manufacturing Districts of Lancashire* (London, 1842).
Edward Baines, *The Social, Educational and Religious State of the Manufacturing Districts* (London, 1843).
Charlotte Tonna, *The Wrongs of Women* (London, 1844).
R. W. Cooke Taylor, *Factories and the Factory System* (London, 1844).
Mrs. Gaskell, *Mary Barton* (1848).
The Works of Charlotte Elizabeth (2 vols.; New York, 1849).
The Establishment of Day Nurseries in Manchester and Salford (pamphlet; Manchester, 1850).
Public Nurseries (pamphlet; London, 1851).
Rev. Wm. Parker, *The Destitute and Criminal Juveniles of Manchester* (pamphlet; Manchester, 1855).
Mrs. Gaskell, *North and South* (London, 1855).
R. K. Philp, *The Practical Housewife* (London, 1855).
Household Truths for Working Men (London and Norwich, 1857).
Life of Robert Owen by Himself (1920 reprint of 1857–8 edition).
Household Truths for Mothers and Daughters (London and Norwich, 1858).
Mary Merryweather, *Experience of Factory Life* (London, 1862).
P. Kay-Shuttleworth, *Four Periods of Public Education* (London, 1862).
Ellen Barlee, *A Visit to Lancashire in December 1862* (London, 1863).
J. T. Arlidge, *On the Mortality of the Parish of Stoke-on-Trent* (London, 1864).
James Whitehead, M.D., *The Rate of Mortality in Manchester and Other Manufacturing Towns compared with that of Cathedral and County Towns* (London, 1864).
Lucien Davésiès de Pontès, *Social Reform in England* (London, 1865).
Edwin Waugh, *Home Life of the Lancashire Factory Folk during the Cotton Famine* (London, 1867).
Opening Address by W. S. Jevons, British Association, September 1870.
Infant Mortality—Its Causes and Remedies. Published for "The Committee for amending the Law in Points where It is Injurious to Women" (Manchester, 1871).
Infant Life Protection Society: Prospectus (London, 1871).

Reply of the Infant Life Protection Society to a Memorial of Members of the National Society for Women's Suffrage objecting to the Proposed Measures (London, 1871).

London to Lancashire, with a Preface by Sir C. Trevelyan (London, 1872).

F. Marbeau, *Crèches pour les Petits Enfants d'Ouvrières* (8th edition, Paris, 1873).

C. Ansell, *The Statistics of Families in the Upper and Professional Classes* (London, 1874).

Homes Homely and Happy (Religious Tract Society, London, 1874).

W. S. Jevons, "Amusements of the People", published in *Contemporary Review*, October 1878, vol. XXXIII, pp. 498–513.

W. S. Jevons, "Married Women in Factories", published in *Contemporary Review*, January 1882.

E. Hodder, *Life and Work of the Seventh Earl of Shaftesbury* (London, 1887).

Richard Heath, *The English Peasant* (London, 1893).

George Reid, *Infant Mortality and the Employment of Married Women in Factories: a Paper read to the Public Medicine Section at the Annual Meeting of the B.M.A.*, 1892 (Stafford, 1892).

John Simon, *English Sanitary Institutions* (London, 1897).

Allen Clarke, *The Effects of the Factory System on Health* (pamphlet; Bolton, 1899).

MORE RECENT PUBLICATIONS

Edited by Thos. Oliver, *Dangerous Trades* (London, 1902).

Anna Martin, *The Married Working Woman* (pamphlet; National Union of Women's Suffrage Societies, 1904).

G. F. McCleary, *Infantile Mortality and Infant's Milk Depots* (London, 1905).

G. Newman, *A Special Report on an Infant's Milk Depot* (London, 1905).

Papers of the 1906 Conference on Infantile Mortality (London, 1906).

Records of the Second Conference on Infant Mortality (London, 1908).

Sir George Newman, *Infant Mortality—A Social Problem* (London, 1906).

Hasbach, *A History of the Agricultural Labourer* (London, 1908).

G. M. Tuckwell, C. Smith, M. R. MacArthur, *Women in Industry from Several Points of View* (London, 1908).

E. C. Harvey, *Labour Laws for Women and Children in the United Kingdom* (Women's Industrial Council, 1909).

W. S. Jevons, *The State in Relation to Labour* (4th edition; London, 1910).

Allen Clarke, *The Effects of the Factory System* (3rd edition, London, 1913).

B. L. Hutchins, *Women in Modern Industry* (London, 1915).

Edited by the Women's Industrial Council, *Maternity: Letters from Working Women* (1915).

Edited by Clementina Black, *Married Women's Work*: report of an enquiry by the Women's Industrial Council (1915).

Ellen Smith, *Wage-earning Women and Their Dependants*. (Women's Fabian Group, 1915).

G. W. Daniels, *The Working Life of Women in the Seventeenth Century* (Manchester University Press, 1920).

M. Dorothy George, *London Life and Labour in the Eighteenth Century* (London, 1925).

G. Talbot Griffiths, *Population Problems of the Age of Malthus* (Cambridge University Press, 1926).

B. L. Hutchins and A. Harrison, *History of Factory Legislation* (3rd edition; London, 1926).

W. F. Neff, *Victorian Working Women* (London, 1929).

J. H. Clapham, *An Economic History of Modern Britain: The Early Railway Age, 1820–50* (Cambridge University Press, 1930).

Ivy Pinchbeck, *Women Workers and the Industrial Revolution* (Routledge, 1930).

G. F. McCleary, *The Early History of the Infant Welfare Movement* (London, 1933).

W. O. Henderson, *The Lancashire Cotton Famine* (Manchester University Press, 1934).

G. F. McCleary, *The Maternity and Child Welfare Movement* (London, 1935).

N. E. Himes, *The Medical History of Contraception* (Allen and Unwin, 1936).

Phoebe E. Curden, *The English Nursery School* (Kegan Paul, 1938).

J. C. Drummond and Anne Wilbraham, *The Englishman's Food* (Cape, 1939).

G. F. McCleary, *The Development of the British Maternity and Child Welfare Services* (London, 1945).

C. Driver, *Tory Radical* (Oxford University Press, 1946).

Henry Hamilton, *History of the Homeland* (Allen and Unwin, 1947).

G. E. Fussell, *The English Rural Labourer* (Batchworth Press, 1949).

H. Grisewood (ed.), *Ideas and Beliefs of the Victorians* (Sylvan Press, 1949).

F. Zweig, *Women's Life and Labour* (Gollancz, 1952).

INDEX